Praise for
dreamseller

"Brandon's story is a cautionary tale interspersed with moments of hilarious despair. You can't make this stuff up!"
—Tony Hawk

"Entertaining, shocking, crazy, unimaginable!"   —Bam Margera

"Skate, drugs, and rock 'n' roll!"   —Kat Von D, *LA Ink*

"I love it, but it's unfortunate that it's true."   —Bucky Lasek

"Brandon Novak could have been one of the top professional skateboarders in the world. He had the talent, and the door was wide open for him to walk in and claim his place. Instead, he choose drugs and robbed himself and skateboarding of some of the best years of his life."   —Mike Valley

"Novak's riches-to-rags saga may amount to a depressing life...but is makes a pretty damn good book! Fantastic! I couldn't put it down!"   —Rocco Botte, Mega64

"The best book we have ever read! Wait...the *only* book we have ever read!"   —Don and Murph, "The Don and Murph Show"

"What a great book! It's a shame Novak can't read! HAHA!"
—Jimmy Pop Ali, of the Bloodhound Gang

"Brandon Novak is the illiterate bastard son of fellow Baltimorean Edgar Allan Poe."   —Ville Valo, of HIM

"Novak has been through Hell (*Perkele* in Finnish) and made it back! Rock 'n' roll lifestyle gone bad...
—Jukka, from *The Dude*

dreamseller

brandon novak
with JOSEPH FRANTZ

CITADEL PRESS
Kensington Publishing Corp.
www.kensingtonbooks.com

CITADEL PRESS BOOKS are published by

Kensington Publishing Corp.
119 West 40th Street
New York, NY 10018

All Kensington titles, imprints, and distributed lines are available at special
quantity discounts for bulk purchases for sales promotions, premiums,
fund-raising, educational, or institutional use. Special book excerpts or
customized printings can also be created to fit specific needs. For details,
write or phone the office of the Kensington special sales manager:
Kensington Publishing Corp., 119 West 40th Street, New York, NY 10018,
attn: Special Sales Department; phone 1-800-221-2647.

CITADEL PRESS and the Citadel logo are Reg. U.S. Pat. & TM Off.

First Trade Paperback Printing: October 2009

10   9   8   7   6   5   4   3   2   1

Printed in the United States of America

Library of Congress Control Number: 2008929358

ISBN-13: 978-0-8065-3004-8
ISBN-10: 0-8065-3004-9

This book is dedicated to my mother, Pat Novak, whose love, kindness, and forgiveness provided strength, hope, and inspiration.

Contents

Foreword
by Tony Hawk

The lure of celebrity is strong at a young age. This is especially true in the world of skateboarding. Kids who show a hint of talent usually do so just as they are becoming teenagers, and there are plenty of companies that will promise fame and fortune to these naïve souls. It is hard to keep your head clear when you are suddenly thrust into the spotlight for your skills and puberty is still something you've only heard about in health class. It is all too easy to get caught up in the hype, join the party scene, get the girls (who never gave you attention until you got your picture in the skate magazine), and let your skating take a backseat to your celebrity status. You are soon forgotten because your skating is no longer on point, but in your (drug-fogged) mind you are still the shit. Only when the money stops coming in and the attention dries up does reality come crashing down: you love drugs more than you love skating (or even yourself). I have seen it too many times, but one of the biggest offenders in this cliché scenario is Brandon Novak.

Brandon was a prodigal skater in the '90s. He was well on his way to a successful pro career until he got caught up in the party scene. For a while, the only amateur name you heard about was

Brandon. "This kid from Baltimore is amazing! . . . the next Bucky Lasek!"

And suddenly he was gone. There were plenty of rumors about what became of this young hopeful. He stopped skating; he was doing heroin; he died. I didn't know what to believe, but I knew whatever he was doing . . . it wasn't good. I knew Bam was trying to help, but it seemed like he was unknowingly becoming Brandon's source of income—just so he could get a fix. Skating was just a memory for him; he now lived for the needle.

I only got to see Brandon skate a couple of times, but there was no denying his natural talent. He could have learned anything he wanted and made a decent living in the process. Now he is a likely candidate for a *Behind the Music* (Behind the Board?) episode, but his story is one of the few that has a silver lining. Through these experiences and his subsequent sobriety, he now serves as a cautionary tale. Sure, we can laugh at his stories and make fun of his poor choices, but we have to realize that this stuff can happen all too easily when you have these opportunities at such a young age.

So enjoy these tidbits, but take warning. Don't forget what you love doing if success falls on you early in life. Keep it all in perspective by keeping a clear head along the way. Don't become a cliché. Remember that Brandon is one of the few who made it out by cleaning up. The only other endings to this story are jail or death, and there is no skating in either of those scenarios.

Introduction
by Bam Margera

I met Brandon Novak at a skatepark when I was a kid. Basically, he was my friend as well as competitor whenever I saw him at the skatepark, which was a positive thing because he forced me to be my best and I forced him to be his best. Soon Brandon earned a full-on sponsorship by Powell Peralta. As time went on, I saw less and less of him.

One day I ran into Bucky Lasek, our mutual friend. I asked, "What happened to Novak? Do you still skate with him?"

Bucky looked at me, completely bummed out. "I think he's on heroin." I laughed at this, but Bucky said, "No, seriously, I've heard some things and he's definitely on drugs. I'm pretty sure it's heroin. He quit the team and basically threw away his whole life. It's a shame. He really had something."

Bucky was right. Brandon should have been a famous skate-boarder. That's what was supposed to happen, that's what was meant to happen. It just didn't seem to make any sense.

One time, I was going through some old videotapes and found some footage of Novak. He was about ten years old, dressed in baggy clothes that were about ten sizes too big for him, with gold jewelry just like a little gangster rapper. I had a laugh at this, and then I got bummed when I started to remember all the talent in this kid that had gone to waste. I was on the phone with his mom in five minutes, and she told me he had just gotten out of rehab and could use my advice. I didn't know what I could tell him that could help, but I left my number for him.

That night in bed I kept thinking about Mrs. Novak asking me to give him advice. Could I really help him? Could I actually make a difference? It felt strange that we both had started out at the same level yet ended up so differently.

By the time I got hold of Brandon the next day, I had made my decision that he should come to live with me while he cleaned up his act. At least I could look after him and give him a hand up and help get him back on the right track.

We filmed *CKY 3,* and a movie called *Haggard.* In *Haggard,* I gave Brandon a part where he played a drug dealer. I also made a behind-the-scenes documentary for *Haggard.* Half of it became about Brandon's drug addiction. Before I knew it, I was getting fan mail about the movie, and everyone asked, "Whatever happened to Brandon Novak?" I'll tell you what happened. He went right back on the heroin as soon as he had the chance.

While he lived at my house he was always acting shady. And soon, all the skateboarding gear that my sponsors were sending to my house was disappearing: skateboards, wheels, trucks, decks, sunglasses, clothes. Brandon swore he wasn't stealing them, but who else would have? My parents?! Soon enough, everyone at Philly's FDR skatepark was telling me that Brandon was selling all my gear for cash.

Soon he started borrowing money from my friends and never paid them back. Then jewelry started disappearing from my mother's room. Then my brother Jess's CDs started to disappear. And everything that had once been in the medicine cabinet was gone except for a box of Band-Aids. Soon, my mom had to hide her purse, and the whole family had to find hiding places for anything that was valuable.

Meanwhile, Brandon was taking the bus back to Baltimore on a regular basis, for the most unbelievable reasons in the world. I can still remember a few:

- He had to help his mother move a heavy piece of furniture.
- His mom was sick so he had to go look after her dog.
- He had to go back to get his favorite pair of jeans. Your favorite *pair of jeans*?! Are you fucking kidding me?!

Whenever he returned from Baltimore, he had a glazed look in his eye that told us the real reason he went home—obviously, to buy more heroin.

At that point my parents and I realized that you can't get a junkie off of heroin unless he is ready to make the decision to quit. And Brandon clearly hadn't made that decision. We soon realized that it would be the best for all of us if he left our house before something happened that ruined our relationship for good.

Three years later, I got a call from Brandon. He told me he had been clean for a few months, and for some reason I believed him. He came to my house and I let him live with me for a while. He really did seem clean, and I put him on *Viva La Bam* and on my weekly radio show.

Having Novak around was entertaining because he always had crazy insane stories about being strung out. These stories would usually leave his listeners with their mouths open and in shock, saying, "Are you serious?!" Eventually, they would approach Novak and ask him to retell his tales for their friends. I never got tired of hearing the hundreds of insane stories. I still don't think I've heard them all. Apparently, when you're a junkie, you're prone to a lifestyle that is unimaginable to most. Well, at least when you're as bad off as Novak let his life get.

After living with me for a few months, Brandon started to stagnate. He was doing nothing to improve his well-being, and still didn't have a job. He was doing a lot of drinking.

Finally, one day when he was telling his crazy heroin stories at my house, my mother Ape said, "You know, Brandon, you should write a book!" It hit me; I had an idea that would keep Brandon motivated and bring purpose to his life for the first time since he quit skateboarding. I told him, "That's it, Brandon! That's what you're meant to do!"

"What do you mean by that?" he asked.

"From now on, you're going to stay productive! While you stay here, you don't have to pay rent, you don't have to get a job, but you're going to write down all your experiences on paper and it's going to be a book!"

Brandon's face lit up. At that point, I think he realized this is what he was meant to do, the reason why he had all his experiences as a junkie. To write a book, and to inspire other people not to ruin their lives and careers like he had once ruined his.

Acknowledgments

Brandon Novak and Joe Frantz wish to extend a heartfelt thank-you to those whose special advice, efforts, guidance, and friendship helped bring the *Dreamseller* project to fruition:

Mandy Buchanan, Richard Ember, Ted Field, Terry Hardy, Todd Hastings, Tony Hawk, Jody Hotchkiss, Bucky Lasek, Guy Leeper, April Margera, Bam Margera, Phil Margera, Scott, Mike Vallely, Keith Yokomoto, Howard Yoon.

Brandon would also like to extend a warm thank-you to his loving brother and sister, who gave him his first skateboard.

dreamseller

chapter one
The Last Day of Using

I am a twenty-five-year-old junkie, sleeping in an abandoned garage in one of the worst parts of Baltimore City. My eyes open.

It is August 11, 2003. I can't tell you the time because I don't own a watch, but judging by the angle of the sun's rays shining through the cracks of the abandoned garage door, it is about eight-thirty a.m.

As soon as I am conscious enough to think, panic consumes my body. My mind searches desperately for the answer to the question, "Did I leave a gate shot for myself last night?" A "gate shot" is what we junkies refer to as the first fix of the day, which draws the user "out of the gate" until they can pull a hustle that will lead to the next fix. I suppose this is a term borrowed from horse or dog racing, which conjures an insightful visualization of a junkie's lifestyle: a fixated animal running a desperate, circular sprint.

My hands strike out, searching, reaching, grasping. Not in my shoes, not in my pockets, not on the floor . . . I arrive at the terrible conclusion: no gate shot, not today.

I am dreading the chain of events that are rapidly approaching, and I want so bad to reject the responsibility of having to scrounge up ten dollars for a pill of Dope, but Heroin is calling. I know I have to make it happen somehow, some way.

I take a deep breath, and stagnant air fills my lungs. My eyes, adjusting to the sunlight, fix on the cracks on the ceiling, the peeling paint, the broken light fixture, the cement beams, all the exterior details which express my inner condition.

My body shivers from the chill of the cold cement floor beneath my "bed," which consists of three moldy dingy-yellow cushions. A few days prior, I had taken them from a sofa that was sitting in the rain next to some trash cans I happened to be picking through. I thought they might bring comfort after a long day of stealing, lying, and hustling, so I took them to the abandoned garage I call my "home." I had arranged them in a symmetrical line, spacing them three inches apart so they might almost accommodate the length of a five-foot-six body. That night, as I drifted off to sleep with my feet resting on the cold cement, I found pride in my accomplishment—the acquisition of these three dank cushions, stinking of mold and mildew, which I now I refer to as my "bed."

I sit.

I unwrinkle my makeshift pillow, my hooded sweatshirt. I wear this sweatshirt for one good reason: the hood conceals my white skin. You see, I buy my drugs in an all-black neighborhood, and there are stick-up boys everywhere who look to prey upon white-boy junkies like me. Also, being the only white person in the area makes me a prime target for cops, who know that any white person they see here is a drug addict.

I slip my shoes over the socks I have worn in my sleep. I wear my socks to bed because I have not showered properly in a few months, and the barrier of crust imbedded in the fabric helps contain the stench of my feet.

I stand.

I have slept in many depressing, deathly places, but this one is the unrivaled worst. The floor, covered in muck and grime, is littered with used needles, bloody ties, candle nubs, burned match packs, empty lighters, crushed water bottles, and blackened cookers of all forms—spoons, cans, bottle caps, tins, and other dish-shaped metal scraps. In the center of the floor a refrigerator on its side functions as a "coffee table" for the junkies who reside here. There have been days when I wondered whether it might actually work when plugged into a live outlet, and others when I contemplated somehow transporting it to the junkyard in exchange for cash. But it's heavy, which means I would have to divide the work, as well as the proceeds, with another junkie, and that wasn't a possibility. Sharing is a concept foreign to addicts.

Piles of broken drywall, which once divided a corner of the garage into a bathroom, surround a toilet that hasn't worked in years. But junkies who sleep here use it anyway, and it is overflowing with urine and feces. Standing within a two-foot proximity will cause me to vomit from the sight and stench.

It is sick that the content of this garage represents the person I have become, and what is worse is that I have become accustomed to it.

As I stagger toward the door, each step intensifies the sinking feeling that today is going to be my day to die. But this idea does not deter my attention from the task at hand, the hustle for ten dollars, the price of a pill of Heroin, a small gel capsule full of Heroin powder that can either be snorted, or cooked then injected.

Where? How? I race through a mental catalog of scams. How can I get ten bucks through a minimum amount of effort? It comes to me: Mom.

Mom is a resource I tap only when all others have run dry, because I am ashamed for her to see me in this condition. But this morning I am desperate. I'll offer her one of my stock alibis such as, "I need to borrow lunch money until my next paycheck clears," or "I just got a job as a busboy, but I need to buy a new shirt for my first day of work." These fabrications never fail to extract money from her purse. This is not because she will believe them. Instead, Mom will hand over the cash just to rid herself of this twisted vision of the filthy junkie who is her beloved son.

The garage door. My opponent. When unlocked, tension from two industrial-strength springs allows it to glide open almost effortlessly. But with the handle in its present "locked" position, the springs act as a fulcrum securing the door to the ground. Yet, the door can be heaved open with a great amount of effort from a desperate junkie.

I grab the handle and begin to lift, straining. I am frail—weight: one hundred fifteen pounds, eat: two or three times a week. I can only call upon as little energy as one would imagine a person of this description might possess.

My legs begin to tremble, and I manage to raise the door almost three inches before it slips from my grasp and slams shut: *Bang!* As the sound resonates, I wince, fearful that the people who live above this garage might call the police if they discover that every night a junkie sneaks in and sleeps like an abandoned dog.

I step back, take another breath, and analyze the situation: I'm sick, I need ten dollars now, and goddamn it, this door is going to open! Again, I grab the door handle and pull. My knees are buckling, my arms shaking, my back is about to give out, but I am motivated by the thought of my next fix: inspiration! Finally I manage to create a three-foot slot, underneath which I cram my shoulder and apply it as a brace to hold the door up.

I look outside, to the far end of the two-story valley of red-brick row homes, where the mouth of the alley touches the street. There, the sunlight almost washes away the images of pedestrians, cars, stores. To most people, this is scenery. But to me, in these things I see opportunities to steal, lie, hustle, scam, and create victims. I swiftly slip out from under the door, letting it strike the concrete with a *slam!*

I hit the streets, motivated by my plan to scam my mom. Suddenly behind me, a familiar voice rings out. "Yo, Brandon! What's up?"

I turn toward my old friend Scott, who glances over my condition. "Yo, Scott," I say in a shaky voice.

Scott is four years clean. As teenagers, we rode skateboards together. As we grew up, we became addicts together. The difference is, he went clean, I got worse, and he became my NA sponsor. It is an indisputable fact that we could always depend on one another; however, in this case, an unspoken code of ethics dictates that I cannot ask for money. This is for my own good—we both know it, and we both know why: obviously, any funds extended to me would be spent on Dope.

Scott looks me up and down, scrutinizing my condition. "You don't look so hot, friend."

"Yeah . . ." What else is there to say?

Scott looks at me with pain in his eyes. "Look, Brandon, I have to get going to work. But here. Take this." As he speaks, he jots down his phone number on a scrap of paper. "I know I always give you my number when I see you, but I want you to know, the offer still stands. Anytime, anywhere, if you ever feel the desire to clean up, call me, and I promise I'll stop whatever I'm doing, come get you, and take you to rehab, okay?"

"Okay. Thanks, Scott."

"Promise you'll call me if you need a ride?"

"I promise. Thanks, Scott."

"No problem, Brandon. Good luck."

Scott's current occupation is real estate, and he is apparently doing very well at it. He steps into his white Mercedes and pulls away. I pocket the phone number, not because I intend to ever need a ride to rehab, but perhaps I can use Scott for something at a later time: a place to sleep, a change of clothes, a shower, whatever. A junkie always has to consider his resources. Okay. Mom's house. Here I go.

As I walk the six blocks to Mom's house, my pace quickens, faster and faster. Her house is now in sight. I see her car and I know she's there. Excitement shoots through me. I am trembling, as I can almost feel the sweet Heroin surging through my veins.

Then I see it. I stop dead in my tracks, as my hope of obtaining ten dollars vanishes. The front door of Mom's house opens, revealing my half brother David, a thirty-two-year-old lawyer who works for the State. He is the proverbial "brain" of our family. Behind David follows our older sister Lisa, who, at a young age, voluntarily assumed many of the parenting responsibilities necessary to raise me while Mom worked her way through medical school in order to provide a better life for us. With my sister are her children, my seven-year-old niece Cindy and eight-year-old nephew Nicholas. Cute little kids, innocent, not yet aware of the world's evil. The last to exit the house is my mom. In raising us, she had done her best, especially under the circumstances of being separated from our father.

As they gather in front of the house, I hide behind a tree, struck with jealousy, envy, and remorse as I watch them standing in a circle of laughter and joy.

I grit my teeth at a memory of my childhood, when I was seven and won my first skateboard sponsorship. I remember the pride I felt in watching my mother cry with joy, and in the celebration that followed, when brother, sister, and mother surprised me with a cake on which was written in icing, CONGRATULATIONS, BRANDON! and a little skateboard, sculpted in pieces of chocolate candy. . . .

Hidden behind the tree, I ask myself if I am willing to suffer the humiliation and looks of disgust from my family. I contemplate turning back, but my subservience to Heroin makes my decision to proceed, slowly and cautiously, reciting the lies that I will use to deceive those I love most.

David notices my approach and calls out, "Hey! Brandon!" At first, happiness is his instinctive response, but in recognizing the familiar signs of my condition, he then recollects the emotional pain I have caused him and my family: deceit, lies, and betrayal. At once, bitterness washes the pleasantness from his face.

Lisa takes notice of me, hides her pain for the sake of her children, and calls out, "Hey, Brandon!" I give her my biggest smile possible and rush to her in hopes that I might win sympathy from my brother and, ultimately, the money from my mother.

Lisa embraces me, and her nose retracts, wrinkling her face with disgust as she inhales my terrible stench. Breaking the hug from Lisa, from the corner of my eye I glance sideways to see if Lisa's kindness is evoking any positive sentiments from David. One look tells me it is not.

As I close in on my mother, I notice a sad disappointment in her eyes, which she quickly hides in order to make this occasion the least painful possible.

My mother asks, "So, Brandon, what are you doing here?"

I reply, "Oh, I had off work today so I figured I'd stop by to say hi." Lies: I haven't worked in years, unless you can refer to hustling for Dope as "work," and I certainly did not come here to say hi.

Mom hugs and kisses me, tolerating my stink because, although I am a junkie, the fact remains I am her son.

Mom says, "We're going to look at your sister's new house; do you want to come?"

In my head, I cry, "No! I just want to get my Dope money and get the fuck out of here!" I do not want to spoil this day for my family, to force them to look at me or smell my putrid stink. But, as sick as it sounds, enduring this discomfort is preferable to walking downtown, stealing, and risking arrest, so, I go against all better judgment and answer, "Lisa, that's awesome; you got a new house? I'd love to see it."

My brother glares at me as if to silently scream, *Get the fuck away from us!* but he keeps his composure for the sake of my mother, and because, ultimately, he does love me.

I turn to my niece and nephew. "Cindy! Nicholas! Come here, let me look at you!" I give them kisses on the head, telling them, "Mommy has been telling me how good you two are!"

A vivid memory fogs my perception as I recall that not so long ago these beautiful children once came with Lisa to visit me in a rehab center.

"What is this place? Why are you here?" they had asked.

I remember how naturally my answer, a lie, was issued forth. "This is where I work."

We load into my brother's van. I want to take a seat in the back, to spare them from my stench, but Mom insists I sit up front with David. He clearly does not want this, and I do not want it, but we do it anyway.

I know that before long, Mom will begin to carry on a casual conversation, a social skill I haven't practiced in years. At this point the only thing I am used to conversing about is where good Dope can be found and what makes of undercover cars the police drive. My mind races as if I had just snorted half a gram of coke, as the barrage of questions, and the subsequent lies, ensue:

MOM: So where are you living?

ME: Well, I'm living in Fell's Point; I have an apartment with a friend. It's pretty small, but it's okay.

MOM: Oh, that's nice. And where are you working?

ME: I'm bartending part-time at a couple places, filling in different shifts. Soon one of the places will hire me full-time, once someone quits . . .

MOM: Well that's good. . . .

Before the next question is asked, my brother, who has the opposite personality of my mother, interrupts. "So, Brandon, where did you sleep last night?"

A setup. This is a question that, if answered truthfully, will confirm that I have lied, and if answered untruthfully, will be met with a challenge. Whichever answer I give will be the wrong one. I answer anyway. "At a friend's house."

Here we go. "That's a fucking lie!" He points out the window, at a park bench. "You look like you slept on that bench last night! And you smell like a goddamn bum!" Correct on all three counts.

My mother screams, "David, don't!"

His voice raises a decibel. "Mom, stop protecting him! Let's get real! He smells like a fucking bum from the streets! If we have to spend the day with him, we're gonna have to stop at a hotel or somewhere to get him a shower! This is disgusting!"

My sister remains silent. My mother pleads, "Please, David, stop it!"

David insists. "I will not stop it! Enough is enough! I want him out of this van!"

"Fine!" I snap back. "You want me gone? No problem! You'll never see me again! I guarantee you that!" The van is traveling ten miles per hour as I fling open the door, stumble and fall on the asphalt, scramble to my feet, and run away in tears and disgrace.

Behind me I hear the sound of grinding gears as the vehicle is thrown into reverse before it comes to a full halt. David, now driving backward, is beside me, pleading, his anger for my addiction now overcome by his love. "Wait! Brandon, wait!"

"Fuck you!" the only response I could muster.

"Brandon! Look, I'm sorry! Get back in the van! Please?"

For a moment I consider this, only for the purposes of pitting my family's affections against their judgment in order to procure the money for my fix, but what little pride I have will not allow me to do so.

As they drive away, I turn and examine this mess I've caused. My mother is apologizing for my brother. My sister is crying, hiding her face in her hands. And a heartbreaking vision engraves itself into my memory: my little niece and nephew, turned around in their seats like puppy dogs, with tears running down their faces, waving good-bye. And somehow, through their sobs, I could hear one of them call out, "Grandmom, please, just give him the money . . ."

Hearing this, I realize I have not even asked my mother for the money yet, and I arrive at a conclusion horrible to consider: that, in my niece's and nephew's limited experiences on this earth, although they could not yet comprehend my addiction, their knowledge of what follows my visits includes an inevitable consequence: I ask my mother for money.

As I walk toward the city in search of the Heroin money, I consider the lesson that had been inflicted on my niece and nephew: In trust, they will find lies. In relationships, they will experience manipulation. In love, they will encounter pain. And this is what they would forever remember, that I, their mother's half brother, Uncle Brandon, had taught them about life.

chapter two
A Prayer Answered

I advance my mental Rolodex of hustles until I turn up the address of a CD shop from which I might liberate several albums. When I arrive, I am met by a large black security guard who shakes his head as if to say, "Do yourself a favor and keep walking." To protest would be a waste of time and energy. My intent is obvious; I harbor no resentments and accept reality: people perceive me as another junkie trying to get over. I turn away, becoming increasingly ill, contemplating my next option: Kmart.

A Junkie's Guide for Shoplifting at Kmart:

- Most Kmart employees are not paid enough to exert the energy to spot shoplifters.
- Undercovers are the effective deterrent to the shoplifter.
- An increased number of shoppers create distractions for undercovers, hence opportunities for the shoplifter, but, an increased number of shoppers also indicates an increased number of undercovers.
- Undercovers can be easily spotted, as they are the only shoppers unaccompanied by nagging children and/or arguing

spouses, and they are among the few in the store who demonstrate acceptable hygiene practices.

I arrive at the Electronics department, and to my disheartenment, I see several undercovers detaining a white woman and a black man, emptying the contents from the suspects' handbag and pockets on a counter. Immediately I turn and exit, hearing behind me the *click-click-click* of handcuffs as they close around the wrists of the shoplifters. Goddamn it, can today get any worse?

I make my way toward the Baltimore Inner Harbor, or what money-scrounging junkies refer to as "the tourist area." I spot a tour group of about twenty people, and for my own amusement, I alter the tour guide's speech in my mind. "Welcome to Baltimore's Inner Harbor, one of the most prominent seaports in the United States since the 1700s. . . . Here, the National Aquarium is the city's leading attraction and is home to more than ten thousand specimens. . . . Over here, students and scientists frequent the Maryland Science Center. . . . For a grand view of the city, one might visit the observatory in the Baltimore World Trade Center, which is the world's tallest even-sided, pentagon-shaped building. . . . And finally, this is Brandon Novak, a once-prominent skateboarder who senselessly threw away his career because he became addicted to heroin. You might note that he is now a sick junkie with a disgusting presence and a putrid stench, and he is planning to ruin the good time of all the tourists in the vicinity by begging and badgering them for money." The tourists then click photos of me, which will later be placed in albums next to landmark photos of Fort McHenry, the USS *Constellation*, and the grave of Edgar Allan Poe . . .

Surely, if I ask enough tourists for a dollar, and one out of ten pays, then, one hundred questions later, I will have my ten bucks,

I think. But in my optimism, what I failed to take into consideration is that I look and smell so horrible, no one will even stop long enough for me to ask them for money. As time passes and my desperation increases, my approach changes:

- First, *delicate diplomacy:* "Excuse me, sir, could you please spare some change so that I might get something to eat?"
- Then *assertiveness:* "Hi, look, I hate to bother you, but I really need a dollar and sixty cents to catch the bus. Can you spare two bucks?"
- Finally, *aggressiveness:* "Hey, man, I'm in a bad way! Give me five bucks?!"

Hours later, nothing, not one red cent, just a cigarette given to me by a twelve-year-old girl who would brag to her friends that she "felt cool" because she had talked to a "squatter."

The bell in the tower above a neighboring church rings out, and as I count the chimes, I consider that the bell was probably manufactured to toll for the glory of God in the late 1800s. Now, over one hundred years later, I feel as if it had been constructed for the single purpose of increasing my frustration with each ring . . . *Dong. Dong. Dong. Dong. Dong.*

"Five o'clock?! Already?! Fuck!" In a few short hours, the Dope dealers will start to pack up shop, forcing me to spend the night in that horrible garage, in a state of sobriety and complete awareness.

My brain is pounding as I again race through an index of scams and hustles for a solution. . . . Then I see it, literally right in front of my face.

I am sitting on a corner adjacent to an antiques store, and on the sidewalk, on display, is an array of handmade, sheet-iron furniture. . . . It's lightweight, expensive-looking, and most important, unguarded by the employees who are inside the store preparing to close for the day.

I sit and finish my smoke in careful analysis, noting the frequency of pedestrians passing by and customers walking in and out of the store. By the time I finish my smoke, I am able to conclude that, if I exercise a reasonable amount of caution, this might go smoothly.

I cross the street and walk past the furniture, mimicking the mannerisms of an interested customer. I glance at the price tags, scoping out the items that might yield the maximum profit for minimal effort. I spot them: an end table worth four hundred dollars and a small statue worth two hundred. Perfect!

I continue to the corner and give one final look around. I take a deep breath and remind myself that, being too sick to go to jail, I cannot afford to *not* do this correctly.

Waiting for the moment when conditions will allow me to walk away with the merchandise in a nonchalant manner, I see an opportunity arise. A group of suit-and-tie-wearing men pass, and I follow closely behind them, trying to appear to be one of the men's younger brother. But I am cautious not to follow *too* close, because I want to avoid being noticed by the businessmen. As I follow, I am struck with the irony that today I have been through more stress than the combined sum of this entire group of office-working nine-to-fivers.

Okay, here I go; my eyes are locked on my target, the four-hundred-dollar table. I draw closer, picking up speed, and in one smooth motion I scoop up the table and swiftly walk away, with a prayer that I will not hear a voice screaming for me to come back.

I turn the corner, and as it is my nature to test the boundaries of risk, I place the table on the ground, then return to the sidewalk display, grab the two-hundred-dollar statue, again turn the corner to my awaiting table, scoop it up, and haul ass!

Blocks and blocks later, I find myself asking anyone and everyone in my path if they would be interested in the purchase of this furniture. Why would they, especially from me?

Again, I hear the bell from the neighboring church. I pause and count the chimes . . . six o'clock?! That leaves me only one hour until the closing time of the antiques store that pays at least ten percent of the tag value on stolen goods. By the final stroke of the bell, I am running at full speed down the street with the furniture.

Set within the hand-carved molding of the antiques store's door is a pane of glass, blurred with age, through which can be seen the standard orange-and-black sign that reads, in large capital letters which seem to intensify its implication: CLOSED. Closed?! Hopeful that the owner might have forgotten to flip the sign to read: OPEN, which to my knowledge he has never done, I turn the door handle. Locked. And then I see it, a note in shaky handwriting taped to the door. "Closed early due to a family emergency."

I collapse to the ground, laughing and crying all at once, prepared to sit and rot away in my own self-induced filth and smell, exhausted and defeated. Hopeless. And suddenly, as if God had heard a prayer and reached in to grant me the favor, the sound of a car horn captures my attention. *Beep!* I turn, seeing a brand-new cherry-red Cadillac Seville. A voice from within calls out, "Hey kid, what are you doing with that furniture?" In a split second, my hope is restored.

I reply, "It's for sale, you interested?" The man steps out of the car; I carefully analyze him from head to toe. Five-six, two hundred and forty pounds, slightly balding with hair freshly cut and parted to the side. Pressed charcoal-gray pin-striped suit. On his right pinky is a gold ring studded with diamonds, on his left hand a wedding band. Are those alligator-skin shoes?

This guy definitely is not a cop; maybe he's a lawyer or a character involved in some kind of shady business. Whatever the case, I am fairly certain that I can assume two things: one, this man is married, and two, he has money.

"That furniture would go great in my summer house at the beach. What's the price?"

"Give me forty bucks and it's yours," I tell him.

As he steps closer, I realize he is closely evaluating me just as I had evaluated him. He tells me, "I like the furniture, all right, and I have forty bucks to spend, but I really want to spend it on something else. . . ."

I know exactly what that "something else" is. Not far from this neighborhood, there is a strip where young boys stand on the corner and let old men pick them up for quick cash. I used to pass that strip on my way to the Dope shop, and wonder, How the hell could they let things get *that* bad?! But now, today, this very second, I have come to understand them. And if how *I* feel right now is an indication of how *they* usually feel, then God help them, and forgive me for judging them.

"How about it?" the man says. The weight of the moment grows heavier. Reality sets in. I am sick, broke, and the Dope shops are rapidly closing for the night.

It hits me. This drug is so powerful that I am going to make the decision to break the only moral code I have stood by through seven years of addiction.

Can you even imagine being a twenty-five-year-old junkie, and, and in the blink of an eye, letting a fifty-year-old married man suck your dick while you are completely sober, with no drugs or alcohol in your system to numb the feeling? Well, I am about to tell you *exactly* what it is like.

chapter three
The Last Night
of Using

The man stares at me, still waiting for a response. "Well? You interested?"

In a flash, I am struck with several past-tense reflections: I *was* once a skateboarder with a promising career; I *had been* engaged to the most beautiful girl; I *did* live in a nice home with a mother who loved me. And now, in the present tense: I *am* selling my body to a middle-aged married man. This is what I have become.

These thoughts are interrupted by two words ringing clearly in my head: Scott! Rehab!

A conviction reveals itself: Tomorrow, I will call Scott and go to rehab. . . . A dilemma arises: Tonight, I need a fix . . .

I am brought back to reality by this disgusting man's voice: "This is your last chance, kid." This dirty old fuck is getting frustrated that I am stalling on letting him buy my body. And so, I make my decision: Tomorrow, I need to end this. But right now, I'm sick, I need Heroin, and I will sell myself.

I go completely blank, cold.

I drop the two pieces of furniture that seemed so valuable only a moment ago and walk directly to the passenger side of the car. The man opens the door for me, I sit, and he slams the door in my face, shutting me in.

Within a minute, the car is in motion. Billy Joel's "Piano Man" plays on the stereo. Besides this morning's debacle in my brother's van, it has been months since I have ridden in a car, and, with the sounds of the outside world muffled, for a few moments I actually find the experience peaceful, warm, comfortable. Suddenly I snap out of it, now fully comprehending the situation, as the time draws near that my obligation to this man must be fulfilled.

He looks at me, sensing that something is awkward, difficult, wrong, and asks, "You all right, kid?" I just sit, numb, staring forward, about to allow this old fuck to take complete control of everything. Take control of me. I want no part of this, yet I have to go through with it. I'm no longer an individual. I am a slave to this man and my addiction.

This old fuck is no stranger to the prostitution game. Within only a few minutes, we are parked in a shadowed, desolate lot next to the Chesapeake Bay. As I stare into the water's rippling reflections, I consider that, under a different set of circumstances, this might be an all-time perfect make-out spot for a guy and his girlfriend. Yet, as fate would have it, I find myself here with a middle-aged, overweight, married man who is about to do with me exactly as he would desire. What did I get myself into?

He turns the key, shutting off the engine. He presses the UN-LOCK button on his seat belt. *Click.* His bloated body sways slightly to the left, and he reaches under himself to produce his wallet, in a motion that resembles a fat man wiping his ass. I somehow smell it.

He flips through the bills, liberates two twenties, and slides them in my sweatshirt pocket. I stare into the river. I feel his meaty hand fall on my knee in a deliberate manner, as a man might console a female friend who is under emotional distress, with the intent of coercing her into his sexual favor. He announces, in a patronizing tone, "See, kid, I told you I wouldn't do you wrong," and, as sick as it sounds, the forty dollars succeeds in making what is about to happen almost bearable.

Again, the voice in my head rings loudly. *Tomorrow I'm calling Scott and going to rehab!* The man's restless hand slides down to my belt: a shoestring wrapped tightly through the loops of my jeans, which doubles in purpose as a tie for constricting the blood flow within my vein prior to shooting up.

I twitch as his hand makes contact with my torso.

He licks his lips and says, "Just relax, it will be done before you know it." God, I hope he is not lying. He pulls loose the shoestring / belt / arm-tie, then undoes my button. No need to unzip my fly, it is broken.

"It," whatever "it" might be, is about to happen. I know it, he knows it, and I stay focused: there are forty bucks in my pocket. Dope.

My eyes are closed and, no matter how hard I try to ignore it, I feel a warm wet mouth on the head of my dick and bristle of five-o'clock shadow around the lips of the perpetrator. The thought of Dope is now not enough to distract my consciousness. Instead, I imagine a beautiful woman performing this act. He continues to penetrate his mouth with my dick, which, to my surprise, is getting hard. I do not understand how or why, but it is.

The man and I are of complete opposite sentiment: I detest every moment of this, every millisecond; I resent this very time and place in the universe, and he could not be happier. He is, in fact, moaning with delight, his entire body in a full continuous motion, pacified. Does my apparent discomfort excite him? And, I wonder, exactly *how* this man can stand the stench of me!

The dashboard clock reads 9:37. Panic sets in! My situation has now become more desperate. You see, by 10:00 P.M., the squad cars start patrolling the streets, the reputable dealers pack up shop and go home, and the low-life druggies come out. There are a few legitimate all-night shops, but they do not serve white people. The later it gets, the harder it is to get Dope, and time is running out.

I am calculating how long it is going take to finish my business with this sick fuck, and for him to drop me off exactly where I need to go. If I hurry, I can make it. I push his head off my dick and pretend to cum on the inside of my shirt. For the first time, I look at his face, which has a sick grimace of complete satisfaction. I am sure that my expression conveys disgust and demoralization as I tie my shoestring belt.

The sick fuck asks, "Where do you want to get dropped off?"

"Patterson Park and Fayette Street." We drive away.

It is now 10:05 P.M. and we are nearing my destination. With each passing block my anticipation increases, the excitement pumps my endorphins and adrenaline, and in some strange way the chemicals satisfy the sharp pain brought on by the appetite of my addiction. It's as if my vein somehow understands that I am bringing it closer to a fix, and in appreciation, is granting me temporary alleviation.

The sick fuck pulls the car to our destination, hits the UNLOCK button, and asks, "Can I see you again?"

Now that I have what I need—the cash—my confidence has returned. I open the door and before I step out, I look him in the eyes and yell, "Fuck you, you sick fuck! Why don't you go home and tell your wife what you just did?!" I slam the car door and retreat into the darkness.

I have already decided how I am going to spend the forty dollars. In my head is inscribed a forty-dollar version of a junkie's grocery list, which reads: three dimes of Dope, one nickel of coke, and a pack of smokes. But now I am faced with a new dilemma: I see no reputable dealers.

The street, illuminated by flickering-yellow sparsely placed streetlights, is scattered with darkly dressed thugs. One approaches and follows close behind me, with his jaw close to my ear, loudly whispering in repetitive monotone, "Blow-blow-blow-blow-blow!"

Meanwhile, two bearded hoods pass me on either side, each brushing against one of my arms. I know they are contemplating jumping me, but each one waits for the other to act first, and neither does, so I press on.

I pass another man, even filthier than me, whose breath is so awful, whose armpits so pungent, I cannot describe the magnitude of their stink. "Yo, snort! Snort! Snort, man, snort! Back here, man! *Git back here!*" His tone is angry, intimidating. I hear him spit in my direction, but I hear nothing land on the ground. Is it on my back?

On the next block, I see a small midnight Dope shop. They holler to me, "Boy and girl! Boy and girl!", slang which translates, "Dope and Coke! Dope and Coke!" At this point this offer looks as good as any I might get, and afraid it might be my last, I cross the street and make a beeline toward the pushers.

"Three boys and one girl," I request. One guy steps up, and I give him forty; he returns ten in change and three gel caps. A second guy steps up, and I hand him the ten; he hands me one glass vial and a five in change. As I turn and walk, I review my day: I have destroyed what remained of the relationship I had with my family; I have demoralized myself and sold my body to a married man. Now that I have my drugs, however, none of that matters.

Finally, in a run-down convenience store, while waiting in line to buy my smokes from a Korean man behind bulletproof Plexiglas, as the rush of the score subsides, I come to a realization. *Wait a minute. . . . I didn't know those thugs who sold me the Dope. . . . Maybe there's a chance I got burned.*

While still in line, without concealing my actions, I pull the vial from my pocket, remove the red cap, touch my finger to the powder, and taste. To my immediate distress, I do not experience the numb feeling that should be induced by coke. My defenses kick in, and I convince myself that I did not have enough on my finger. I try again, this time placing a greater quantity of the powder to my tongue . . . fake.

Okay, they burned me on the coke, but the Dope, I'm sure, must be real . . . I silently rationalize. After all, coke is like the dessert at the end of the meal. But the Dope, the main course, the sustenance, I absolutely cannot do without!

"Next!" The Korean cashier interrupts, his voice muffled through the small holes in the half-inch bulletproof Plexiglas. I turn and march out the door, unable to spend another cent until I know for sure if this Dope is real.

I break open a pill; the color looks off. But I rationalize that the hue of the streetlight may be playing tricks on my vision. I touch a bit of it to my tongue. It leaves no bitter taste, as does Heroin. . . . And as I taste and examine this powder again, and again, I am unable to deny that this substance has a flavor and texture like chalk. . . . It's fucking drywall! Crumbling dust, pinched from a filthy floor of one of these decaying buildings!

I cling to the hope that the other two pills may be real. I pull the second one out, taste it. Drywall.

Before I taste the last pill, I pray to the Lord to grant me one request. "Please, God, hear my prayer. I have heard your call, and I am abiding by it! Tomorrow I am going to rehab, and finally I am going to sort out this mess that is my life! But tonight I *need* one last fix! Lord, if you exist, if you will ever answer one single prayer in my life, let it be now! I swear, I will never ask you for anything again, if you just grant me this one wish. And so I ask, *"Please let this pill contain dope!"*

Obviously, drywall.

My body goes limp as the pills fall to the ground. This is morbid. After this whole day of dreadful events, I just got ripped off.

I make my way up the street to another group of thugs who have the reputation of selling the worst Dope in town. This Dope is absolute garbage, but at least I know it is real. Why didn't I just buy from these guys in the first place?

I purchase my pill and retreat to the abandoned garage I call home. After I sit on my bed of three moldy sofa cushions, I cook up my shot, tie my shoestring / belt over my arm, find a vein, and inject the needle.

As I watch my blood squirt into the barrel of the syringe, I rest with the satisfaction that my goal has been accomplished.

chapter four
The Phone Call

Morning.

My eyes open.

Here in the abandoned garage, several junkies are with me preparing their morning fix like so many people cook bacon and eggs.

As I gain consciousness, I deceive myself that the prior day's events might have been nothing more than a nightmare through which there was one glimmer of hope: Scott's offer to be my guide to rehab.

I stand, slip on my sweatshirt / pillow, glide my shoes over my yellowed-crusty socks, approach the garage door, then grasp the handle and lift. But I can hoist it only a few inches. It slips and *slams* shut, followed by hushed screams from the other junkies, paranoid that someone living upstairs might hear the disturbance and call the police.

JUNKIE #1: Shut-da-fuck-up, man! What's you thinkin?!

JUNKIE #2: Keep-it-cool! Damn, you-a-stupid-muthafucka!

JUNKIE #3: Chill-chill-chill-chill!

I take a good, hard look at the junkies, who are like me. My eyes focus on this image of three men squatted on a floor, huddled around a spoon, arguing about which one deserves more Heroin in their needle than the rest:

JUNKIE #1: Back off wit dat! This is my game! I got the score!

JUNKIE #2: Naw, naw, naw, it ain't like dat, it ain't like dat! It came from mah boy! I was da hookup!

JUNKIE #3: All-yall, better listen! I go first! I brought home all day yesterday! I brought home all day yesterday!

A silent voice: "Fuck it, Brandon! On the other side of this door is a new existence, if you can make it to a pay phone! You have no strength, no muscles, and you forgot to eat yesterday, but it doesn't matter. All you have to do is fucking grab the goddamn garage door and pull!" I turn, grit my teeth, yank with every ounce of strength, finally elevating the door just high enough to squeeze out. Then, once on the outside, I release my grip in one final gesture of defiance of a lifestyle that once was. The door, pulled by the tension from its springs, shoots downward and delivers a *slam* as it strikes the ground, provoking low-spoken shouts from the junkies within:

JUNKIE #1: Chill, dumbfuck!

JUNKIE #2: I'll kick yo' ass, white boy!

JUNKIE #3: He does it again, I'll slap him upside the head!

To the door, I give "the finger." *Fuck you all!*

I advance on foot to the 7-Eleven under the eye-piercing sunshine. I stop to vomit, but there is nothing in my stomach to throw up except bile and a bit of blood. I stumble away dizzy, then stagger into what feels like several people. When the world steadies itself, I find myself face to face with a mother and her two sons staring with a look of repulsion. The mother grabs her children and swiftly crosses the street to get away from me. My initial thought is, Why are they running?! I'm not *that* bad! As I lift my head to wipe the vomit from my chin, in the reflection of a car window I glimpse the image of someone my approximate age. *Wait, who am I seeing here? Is this me?!*

For the past half year, I have gone to great lengths to avoid my own reflection. I have turned my head when passing clean storefront windows, crossed streets to avoid reflective objects of every sort, and, when using a mirror-mounted bathroom sink, fixed my line of vision to the drain. In this way, I could escape what I had become. And so, I have avoided this very situation for six months. But now, finally, I am facing "it"—myself: matted, oily hair, chunks of dandruff on my shoulders, lines of white on my face where dripping beads of sweat have acted as a solvent to the layer of dirt revealing strips of my pale, sickly skin. Clothes: absolutely filthy.

Now standing, I turn my attention back to the mother and children: *Why wouldn't a mother take her children across the street to get away from me?*

In the distance, mounted to the wall of the 7-Eleven, is a pay phone, surrounded by a dozen Mexicans waiting for a truck to pick them up for work. *Man, even illegal immigrants are better off than me.*

My last fifty cents. I pump in the quarters.

The phone number. I dig through my pockets, then a scrap falls to the ground on which is written "Scott." A sense of calmness and peace washes over me.

I dial and allow the phone to ring three times then disconnect the call, fearing that Scott's answering machine will interrupt and cause the phone to swallow my coins.

God, please let him answer. I don't want to end up back at the garage, arguing with junkies over ten ccs on a hypodermic needle.

I reinsert the coins and dial. Three rings and I hang up, and again I retrieve my fifty cents from the coin return.

As each call goes unanswered, so does my prayer. Slowly, a junkie's defenses kick in, and I explore the possibility that perhaps this is not meant to be. . . . Okay! I'll call one more time. If no answer, I go back to my junkie lifestyle, my mindless existence. It is a horrible life, but nevertheless familiar, and might actually be easier than facing sobriety, anyway, I rationalize.

And so, this pay phone has turned into somewhat of a slot machine. Not unlike a desperate gambler clinging to the astronomical chance that he might strike the jackpot, allowing him to win back the fortune he has squandered, I insert my last coins. *Dial.* The phone rings once, twice, three times. Then, at the far edge of the third ring, I hear it, fate has stepped in: a *click,* followed by Scott's voice. "Yo, who is this?"

"It's Brandon." A sense of confusion produces a profuse heat within my neck and swells my throat with pure emotion. Choking.

"Oh, hey man, how are you?" Scott asks.

I force out the words in between deep sobs, fighting the painful contortions in my throat, as years of suppressed emotions take vengeance. "I'm . . . not . . . too . . . good, brother . . . I . . . need . . . help! . . . Please . . . help me . . ."

Urgency in Scott's voice. "Where are you?"

I am unable to speak, convulsing, wiping away the sheets of falling tears.

Scott demands, "Brandon, *where are you?!*"

Finally, "The . . . Seven . . . Eleven . . . on . . . Broadway. . . ."

"Wait there! Let me put some clothes on and I'll be there in ten! Brandon, are you there?!"

"Yes . . . Scott."

"I love you."

I reply, "I . . . love-you-too . . ."

I hang up the phone, collapse into a squatted fetal position, and take a deep breath. Shaking. "Hey, Brandon!" I turn to my left: Alexia. She asks, "What's going on?"

I shut off the emotion and collect my thoughts. Alexia plucks two smokes from her purse, hands me one, lights it. I inhale and answer her with honesty. "I'm getting ready to go to rehab." Laughter emanates from her lips, like wind chimes in the breeze. Laughing is the initial reaction we junkies have when another makes known their intention of rehabilitation. This response is not meant to discourage another human's aspirations. The laugh is a default mechanism that expresses the absurdity of man's innate will to heal, which to the junkie is as incomprehensible as the concept of infinity.

When Alexia is finished laughing, she expresses her sympathy toward my condition. "Look, Brand, I know how you feel. Tell you what, I'm on my way to turn a trick. I'll be back in about an hour. When I'm done, I'll split a pill with you, okay, sweetie?"

"Where were you yesterday?!" I chuckle through my shaking lips, still struggling to hold back a wave of emotion. This is the ultimate test, but somehow I find the strength to tell her, "No thanks, Alexia. Enough is enough."

"Okay, if that's the way you want it, Brandon. Are you sure? You look like you need it."

I shake my head. "No."

Alexia shrugs. "Okay, well, I'll see you around, I guess. . . ." Alexia turns and walks away. When she reaches the corner, she

stops and looks at me, lifting her eyebrow, extending one final opportunity to accept her offer. Again I shake my head with a silent,
"no," and take a drag from my cigarette. Alexia winks her eye,
blowing me a kiss. I know her love for me is as sincere as it could
possibly be in a junkie's world.

Alexia is a twenty-six-year-old blond-haired, blue-eyed girl
from the neighborhood. She has a walk that just sways. There is
still innocence in her eyes, despite the fact that she is a junkie. She,
like me, knows better and comes from better, but once again, this
Drug took something so beautiful from this world. . . . Alexia was
nearly perfect, but Heroin exposed all her flaws and intensified
them until only they remained.

This girl is more than just a hooker I know, more than an old
street-running partner. She was my high school sweetheart, my
best friend, my first true love, and my fiancée. At one point, she
was my everything.

chapter five
The Story of Alexia

I met Alexia almost ten years ago. I was skating with a few friends, trying to varial heelflip nine stairs, paying more attention to the trick than to the pedestrians. Suddenly, someone I had not seen a moment before was underneath me and the board as we soared through the air. I bailed on the trick, tumbling over myself onto the concrete. Now, usually when you almost kill someone with a skateboard, at the very least an argument ensues. However, I was now lying beneath a beautiful blonde with opal-blue eyes and tan skin, who seemed to be more concerned for my well-being than her own.

"Are you okay?!" she asked with her hand over her mouth.

"Yeah, I'm fine," I lied. I thought for sure my knee was broken.

"I'm so sorry; I didn't see you coming," she told me as she picked up my skateboard and handed it to me.

Why the hell is she apologizing to *me?!* It was totally my fault! I could have seriously hurt this girl! I thought.

As my friends skated on to the next spot, I stayed and talked to this girl, Alexia. In the hours that followed, I came to understand several things about her.

Alexia was new to Baltimore, its freezing winters, the confinement of narrow low-roofed living spaces, the two-hundred-year-old red-brick row-homes. She was from L.A. and having trouble adjusting.

Alexia was vulnerable. An undeniably beautiful, eleventh-grade honor-roll student who played on the basketball team of a prominent private school, Alexia had scouts interested in her and scholarship deals on the table. Alexia's allure, athletic abilities, and intelligence filled the other girls in her school with envy and vindictiveness. Consequently, Alexia was in most respects ignored and excluded, and was left feeling very alone.

Alexia had no mother and no one to share her feelings with. Her father, a union sheet-metal worker, did the best he could in his own way.

I found myself entranced by this girl Alexia, and I had to have her. So, I tried for her, and before I knew it, she was mine and we were in love.

We shared several months of passion and affection in its purest form. Then one weekend my mother went out of town, and in my mother's bed I lost my virginity to the first love of my life, and Alexia had chosen me as the first person to give herself to. I was in love with a girl with golden hair and a pair of blue eyes you could get lost in.

Then the party began. . . .

Social Drinking

I began to cut school, often. So did Alexia. Her grades suffered, but not by much, at first.

Overdrinking

Alexia's father began to notice changes in her social life. She was no longer reading for recreation. Now she was going with me to parties. Coming home late. One night she did not come home at all, claiming she had slept over at a friend's house. Alexia's father tried grounding her, but the punishment made her more rebellious.

Drug Use

Until Alexia met me, she had never once gotten high, and neither one of us had ever considered the possibility of using Heroin. We smoked pot here and there, and popped pills when they were supplied by my friends. Later, when I became a Dope user, she would drive me to score. After a few months, she started asking questions about this mysterious drug. "What does it make you feel like? What's the attraction? How good could it possibly be?" Perhaps she felt excluded, jealous of the relationship Heroin and I shared. I always discouraged her curiosity, threatening that if she even thought of trying it, I would break off the relationship. Then one day, she asked to snort a bit of it, just to find out what it was like. That is all it took, and within a few weeks she was pulled into my sick world.

In time, the number of days Alexia had not attended school began to outnumber the days she attended. Alexia's grades dropped to just above passing. Her adviser warned that, if she did not soon make an effort to improve her performance, she would be kicked off the basketball team. Her father finally became strict with her, but he was far too late.

Drug Abuse

Within one year, our once-bright futures transformed into faint, distant memories. Alexia's grades were failing, she had quit the basketball team, and her scholarship deals were revoked. And soon, the Drug became bigger than the both of us.

Addiction

No junkie has ever made the decision to become an addict. Addiction is a state of progression. It develops gradually and expands in geometric proportions until it finally consumes the user.

When I think of Alexia, my mind takes me to that one perfect day when our lives still made sense, when we still had families who cared, when we still had each other's love and respect, and when all these things suddenly became meaningless.

It was a perfect sunny Sunday afternoon at Druid Hill Park. Every storybook-like element seemed to exist for the benefit of our romance: a cloudless sky, chirping birds, leaves swaying back and forth on a gentle breeze.

I looked over at my precious Alexia as we walked together, bound by clutching hands. Alexia was swinging a picnic basket she had packed. I had brought the blanket and the bag of Dope. What an afternoon we had, high as kites, on top of the world, lying blissfully under the afternoon sky.

Later . . .

As my eyes open, an excruciating pain shoots like an electrical impulse through my skull, down my spine, and into my hands and feet. My eyes slowly make their way around as I take in the industrial-grade fluorescent light fixtures, the institutional-floral-patterned wallpaper, the stainless steel bed . . . the details that reveal my current setting, a hospital.

I glance to my side and see Alexia sitting in a chair. This girl, who, such a short time ago was so vibrant, so delightful, now looks worn down, miserable, depressed.

My mind is bombarded with the natural progression of questions inevitably asked by those in my current position. What's wrong with me? How long have I been unconscious? Am I paralyzed?

And so, I ask Alexia, "What happened?!"

She replies, "You were driving home from Druid Park and I fell asleep, and I guess you blacked out. . . . We hit a tree and your head went through the windshield. They had to put twelve metal staples into your head."

I glance at the bedside table to see a clear plastic bag containing my clothing, caked with dried blood. Alexia continues. "The doctors said the only reason you survived is because you were so high that your body just went completely limp at the time of impact. You're fine, other than that footwide gash in your head. I somehow managed to make it through the accident okay. There's not a scratch on me."

Any other person would now thank God to be alive, take inventory of himself, and make amends to lead a virtuous existence. Not me, though. I ask, "Do we have any Dope left?"

"No," Alexia replies in a desperate tone. "But we need to get some! I'm getting sick."

"Well, do we have any cash?" I ask.

"No!" she cries, and I come to understand that she is more upset at this fact than about my condition. I don't mind. I feel the same way. In fact, I am glad that she shares my sentiment, because two motivated junkies are twice as likely to score as one.

"Who can we call?" she asks.

Think. I need a special individual with specific character traits: One, he must be a Dope fiend who can sympathize with my current disposition. Two, he must be willing to spot me a bag. And three, he must have a car and be motivated to deliver the Dope to the hospital. These are three qualities which few Dope fiends hold. *Think!*

"Bill Carson!" I exclaim. Bill is a functioning drug addict. He owns a construction business and still manages to shoot Dope part-time. "He'll definitely do it because I've hooked him up in the past! He owes me one!"

I grab the phone next to my bed . . . *goddamn it!* A sharp sensation like a chain saw cutting into my skull blasts through my nervous system! I was so excited about the Dope that I completely forgot about my head wound and apparently had pressed the phone against it! I look at Alexia, who winces as she imagines my pain. "Jesus, take it easy, Brandon!"

"No shit!" I snap. It takes a few seconds for me to recuperate.

Alexia takes the phone. "Here, I'll call. I'll set it up and make it seem way worse than it is. I'll get his worry level up and pass the phone to you, then you ask him for the Dope."

That's my girl, always thinking! I dial . . .

Soon, she has Bill on the phone, and her performance is as flawless as any Academy Award–winning performance in the history of motion pictures: "Hello, Bill? This is Alexia . . . Brandon Novak's girlfriend. . . . Well, Brandon's . . . had a bad car accident. . . . Yes, he's alive, but it was very close. I'm so upset . . ." Alexia breaks down in tears that seem so real that, for a moment, even *I* am fooled into thinking they are for her pity of my condition rather than for her want of Dope. She feigns the inability to continue the conversation, hands me the phone, smiles and shoots me a wink, which I return with a "thumbs up."

I make my voice sound as pathetic as possible. "Hello? . . . Is this Bill . . . ?"

"Yeah, Brand, it's me, Bill! Are you okay?!" From the urgency in his voice, I can tell that he is now properly motivated to bring us some Dope, thanks to Alexia! I love this girl!

"Well, I could be worse, I guess, I'm still alive. . . . But, I'm so sick . . . real sick. . . . Do you think you could bring me something? You know what I mean?"

"Yeah, buddy, I got you. Where are you?" he commits.

I tell him the hospital and room number.

"No problem. I'll be there; okay, Brandon?"

"Thank you so much, Bill. I owe you big time."

"Sure, buddy, just hang in there."

I hang up the phone, and we give each other a high five, as if we had actually made an accomplishment worth noting. Now the countdown begins . . .

One hour and a half later, Alexia sits glaring at me. She is irritable, short tempered. I am filled with anger and hate, and can't even stand to look at her. After all, we are sick and have nothing to focus our negative energy on but each other. Soon, I find myself concentrating on *not* looking at the clock, *not* hating Alexia, *not* thinking about the Dope, trying to shut out everything until the time when I will have the ability to transform this world into one worth living in, an existence in which I am high.

The situation changes as Bill walks into the room. Alexia and I perk up, our moods altered, and we are now two of the happiest, most delightful junkies in the world.

Bill hugs Alexia as he looks over my condition. "Man, buddy, you got fucked up. I bet you could use a blast!" Then, he examines my IV and says, "Man, that's a junkie's dream."

"What to you mean?" I ask.

"This intravenous tube is injected right into your bloodstream. I know junkies that would trade their right arm to have a permanent IV stuck into their left one. Too bad you don't shoot this shit 'cause you already got a main line going right into your vein," Bill explains.

Until this time, I had never shot Dope. I was only snorting. Piercing my vein with a needle to get high had never even crossed my mind. But since the needle was already in my arm, I figured, "What's the big deal? Let me try shooting it."

Bill smiles as he pulls out his bag of Dope. "Okay then." He holds up a brand-new needle. "The doctor is in!"

Three minutes later, Alexia stands guard in the hallway, keeping a lookout for hospital staff. Meanwhile, in the room, I watch as Bill pours a few drops of water onto a spoon, adds a few pinches of raw Dope. He holds a lighter flame under the spoon, bringing the mixture to a boil, and places a small piece of cotton in the center of the brew, which absorbs the liquid and filters out the impurities. He then touches the needle to the spoon and pulls up on the plunger, filling the barrel, then injects the needle directly into the feeding valve of the IV tube. "There you go; enjoy."

Several seconds later I am in the midst of the most intense high I have ever experienced in my life. Words cannot describe this feeling. From this point on, I would be committed to the needle.

When I regain consciousness, I am in the passenger seat of my mother's Ford Escort. Alexia is in the back. My skull is aching, pounding with every pump of blood that surges through my head wound. As we pull up in front of Alexia's house to drop her off, Alexia gives me a kiss and tells me, "I love you, baby. I'll call you later." Obviously, Bill was kind enough to get her high, too; I could tell by her smile. "Bye, Ms. Pat," she tells my mom. "If you need anything, give me a call."

As Alexia exits the car, her dad storms out of her house followed by three big friends, all furious. Alexia's father, with a beet-red face and veins bulging from his neck and forehead, points to me as he crosses the lawn. "You! You fucking drug addict! Don't ever step foot near my daughter again!" No doubt this man has been sitting in the house for hours awaiting my arrival while his friends instigated his anger. His sleeves are rolled up and his biceps are pumped with energy, each arm slightly raised from his body, like a street fighter ready for a brawl.

I reply, "What are you talking about?"

"Don't gimme that bullshit! Get out! Get out of the car, you little fucker! I'm gonna teach you a lesson, right here, right now!"

His buddies cheer, inciting his temper. "Get him! Fuck him up!"

Alexia's father reaches through the open window and grabs hold of the only part of my body he could reach: my wounded head. As he tries to yank me from the car, I experience what I can honestly say is the worst pain I have ever felt in my life. My head, which is literally held together by staples and throbs with every breath, is now being pulled hard enough to separate from my neck!

My mom begins screaming and nails the gas, causing Alexia's father to fall to the ground. He springs to his feet, and as he sprints alongside the car, he manages to punch me in the face. Finally, as my mom drives away at top speed, his voice booms over the suburb, echoing, "You little piece of shit! If I catch you again I'll kill you! I'll fucking kill you!"

Now, when a memory such as this is shared, it is usually either prefaced or concluded with a quote such as, "This is the worst it ever got." But, this was not the worst it ever got. It gets worse. Way worse.

chapter six

Deceit and Betrayal

It is approximately one year later. By this time, I have gotten kicked out of high school, been arrested several times, and forgotten my lifelong dream of skateboarding. I have quit the Powell Peralta team for which I once skated. Alexia has taken up waitressing. My current occupation is full-time Heroin addiction.

On this particular afternoon, I am in my bedroom at my mom's house, staring out the window, awaiting the arrival of Alexia's car.

Questions

- Where the hell is she?
- Why is she late?
- If she knew she was going to be late, why didn't she call?
- How could she do this to me?!

These questions are typically asked by a male in contemplation that his girlfriend may have been unfaithful. But, of course, the reason I am upset is because I am sick, and she has our Dope! The lack of consideration she is demonstrating is unacceptable! Alexia has now forced me to break a taboo of the restaurant business, to call a waitress who has already started her shift.

"Fine! If that's the way she wants to play it, I'll play that way, too, and if she gets in trouble with the manager, it's her own fucking fault!" I say as I grab the phone and furiously dial, striking out at each button with my index finger.

"Good afternoon, how may I help you?" the female on the other line asks.

"May I speak with Alexia please?"

The hostess replies with an air of arrogance, "Alexia? She's on the floor. She's working."

No shit, bitch! I insist, "It's a personal emergency, no one's dead or anything. But I do need to speak to her."

"One moment please." I can tell the hostess is annoyed. Good! I tap my foot as I wait.

Alexia picks up. "Hello?"

I start in on her. "Are you fuckin' kidding me?! I'm sick as hell and you didn't even call to let me know what's going on?! What the fuck?!" I am as resentful as a husband who is on the hallway side of a bedroom door, listening to his wife with her lover as she screams with a lustful intensity that he has never heard before.

"We took a loss," she says.

"What are you talking about?" I shout.

"Kaitlin set me up!"

Kaitlin was a junkie, a black girl from Park Heights who would sometimes cop Heroin for us when we were in need. She would, as per our agreement, provide these services in exchange for a small cut of Heroin, which she would extract from each bag she scored for us. Fair enough: she gets dope for us, and she gets a cut.

However, it soon came to our attention that Kaitlin was taking not *one* cut, but instead, *two* cuts. First, Kaitlin would take a cut or "pinch" from our bag when it was scored in our absence. Then, in our presence, she would extract a second cut, acting as if it were her first and only. The fact that Kaitlin was double-dipping became known to us one day when we arrived at her apartment sooner than expected, before she had a chance to pinch. The amount in our bag was far more than had been in prior scores, and Alexia and I concluded that Kaitlin had been stealing from us all along.

To avoid a confrontation with Kaitlin (because one, given the opportunity, we would have done the same to her, and two, we needed her for future scores), Alexia and I made it a point to be present at each and every future score, thus ending the problem.

One day Kaitlin told me she could score pounds of weed if I ever needed it. I was not a smoker, but I did require money to support what I then referred to as a habit. Kaitlin said that a pound of weed went for eighteen hundred, and she wanted an additional two hundred for setting up the deal. "Fair enough," I said, calculating that a pound of compressed brick weed, broken up and divided into quarter ounces and sold to college kids, minus the two hundred dollars given to Kaitlin, would almost double my investment. But, my trust for Kaitlin was at a minimal level for the above stated reason, so I told her I would be interested in buying one pound of the weed and would wait at her place until it came. She agreed, made a call, and sure enough, within the hour there was a knock on the door.

This was the first time I ever set eyes on a man named "Jah," and it was clear why he had been nicknamed after the Rastafarian Jehovah. Jah was a six-foot-five, two-hundred-forty-pound, thirty-five-year-old, broad-shouldered, slender-waisted, thick-dreaded Jamaican, whose presence filled me with awe. His eyes could, if his emotions rose, fill any room with uncomfortable intensity, like the blast of heat from an open furnace. His patois accent was so thick that neither whites nor blacks could quite understand his every exact word and had to rely on the thread of the conversation to grasp his meaning. However, Jah had managed to overcome this language barrier effectively enough to have a hand in every kind of racket imaginable: used car lots, horses, and real estate, to name a few. Jah ran a small Maryland empire, and considered himself just another drug-dealing entrepreneur living the great American dream.

Jah's weed was very high quality, and the deal went down without a hassle. Every week I continued to go to Kaitlin's apartment to buy quantities. This setup was perfect, because Alexia worked at a restaurant, and almost all waiters get high; therefore her co-workers became her clients. In time, Alexia accompanied me to Kaitlin's house for pick-ups. But this morning, she went alone for the first time. The plan, in my mind, was simple: Alexia was to go to Kaitlin's house, buy a pound of weed from Jah, drop it off to a waiter friend, and use the profits to score Dope, at which time she was to come back home and shoot up with me before she went to work. To me, this highly illegal drug trafficking was a simple morning errand, much like going shopping and picking up a suit from the dry cleaner. The fact that something could go wrong was unfathomable.

I unload my frustrations onto Alexia. "What do you mean, Kaitlin set you up? Where the fuck is the two grand? Did you steal my money?" I demand.

"Fuck you, Brandon! I didn't steal from you, and if you speak to me like that again, I'm gonna hang up!"

"Well, how could you be so goddamn dumb? You know damn right well that Kaitlin is a Dope fiend and will rip you off the first chance she gets! What the fuck?!"

"Brandon, calm down!" she insists, quietly, to keep her customers and coworkers from overhearing. "Listen! I went to Kaitlin's apartment, she called Jah, and just as soon as she did, two black boys burst in her apartment with guns and ski masks and demanded my money. At first I hesitated, but the longer I stalled them, the more violent they got. They started pushing me and pulling my hair, and slapping me. And they were about to start punching me in the face! I had to give them the money!"

By the time Jah arrived with the weed, Alexia was crying. Jah, in the matters of human personality, was wise. He knew Kaitlin's ways and that something was not quite right. He ordered Kaitlin to wait in her bedroom behind a closed door, separating the two women. Then, alone with Alexia, wiping her tears, Jah asked to hear her side of the story:

"Well, we were waiting for you when two thugs with guns and ski masks kicked the door in and demanded my two thousand dollars . . ."

Jah stopped her. "Whait ah seh-cond, 'ow did dey know 'ow much money you 'ad, ghirl? Or dat ya 'ad money ha-tall?"

"I don't know how they even knew, but somehow they did know I had two thousand dollars. They knew the exact amount," she said.

Jah understood. "You been sed up, ghirl. Mah 'eart ghoes oud to ya. Ere, take dis, dis is ahn da house, ghirl." Jah gave her half a pound of weed for free, which would help us recoup our losses. He also gave her his pager number. "From now ahn, use dis number to call me, and don' come roun' ere noh-more. You go now, ghirl. You leave ol' Kaitlin to me to deal wit. I'll maka sure she never messes wit people like she did you aghain."

Holding the phone, preparing for my next outburst, I consider that, for some odd reason, Jah had felt responsible for what had happened to Alexia. . . . This tough Jamaican gangster, who is so intimidating, who stands six-foot-five, is capable of feeling sympathy and extending compassion.

Rather than thanking God that Alexia was not seriously hurt, and sighing with relief that the situation might very easily have been so much worse, I am bitter and resentful because I do not have my fix.

I completely overreact, repeating, "Are you fucking serious? Are you fucking serious?"

"I'm sorry, I'm sorry. Please don't be mad . . ." The conversation continues in this manner until she is in tears, because to my demented junkie logic, if I was miserable, she should feel worse.

"Fuck this, just give me Jah's number!" As I take down the number, I sum up the situation from my selfish viewpoint. "I'm here at home, sick as shit, and all I know is, I don't have a fucking fix because you fucked up! You hear?! You fucked up, you little bitch! What about me?"

She yells back, in a shaky voice, "Why is this *my* fault?! What, is it my job to take care of you like a little baby? What am I, your *mother*?" In a final gesture intended to deny me closure, she slams down the phone. I pace, considering that I just might call her back to continue the argument.

Something said by Alexia, "What am I, your mother?" reverberates in my head. This gives me an idea: I am going to run a scam on them both, Alexia and my mother! I squint, my field of vision narrows . . . The three of us, Alexia, my mother, and I, are now interwound in my game. Now *I* make the rules. And I am going to come out the winner.

Slowly, tactfully, I walk downstairs. Mom is in the kitchen. Cooking. Off guard. Perfect. At this point, Mom is still naïve, in denial of my addiction, the ideal candidate for my scheme. I stroll in. The treacherousness of my fake smile generates within me a sense of satisfaction, rendering it genuine. "Hey, Mom. What's you making? It smells great."

"Hi, Brandon. I didn't know you were home. What are you doing? Just hiding out in your room? I haven't seen you in days." She kisses me on the cheek, and I sit on the chair beside her purse. Unzipped. Foolish woman! This is going to be easier than I had thought.

"I'm just making some soup. Are you hungry?" she asks.

"Oh, yeah, soup sounds great . . . Hey, Mom, you know what I like with my soup that you always used to make when I was little?"

"What's that, Brandon?"

"Toast with butter and grape jelly."

She laughs. A pleasant memory of childhood is the most powerful weapon in existence against a mother. This ploy always works when I want to divert her attention. Any statement that invokes the feeling of maternity will somehow allow Mom to forget the current state of my life, littered with arrests and rehab visits, and render her susceptible to my ploys.

"Okay, Brandon," she says.

She turns, opens the refrigerator, and peers in. I calculate. The process of grabbing the items required to make the jelly toast will only take a moment, but a moment is all I need. My hand twitches, preparing itself.

The soup boils. A jet of liquid spits out, falling onto the burner, sizzling, *tsssss!* This masks the sound produced by my hand as it reaches into her purse, drops to her wallet, and discerns the feel of paper bills.

Okay, now I have to time this perfectly. I know that just as she places her hand on the bread, the plastic wrapper will make a crinkling sound. I wait for it, and as soon as it is audible, I swiftly

pull out a few bills and slide them under my sweatshirt. Ha ha!
Got you!

As Mom stands up with the bread in one hand and jelly in the
other, she looks at me. She senses that something is not right, although she cannot quite determine what it is. Did she see a swift
movement from the corner of her eye? Did the shadows in the
room change? I deliver a distraction. "So, what kind of soup is it?"

Five minutes later.

I have never eaten a meal so fast in my life. As soon as I am finished, I compliment her and hurry into the bathroom to check out
my score. I examine the handful of bills. "Oh, no! Ones!" I thumb
through four ones and sigh with comfort as I spot a ten and two
twenties on the bottom. I am so relieved that it takes a few seconds
to recover my breath.

I rush out the front door and jump into the first cab I see. By the
time I arrive at the restaurant where Alexia works, the cab fare is
just shy of fourteen dollars. I pay the driver and explain, "Okay, I'm
going to run into the restaurant. All you have to do is wait here,
in front of the restaurant for three minutes until I come out. If you
wait, I'll give you ten bucks. Got it?" The cab driver agrees.

Now to prepare for part two of my scam. Before I go into the
restaurant, I unlatch my watch, which I always wear. This watch
is very special because my grandfather left it to me, and Alexia
knows this. I hide the watch in my pocket and run in.

Inside the restaurant, Alexia is serving drinks to a family. It is
five thirty, or as it is referred to by casual-dining restaurant employees, the "Dinner Rush," a time when the dining room fills
with customers in a matter of thirty minutes. In this short amount
of time, drinks must be served, orders taken, and the first wave
of appetizers, soups, and salads delivered all at once. For a junkie
like me, this is an ideal time to pull a hustle on a girlfriend whose

mind is concentrating on every detail of waitressing. Chaos can help reinforce any scam. To apply the element of surprise, I wait for Alexia to notice me. When she finally does, she stops dead in her tracks. Hah! She is staring at me, not knowing how to react, waiting for *me* to react, asking herself, "Is Brandon still angry? Did he come here to have an argument? Is this going to get ugly in the middle of my work?" This could not be going any better. I refrain from saying anything until finally, she asks, "Brandon, *what* are you doing here?"

Here we go, time to sell the scam: "Hi, baby. Listen, I need to make this quick. I took a cab here and I didn't have any money to pay the driver, so I gave him my grandfather's watch as collateral. I need to get out there and pay him before he leaves with it. See?" I point out the window to the waiting cab. Proof. Then, in rapid-fire, point-by-point delivery, I continue. "But, also, baby, I'm gonna need to use your car. I shouldn't be long at all. I need to see Jah."

"Jah? Why?"

"I called him with the number you gave me, and he says he feels bad about what happened to you, and told me he has an opportunity for me to make my money back. He says he has something special for me and I'll regret it later if I pass it up."

I can tell she's skeptical. She knows my tricks, so I continue to add more pressure. "Look, I have to go *right now,* because the cab driver is gonna ride away with my grandfather's watch if I don't get out there and pay him!"

"Here," she says nervously as she tosses me her car keys. "Brandon, you better not be long!"

As soon as I have the keys to Alexia's gray Toyota Tercel in my pocket, I hit her up for the money. "I also need thirty bucks to pay the cab driver. I have to go pay him right now!" She hesitantly reaches into her waitress till and hands me thirty bucks. Hah! I kiss her good-bye. As I turn to leave, I hear Alexia call out, "Come back soon, Brandon. I mean it!"

Once outside, knowing that Alexia is watching me through the window, I pay the waiting cab driver the ten bucks, as promised, making sure that the amount of money I am handing him is obscured from her sight (after all, she thinks I am paying him thirty dollars). I then underhandedly slip my grandfather's watch out of my pocket and go through the motions as if the cab driver had just handed it back to me. I then turn to the window, hold up my watch for Alexia to see, and blow her a kiss. Alexia waves with uncertainty.

Now I have sixty dollars and a car! Less than a minute later I nail the gas and speed into town to find a Dope shop. I am driving along, looking into alleys, on the sidewalks. . . . As I glance at the road ahead of me, I realize I am about to run full speed into the car ahead, which is stopped at a red light. I slam on my brakes, screeching and skidding for about seven seconds. Whew! Just missed nailing it by an inch. I look around, and pedestrians are staring. I'd better watch it, I think to myself. I have no driver's license, no insurance, and to top it off, several outstanding warrants.

I spot a Dope shop that is serving in an alley. As soon as I park the car, I pull my sweatshirt hood over my head and place my hands in my front pockets. If a cop spots my white skin in this neighborhood, I will get hauled off to Central Booking and Alexia's car will be towed. I run down the alley, full speed, to the dealer. "Let me get six." This will leave me with no money for a cab ride home from the restaurant after I return Alexia's' car, but Alexia will cover that. Ha! I hand over the sixty dollars and grab my bags. As I walk back toward Alexia's car, I realize my addiction is on par with an abusive relationship. No matter how bad it beats me, physically or mentally, I will always return.

Within a few minutes I am back in the car, returning to the restaurant. On the floor of the car, hidden from a possible police search, in an old cigarette pack are the bags of Heroin. . . . All but one. After all, I need my fix. As I drive down the street, I press the bag in between the steering wheel and my lighter, crushing the rocks into powder. As soon as I hit the first red light, I find a small scrap of paper in Alexia's glove compartment, roll it up, place it into my nostril and snort half of the bag. The bitter drip that hits the back of my throat makes me gag uncontrollably. Relief.

Then, the mentality of an addict kicks in. *Why bother to save half a bag? Why not just do the whole thing?* As I hit the next red light, I polish off the rest.

Within two minutes, I am so high that my eyelids will not stay open. I roll the windows down and let the cool air hit my face, praying it will wake me up. This works, but only momentarily. I scan the car for a bottle of water, remove the lid, and douse my hands and face. But soon the weight of my eyelids is becoming too burdensome.

My eyes snap open from the impact of Alexia's car against the Acura Legend sitting at a red light in front of me. A woman of fifty, conservatively dressed, steps out to evaluate the damage.

I am not sure *what* I am saying to this woman. . . . Some kind of bullshit excuse about how I just got finished working my third double shift in four days and I'm on my way to the hospital to see my sick grandmother. The woman seems to receive my story with a degree of doubt, but, by the grace of God there is no noticeable damage to her car, and she tells me, "Maybe you had better go home and sleep this off." I thank her and drive away before the cops arrive and ask for licenses and registration.

As I proceed down a four-lane road, I light up a smoke. *Okay, now everything is fine. I'll just drive along, calm, cool, collected . . . wait, what is that burning sensation? Is that my imagination, or is that real physical pain?* One look downward brings the realization that I have dropped my cigarette onto my lap, and yes, I am on fire.

Swerving back and forth across the heavy traffic fighting the flames on my legs, I realize that I am about to run head-on into a row of parked cars, the closest of which has an unsuspecting gray-haired elderly woman stepping out from its driver's side! Manslaughter! I jerk the wheel as fast and as hard as I can, sending Alexia's gray Toyota tumbling violently as it rolls two and a half times across the four-lane road!

When the car stops moving I find myself in a state of urgency. Panic! Where is my Dope?! Did it fly out the open window?! Oh, my God, where is it?! I search through the mounds of shattered glass on the ceiling of this upside-down automobile until I locate the small cellophane bag. Thank God! I crawl out through the car window.

All the traffic on this four-lane road has now come to a dead stop. Every driver and pedestrian are now gathering around, in shock to see that I am still alive. I wave everyone on, praying that they all just walk away so I can escape before the cops show up. "Okay, everybody. This was no big deal. Don't bother calling the ambulance, I'm fine! You can all just go about your business . . ." Yeah, right! This is the most devastating accident that most of these people have ever seen, and the spectacle is compounded by a driver, who should be dead, trying to rid himself of the gathering audience.

Police sirens can be heard in the distance, and I am still holding my Dope. In the center of the awe-stricken crowd that has formed, I spot three sixteen-year-old girls. I approach them. "Look, I need you to hold this for me until the scene clears or the police leave." I grab the prettiest girl's hand, pull it toward me, and palm her the Dope. At first she is nervous, but I shoot her a wink and her teen-age rebellious side overcomes her discretion. She takes the cellophane bag and retreats to the sideline.

Just then I notice it: a penny-loafer, oxford-blue-shirt-wearing frat-boy, filming me with a video camera! Jesus Christ, can this situation get any worse? If he gives the tape to the cops, I'm done. "Hey, you! I didn't give you permission to film me! Give me that tape!" I yell. I grab for the video camera, but he is about a foot taller than me, with long arms, so he extends his reach, holding it above his head where I can't get to it. He is smiling and laughing at me, and keeps the videotape rolling, filming me as I chase him around the wrecked car. To him this is a game, and he knows this is going to be great footage for all his frat buddies to watch over a few beers. It probably would be pretty funny to watch, actually.

As the police show up, the frat-boy steps off to the side and films from afar, not wanting to run the risk of the cops confiscating his tape. Thank God.

Six cop cars, two fire trucks, an ambulance, and a tow truck line the street. As the police question me, I offer excuses why I do not have my license. One officer writes down my mother's home number and Alexia's work number, and begins to call them. A second police officer says, "Son, would you mind stepping over here to our vehicle while we have a talk with you?" I comply. As I sit in the back of the squad car, the cop asks, "Son, are you under the influence of anything?"

"Like what, Officer?" I ask as innocently as possible.

He looks at me, sternly. "Anything. Drugs? Alcohol? Dope?"

"No, sir, Officer."

"You seem to be acting funny, are you sure?" he asks.

I call on what I know about the psychology of police. Police are trained to observe the insecurities in people. They feed off human weakness and use it to their advantage. If a lack of confidence is shown in the first answer, the questioning continues until the policeman can break down the alibi, expose the flaws of the story, and uncover the truth. So, in answering this first question, I show no weakness as I look right into the cop's eyes and say, "How the fuck do you expect me to be acting? I just rolled a car two and a half times. How would *you* be acting?" The cop raises his eyebrows, unprepared to give a response to this type of answer. He pulls his partners to the side. They whisper to each other, and they glance at me.

I look over at the three girls who are holding my stash; they seem excited, wondering what will happen next.

I examine the crowd, watching with anticipation.

Behind the crowd is the frat-boy, still filming, with a shit-eating grin on his face.

The cops break their huddle and walk toward me, and I think, I'm going right to jail!

The cops surround me. The first officer says, "Well, I guess you're okay, son. We called the girl who owns the vehicle and your mother, and it looks like your story checks out. I'm sure you are pretty shaken up so we'll let your mother take you home."

"Thank you, officers," I say with a smile.

My mother arrives with Alexia in the passenger's seat. As the officers exchange information with them, Alexia stares at me. She doesn't say a word. She doesn't have to. We both know where things stand.

I approach the three girls who are holding my stash. As they hand it back I give them each a hug and thank them for their help.

As my mother drives Alexia and me away from the wreck, I spot the frat-boy who is across the street, still filming. I give him the finger and he laughs at me. *Enjoy the footage, fucker.*

Alexia, Mom, and I sit in silence. I have not even told Alexia I am sorry. I grab her wrist and place two bags of Dope in the palm of her hand. By feel, Alexia knows exactly what she is holding, and her rage is diminished. It no longer matters that I just totaled her car. The only thing that is important is how soon we arrive home so we can shoot up.

chapter seven

Dying Love, Decaying Life

Four months ago, I was kicked out of my mother's house for the last time. Prior to leaving, Alexia and I had secretly opened her checkbook, noted the balance, and cashed checks for the entire sum of the account. Last week, the forty thousand dollars had dwindled down to the very last bag of Dope and vanished.

Alexia has been kicked out of her house as well. Her father did not want to resort to this, but had to. He could no longer keep up with the game she was playing. The lies, the stealing, the conniving. He still loved her, but the pain ran too deep and separated the bond of family.

Alexia and I are now homeless. It is miserable, but in a way I really like it. Even though I have lost everything and everyone, I know I have someone who truly loves me and understands what I am.

Every hustle I once had is dead. I have burned all my bridges. Every person I had once considered a resource has caught on and cut me off. Alexia now pulls the weight. She is the maternal figure who carries both of our habits on her back like a small child. When I shoplift, her beauty is the ultimate distraction to the clerks. When we make a drug trade, she can offer bad product and not get called out on it by virtue of her charisma. When we need a place to sleep or shower, she can charm our way into almost anywhere. And, bright girl that she is, before getting kicked out of her father's house, Alexia had made a spare key to his front door, which she thought she might use sometime down the road. And that time is now, because this week, her dad is on a hunting trip.

A house, any house, is a luxury now foreign to us. When we have access to one, we take full advantage of it. We shower, wash our clothes, brush our teeth, and eat as much as our stomachs can possibly hold.

On this particular day, each of us has injected our gate shot. We are high, but not for too much longer, and time is running out. We have to make a move, and fast.

The sincere and genuine love Alexia and I once shared has evaporated like steam from a cooker. An hour ago we had loved each other. Now we have just gotten through screaming at each other, wishing we had never met. I have heard it said that the love soul mates share never dies. I used to believe that until Heroin was added to the equation.

The love two Dope fiends share is twisted. When they are high, they are warm, compassionate, kind, and considerate. But as soon as the Dope runs out, they transform into two vicious and deadly pit bulls trapped together in a ring. Within hours, "I love you, I miss you, I need you" turns into "I fucking hate you! Why am I with you? It's your fault we're like this!" When two people are strung out together, they see the evil sides of each other. They are at their worst, and they bring out the worst in each other.

I want nothing more than to storm out of the house and leave Alexia behind forever, but I need her to score our next fix. After an hour of arguing and shouting, she grabs the cordless phone and storms off into her father's bedroom, slamming the door.

I sit in silence, pondering what Alexia might be up to. In the quiet of the house, her voice carries as she speaks into the phone. Although the words themselves are muffled, her intonation has changed from malicious and hateful to pleasant and loving. The sweetness of her voice brings me back to a time in our relationship when we had first fallen in love, innocent of the evils of this diseased junkie lifestyle. The wave of comforting emotion diminishes as I face the possibility that Alexia might be trying to score without me!

I tiptoe to the bedroom and press my ear against the door. To my dismay, I hear her ask in a flirtatious voice, "What do you want me to wear?" She responds to the answer with a contrived giggle and concludes the conversation with, "Okay, I'll see you soon. Bye, honey."

No . . . this cannot be. Without thinking, I throw a punch and my fist slams into the door, sending it wide open. Alexia is lying on the bed, staring at me. Caught. Stunned. Trying to calculate her next move.

"Who the fuck was that?" I demand.

"Brandon, stop being so paranoid. That was my friend from rehab." She laughs.

"Sure, like hell it was! I can tell when you're lying! Who was it?!" A very uncomfortable silence falls over the room, and although Alexia tries her hardest to stop them, tears run from her eyes.

"Who the fuck was it?" I draw close to her. "Alexia, I've never placed a violent hand on you in my life, but God help me, in three seconds, that's all going to change if you don't answer me right now!" I am staring at her mouth, waiting for an answer.

Alexia jumps up and grabs her father's bedside lamp, yanks the chord from the wall, and wields it like a baseball bat. "You want to know what that was all about? Okay, curious eavesdropper! Leech! Junkie! Parasite! I tried to protect you, but okay! You asked for it! It was a man on the phone, are you ready to deal with that? It was a man, and it wasn't you! How do you like it? And do you know what he is to me? He's my client, okay? I'm a whore, all right?! Is that what you wanted to hear? Your girlfriend is a fucking prostitute!"

She stands there, crying, angry, hyperventilating, ready to fight. But her words took all the strength out of my legs. I fall to the bed. Now seated, wearily, meekly, I ask her, "How could you?"

Alexia explains in a voice that lies somewhere between that of a mother offering consolation, and a schoolteacher delivering factual knowledge. "Brandon, look, you need to face something. You have nothing, I have nothing, we need a fix, and Dope isn't free. So I have to go now. I have to take care of business." She drops the lamp and walks out the door, leaving me alone, trembling. Just like everything else in life that was once important to me, Heroin had now taken Alexia. But by now, I am used to failure and accept it as normal. I have built such a high wall around my feelings that I no longer recognize them.

Before I get a chance to examine what my life has become, I think of a way to drum up some cash. I have an idea. I pick up the phone and start dialing.

Three hours later, I am in the passenger seat of a 1969 V.W. microbus with a tie-dyed shirt and hemp pants—wearing hippie nicknamed Swimmy. Swimmy is a piece of work. He is an undergrad at Johns Hopkins University and also the resident weed and LSD dealer, which is painfully obvious at a single glance of his Woodstock wannabe gear and stupid-looking peace-sign necklace. He earned the name Swimmy because one day he dropped acid and thought he was swimming through water as he ran around the hallways of his dorm. I guess he took one trip too many. I loathe the fact that he only plays the Grateful Dead on his stereo, as if the 1960s was such a wonderful era that it needs to be refabricated in every possible way. He wears John Lennon–type eyeglass frames, but no lenses since his vision is perfect. What a dipshit.

Swimmy is the least cautious drug dealer I have ever seen. He even smells like pot. Here we are, on our way to a major drug deal, and his car ashtray is full of old joints. He even has pot-related bumper stickers, one of which reads, "Grass or ass, no one rides for free!" Hell, it may as well say, "Pull me over, Pig, I have drugs in the car!" The fact that this guy has never been arrested is proof that God has a sense of humor.

As we stop at a traffic light, right in front of a police station, the idiot begins rolling a fucking joint. I tell him, "Yo, put that away! You should be a little more careful. Aren't you afraid of being arrested?"

"Why?" he asks. That answer describes Swimmy to a T.

In his glove compartment he has $7,500 in a brown paper bag. We are on our way to rendezvous with Jah, who has five pounds of brick weed to exchange for Swimmy's cash. I am to see the deal through, and for my efforts Swimmy is to give me five hundred bucks, a hundred a pound. Sure, if the police catch me I could get a fifteen-year sentence, but this fact matters little right now. "Pull over behind this hospital," I instruct.

"So, this is a lot of money," he tells me. *No shit.* "It's not all mine, most of it's my partner's. He's pretty nervous about this whole thing; he's scared the pot's not gonna be any good."

Okay, here's the part where I reassure him he is not going to waste his money, and I know just what to say. "Oh, don't worry about that. These guys are Jamaican; this shit's direct from the land of Bob Marley!" Actually, I am pretty sure the weed is from

Mexico, but I was just telling him what he wanted to hear, and it worked. He is licking his lips with anticipation.

Jah pulls up to the loading dock in his white cargo van. "Okay, give me the money," I tell Swimmy, who hands over the paper bag full of cash. I peer into the bag and note that the money is not in bundles or stacks; it is unorganized, like Swimmy. Just a paper bag of hundreds. Hmmm. This gives me an idea. I bet I can scam Jah and pawn off the blame on Swimmy here. Sure. All I have to do is grab a handful of these hundreds before I hand the bag off to Jah. True, eventually Jah will count it and realize he has been ripped off. But that will probably be much later tonight when he gets home, and at that point I will be long gone. And when I see Jah again I can just tell him I didn't count the money, either; Swimmy here had shorted him. Yeah, it will work. I know it.

I climb into the passenger's seat of Jah's van. "Hey, Jah."

"Ey, Brahn-don. Ow's id ghoin, mon?"

"Great, thanks."

"Five pounds, rhight?"

"Yep."

"Oh-kay, one seh-cond."

Jah man climbs into the back with Dudly, a five-foot-five, hun-dred-and-fifty-pound dark black man who works for Jah. He is about thirty-five, wears a lot of gold jewelry, and always has on brand-new clothes and white Nikes. He rarely speaks. Together the men open a garbage bag of compressed marijuana bricks and place five of them into a second bag. The van reeks of the pun-gent scent of weed. While Jah and Dudly are occupied, I seize the opportunity to separate a handful of hundreds from Swimmy's money and stuff them into my pocket.

As Jah passes me the garbage bag containing five pounds, I tell him, "Great. Thanks a lot, Jah," and in handing him the bag of

Swimmy's money, I throw him a distraction. "So, I'll call you tomorrow at around noon. I have some buddies who are looking to get like ten or maybe fifteen pounds. Okay?"

"Oh-kay, Brahn-don, tha'd be alright," he replies, reclaiming the driver's seat, and, looking into the paper bag, continues. "Whait ah seh-cond, Brahn-don. Huld ahn, don go no where yet. Led meh cound dis, Brahn-don."

"Okay, sure. I'll be right back. I'll just drop this off to Swimmy first," I tell him. As I start to open the door, Jah grabs a hold of my shirt, looks into my eyes.

Now, in retrospect, I can explain that what I had intended to do was to force down the lump in my throat in as silent a manner as was possible. But what happened, in actuality, was that Jah could, with great clarity and audibility, hear me gulp.

"Wait, wait, Brahn-don, don go no where, I nheed to cound dis."

"Okay, no problem," I comply. As he counts the money, I become increasingly nervous. Every bill he touches brings me closer to the realization that I really fucked up this time. I look at Dudly, whose facial expression is a blank stare. No feelings here. What am I going to say? What am I going to do?

As Jah finishes the count, he looks confused.

"What? What's dis? You're eight hondred short, Brahn-don! Wha da fuck?" He looks at me, enraged. His forehead is wrinkled, his eyes wide and bloodshot.

"Eight hundred short? Are you sure?"

"Of course I'm sure! Coh-mon! Whad da fuck is ghoing ahn?"

Jah man gives me a long, hard, knowing stare. I break the uncomfortable silence. "Look, man, I don't know what's going on, either. I don't, I swear! Look, I'm going to go check with my friend to find out what the hell is going on."

As I reach for the door handle, Jah hits the LOCK button. *Click!*

"You are ghoing noh place!" He tells Dudly, "Git out an tell this
odder guy to ged da fuck oudda ere!"

As Jah begins turning my pockets inside out, I watch Dudly
knock on Swimmy's microbus door. Swimmy hesitantly unrolls
his window, and as he does, Dudly has a few words with him and
pulls up his shirt, revealing a thirty-eight holstered in the belt of
his jeans. Swimmy peels out at a speed I had thought was impossible for a V.W. microbus to travel. Just then, Jah digs the money
from the bottom of my pocket.

"Ow could you do dis to me? Ow could you rip me off, Brahn-
don?" I offer no excuses. There is nothing left for me to say. The
answer to his question is simple: I got greedy. But the question I
have for myself is, Why? Why did I have to push it? Why couldn't
I just have been happy with my five hundred dollars?

Dudly climbs in the back of the van. Jah orders, "Dhud-lee, take
dis modderfocker and give him some licks hee-ll never forghet!"

"Come on, white boy!" Dudly yanks me by the hair and violently slams me to the floor. He then sits on my chest and delivers
a pistol whip to the top of my skull. I see a flash of white; my body
yields and goes limp.

"What were you thinkin', you dumb white boy? What the fuck
were you thinkin'?" yells Dudly in a relentless monotone. He
punches me in the face, over and over. My lips split, the skin of my
cheeks cracks open, my nose flattens. I have to breathe out of my
mouth, which is filling with blood and causing me to choke. Suffi-
cation. Dudly continues. "Where you live, white boy, huh? Where
you live? We know you got a momma! Where she live?"

I beg, "Please, don't bring her into this!"

Dudly cocks his gun and points it in my face. "I'll pull this
shit, white boy! Don't think I won't!" I believe him, I am sure he
has done it before. "Whatsamatter, you too fuckin' stupid to be

scared?" Dudly jams the gun in my mouth so hard that it pins the back of my throat to the floor of the van. "I'm gonna ask you one more time, you dumb white motherfucker! Where your momma live?"

"God save us both," I pray as I give them my mother's address. We drive on.

In twenty minutes, I can tell by familiar scenery that we are close to home.

"Well, well, well! Lookee what we have here!" Dudly announces, pulling me to the window of the van, forcing me to view my mother on her knees, working in the garden.

In my beaten, semiconscious state, my mind tries to escape with a memory, or perhaps a fantasy, in which I am a child riding in the passenger's seat of my mom's car on our way to the park. I am excited, cheerful, happy, and I reach across the seat to hold my mother's hand. Then, when I regain my sense of reality, I realize it was *Jah's hand* I had grabbed. I clench his hand for dear life. "Please, Jah, please! Don't hurt my mother, please! I know you're a good man! Kill me if you want, but don't hurt my mother! Jesus, please let this man, this killer, have some sympathy for my weakness somewhere in his heart!"

Jah stares at me in terror, his eyes holding the expression of a man facing judgment before God. "You'd bedder tank Gohd you did-dent ghet away wid stealin mah money! Dhud-lee, ged im oud of mah sight!" The van is traveling about twenty miles an hour as Dudly throws open the back door and kicks me out onto the street.

When my eyes open, my mother is standing over me with approximately fifteen neighbors. She is in tears, frantic. "Brandon! Oh, my God, Brandon, are you all right? Brandon, you're so beat up, I can hardly recognize you! What the hell's going on?"

There are levels of such vulnerability, such desperation that will compel even a liar like me to come forth with the complete truth. I break down and admit to my mother that I am a drug addict, that my girlfriend has resorted to prostitution, and that my life is hopeless. I weep and cling to her, bleeding all over her clothes.

I wake up in my mother's house, in my old bedroom, lying on my back. My mother is nursing me with ice, bandages, and first-aid cream. I know my mother can not let me stay here; this is temporary, just for tonight.

My forehead is swollen like a basketball. My eyes are black, my cheeks are split, my lips are fat and bleeding, my knees are torn open from being kicked out of the van. But what matters to me the most is the fact that I am sicker than I have been in a long time. I need a fix so bad that I am shivering.

"Someone's here to see you, Brandon," my mother says. The door opens. Alexia. When she sees me, she tries not to cry. I can tell she wants to, but she is strong.

"It's okay, Brandon," Alexia tells me in a sweet, comforting voice. "It's going to be all right." She sits on my bed and holds my hand, secretly palming me a few bags of Heroin, right in front of my mother's unsuspecting eyes.

"How lucky I am to have this girl in my life," I say to myself. I could not wait for my mother to leave the room so I could shoot up.

A month later, in a Best Buy, Alexia and I are stealing some CDs. Although the store employees and security guards know our faces by now, we are too sick to care, so we decide to take our chances.

Alexia and I split up in the store, and I peel the security tags from a few CDs. As I near the front door with the stolen merchan-

dise in my pockets, I hear what sounds like a walkie-talkie behind
me. I turn to see a heavyset security guard on my tail. I break for
the door. I am fast and manage to run away without a problem.

Across the street, I hide behind a parked eighteen-wheeler,
from which I have a view of the store. Twenty-five minutes pass,
and still there is no sign of Alexia. Soon, a police car pulls up and
Alexia is escorted to the backseat in handcuffs. Damn, I feel so bad
for her. I know she is just as Dope sick as I am, but there's nothing
I can do. She has warrants in two counties, so I know I will not
be seeing her for a few months. But that's how it goes sometimes.
We knew the risks of this game called Heroin, and played it to the
utmost.

So this is how I am to part ways with the first love of my life,
I think. It's a sick way to end the relationship, I know, but to a
junkie, it all seems so normal.

As I watch Alexia being driven away in the back of the squad
car, I wonder why, in the end, she had made the decision to throw
her life away. She, like me, once had everything going for her, and
now had nothing. Perhaps she simply was not happy with a life she
once had created for herself, and through her allegiance to me and
my lifestyle, she had finally found escape.

My memories of my relationship with Alexia fade out.

Now my mind brings me back to the 7-Eleven parking lot as I wait
for Scott, who is pulling to the curb in his white Mercedes. Somehow, I feel that all this misery might come to an end.

chapter eight

The Road to Rehab

Scott arrives. In my psychological condition, without the benefit of proper rest and nutrition, I see his white Mercedes as a vision, and Scott an angel. But in the next instant, the hallucination ceases and I am restored to a conscious state.

A big hug. I am repulsed at the thought that another human being might even consider touching my filth. Cleanliness is one of the qualities I am looking forward to achieving with my sobriety. Usually, I pay a black lady in the neighborhood ten dollars for the use of her shower, but my finances have not allowed such luxuries as of late. Sometimes, before I shoot up in a local Burger King restroom, I take a bit of a "bath." I splash water on my face, wash my ass, my hands, under my armpits, my balls, and if there are enough paper towels, my feet. Sometimes, I imagine the voice of an announcer over a loudspeaker, narrating the scene for an imaginary audience.

"Ladies and gentlemen! One and all! Behold! Upon this unfortunate soul has been cast a cruel fate! For, this ex-skateboarder, Brandon Novak, who once held the world in his hands, lived in a nice home, had a car, and a beautiful fiancée, is now, with dampened paper towels, about to clean the filth from his balls and ass! Gaze upon him and consider his misfortune, in this special, worldwide-televised broadcast event brought to you live from the local Burger King restroom!"

After Scott's hug of unconditional love, he releases me and looks into my eyes. His expression conveys sympathy. His smile gives me a sense of hope that I will one day be in an improved state of mental and physical health. He says, "Man, I've been waiting for this call for the last four years! Now I can't believe it, it's actually happening right now! I'm so proud of you. You can do this! Come on!"

Kindness. It's been so long since someone has shown me compassion and wanted nothing in return. As Scott opens his passenger door, I climb in.

As Scott drives, a multitude of doubts race through my mind. He asks, "How do you feel, brother?"

I reply, "Like shit."

As I have mentioned, Scott is four years clean and has been in my position several times, so I take him at his word when he tells me, "Just stay strong. If you do, you'll never have to feel this way again. Just stick it out; it's worth it." Again he forces a smile, a practice which is sometimes necessary for him to draw forth actual sentiments of inner contentment.

We pass a gas station, and Scott asks me if I want anything. I reply in a weak whisper, "I'll take some smokes, man, a pack of Marlboro Reds."

He says, "Is that all?"

I am starving and thirsty, but my pride will not allow me to ask for anything else.

Scott goes to the trunk, takes out a black-white-and-gray striped shirt, and tells me, "Here, take off that dirty sweatshirt you're wearing and put this on. It's clean; it'll make you feel better."

As Scott goes in the convenience store, I change shirts, throwing away the hooded sweatshirt I have used for the last few months to hide the color of my skin.

I sit in the car and take inventory on my life. I am twenty-five. I own nothing besides a needle, a lighter, and a cooker. I have nothing to offer this world. If I died today, it would not make a difference.

Scott exits the store, sipping coffee. My eyes fixate on the pack of Marlboro Reds in his hand, the closest thing to a drug I can get. He tosses me the pack. I take one out; he lights it and starts the car.

Once we are on the road. Scott hands me a bottle of water and napkins, telling me, "Here, use this to clean up a little bit." I pour water on the napkins and begin to wipe the layer of dirt from my hands and face, leaving the napkins almost black.

A look out the window tells me that the rehab is one block away. I know this for two reasons: I have copped Dope on this corner many times, and two, this is not my first time being admitted to this rehab; I have been here several times before.

The rehab where I am about to admit myself is called the Tuerk House. And, like a holy sanctuary in a devil's pit, it is situated in the heart of a neighborhood where street thugs sell Dope in abundance. I look out the car window, watching several men copping on the corner. Now that sobriety has a hold of me, I can see a bit deeper into each junkie's eyes. I empathize with them, understanding how they feel to shoot up their last ten dollars, trying to enjoy the high while it lasts, but knowing they will start to feel sick in another eight hours. So while they are high, they are compelled to hustle for more money. This is the endless cycle of addiction, which continues until the junkie either recovers or dies.

Most people begin using Heroin because they want to escape themselves and the burdens of their lives. However, being an addict is a full-time, twenty-four-hours-a-day, seven-days-a-week obligation for which the responsibilities never end. In a way, this makes sense, because, if a person assumes the slavelike mentality, and his existence is controlled by the never-ending cycle of mind-less tasks he must perform to serve the master Heroin, then he'll never have to face his life, or himself. In this way, Heroin addiction offers the ultimate escape from reality, by replacing it with the worst alternative.

As I take each drag of my cigarette, we proceed closer to my new life. My whole body is shaking. I feel a need to call my mother. But my senses force this urge to subside. It is a common practice for junkies, upon admitting themselves to rehab, to call their loved ones and proclaim their intention to get clean. This can be attributed to several equal and opposing forces acting upon the junkie's mind: First, the junkie is compelled by his innate de-sire to experience the heartfelt emotions of which he has deprived himself for so long. Second, it is the junkie's conditioned reflex to seize all available opportunities to salvage relationships in order to acquire resources for drug money after discharge. I recall several prior rehab experiences during which I was successful throughout the initial fourteen-day program, and how, upon release, I imme-diately scored Dope and shot up by the time the sun had set. And so, I suppress the urge to call my mother, refusing to build her hopes only to decimate them once again.

We pull up to the curb in front of the Tuerk House and head toward the front door. As we climb the stairs, I recite a simple prayer over and over in my head. God, please help me, watch over me and make sure I'm okay!

Scott smiles. "I'm so happy you're going here; I promise you, it will be worth it. I haven't lied to you yet and I'm not going to now."

"I know."

We make it to the door. I look at my cigarette, take one last big drag, throw it down and say, "It's got to be done, and now's the time."

"Well, then, Brand, are you ready for a new way of life?"

I say, "Yep, let's do it!"

chapter nine
Tuerk House

Scott grabs the door handle and opens it for me. I enter first; Scott follows.

The short hallway before me doubles as both a waiting room and a reception area. There are four chairs against each longitudinal wall. At a desk sit two older black ladies. The first woman, with phone against ear and pencil in hand, seems far too occupied to take notice of my arrival. The second, heavyset and wearing glasses, has the presence of a sweet grandmother. She asks, "May I help you?"

Scott replies, "I've brought my friend in for treatment. His name's Brandon."

She looks at me and says, "How do you feel, baby?"

"Not too good."

She says, in an assuring manner, "It's gonna be all right, I promise. My name is Mrs. Evans. If you just have a seat, I'll be right with you; I won't be long."

Scott, who must have a crew on a construction site awaiting his arrival, looks at his watch. "Do you need me for anything else?"

Mrs. Evans replies, "No, we'll take good care of him."

Scott gives me a big hug and says, "I've got to get to work," and in leaving, adds, "you have my number. Call me as soon as you get a chance."

"All right, thank you again for everything, Scott. I couldn't have done this without you."

"Yes, you could have, you're a strong person. Don't ever forget this. You can do it. I love you."

As I watch Scott, my last remaining friend walk away, my loneliness is intense.

"Come on, let's do this paperwork so we can get your cute behind upstairs and make you well," Mrs. Evans tells me, trying to put a smile on my face. She reaches for my hand. I give it to her and she escorts me into an office, where we begin the induction procedure.

"How do you feel, baby?"

I reply, "Like shit."

Mrs. Evans says, "What's your drug of choice?"

I answer, "Dope."

"I know exactly how you feel. I shot Dope for twenty-eight years, so I've walked in your shoes. I've been in your position several times before. And I've been clean for twelve years now, and I got clean by going through this very same rehab. I just hope for your sake you get it this time."

I'm shocked. This sweet old lady, with her soothing voice, once sat in my seat, feeling ill, being asked the same questions.

"Have you brought any personal belongings?"

I shake my head. "No."

"Will anyone be bringing anything for you?"

Again I shake my head. "No."

"How old are you?"

"Twenty-five."

"Oh, son, it's that bad already?" Mrs. Evans asks with a sad but understanding look on her face.

I say in a weak whisper, "Yes."

She then instructs, "You have no choice, baby, you got to get it or you're gonna die a lot sooner than later." I know this and she knows I know it, but she needs to reinforce it anyway. She then says, "I have a nephew your age. I'm gonna get some of his old clothes and bring them in for you."

"Thanks, but I'm okay." Really I'm not, I could use those clothes, but my pride is speaking for me.

She says, "Boy, don't forget, I've sat in that very same chair. You're not okay, you're far from okay, but that's all right 'cause we're gonna do all we can to change that and push you in the right direction. You're gonna make it this time, Brandon. I have a special feeling about you."

She sees something special in me? The very thought that I am actually worth something is foreign. For as long as I remember, if I was treated with respect, it was because I either had Dope, money, or was on the verge of a score. The sense of responsibility that is brought about by another person's respect gives me a feeling of discomfort.

Mrs. Evans continues to ask some basic questions such as: "Who do you live with? Are you married or single? Do you have any family?"

Then the big question hits. "How will you be paying for your treatment?"

I think for a second, and naturally, I make up a lie: "My mother said she would pay, but she's working today and she can't drop the check off until tomorrow evening."

Mrs. Evans gives me a knowing look that implies she has heard this excuse many times before. She answers, "Fine."

I know that if I make it upstairs to detox and treatment, and my mother is able to verify this is the truth and not one of my many lies, she will help me once again. This sucks. I did not even want to tell her about rehab in order to spare her feelings in case I fail once again. But I am willing to do whatever it takes. I need this.

Mrs. Evans then says, "Okay, you're all finished with me here; I'm gonna bring you those clothes tomorrow. You just missed the smoke break. Do you want to go out front with me and smoke one?"

"I'd love to."

For some odd reason, even though my life is an absolute wreck, I feel at peace, and I owe this feeling to Mrs. Evans for making me feel welcome. She is a powerful example that it can be done.

chapter ten

Mrs. Evans

Mrs. Evans and I stand in front of Tuerk House. She lights her cigarette and offers me one.

I tell her, "I have cigarettes; I'm good."

"Save yours; you'll need them. Actually, take the rest of mine, too." She hands me the pack.

"Mrs. Evans, you don't have to be so nice to me. I know you mean well . . ."

She replies, "Sure, I'm being nice, but I'm doing the same things for you that someone did for me when I was in your shoes many years ago. That's what being here is about. It's called the 'therapeutic value of one addict helping another.'"

Not being sure what that means, but expecting to find out, I reply, "Thank you."

Mrs. Evans looks at me as if to let me know what she is about to disclose is intended to bring me strength or inspiration. "Sweetie, I have a story I want to tell you before we part ways. Just something for you to think about, maybe, when things get a little shaky in here. I entered this place years ago in the same exact shape you're in. I had no one left in my life. I had betrayed everyone who crossed my path. I'm talking about this grown lady who stands before you at this very moment was sucking dick for two dollars on the avenue. I've sold my own daughter's body for a quick fix."

Although I was prepared to hear a speech, I was by no means prepared to hear that. This calm, professional, sweet-looking old lady continues on with her story.

"One night at about three o'clock in the morning, I was on the avenue tricking when a man pulled up in a car and offered sixty bucks to fuck, and I took him on his offer. It started out as a normal trick until the guy punched me in the face. He pulled out handcuffs and cuffed my hands behind my back, and wrapped electrical tape over my mouth and around my head. Then he threw me in the trunk and drove to an abandoned house. For hours and hours, he repeatedly beat and raped me."

I have no idea how to react, as sobriety sends a chill throughout my body. Mrs. Evans finishes her story.

"When he was finished with me, he pulled out a needle, cooked up some Heroin, and injected himself, then me. After he pulled the needle out, he informed me that he just shot me up with his AIDS-infected needle. He looked me in the face and said, 'Now you're gonna die just like I am, you dirty bitch!' Then he unlocked the handcuffs and left me to wallow in the sickness that he forced on me. Eight months later, I went to prison, was tested, and the results came back HIV positive. When I was released from prison I used for about three more months before I entered this treatment center."

I just stare at her. What can I possibly say?

"Brandon," Mrs. Evans says, "I didn't tell you that story to make you nervous. I told you because I know when you look at me that's not what you see. But if you really want to clean up your act, with a lot of hard work and determination, you can change from who you are right now to the person you want to be. It's never too late."

She is completely right. When I look at Mrs. Evans I see a sweet, caring, warm grandmother figure, not the woman in the story she just told.

As we wrap up our smoke break, a tall, slender, middle-aged black man opens the door and calls outside, "Mr. Novak?"

"Yes, that's me."

"Your room is ready, just follow me, sir."

I look at Mrs. Evans, not wanting to leave her side, but knowing I have to. In parting, she gives me a hug and tells me she will see me tomorrow. "I have a feeling about you, cutie. Stop this nonsense."

chapter eleven
Kindness from Strangers

The thin man instructs me to follow him, leads me into a small room, and asks, "Do you have any belongings with you?"

I reply, "No."

"Okay, I'm gonna need you to empty your pockets for me."

I comply. From my front left pocket I bring forth two packs of cigarettes and a lighter. From my front right pocket I produce my syringe and spoon, both of which the man instructs me to drop into a trash can lined with a plastic biohazard bag. As I prepare to throw away everything I live for, I note that I am not the only resident of the Tuerk House who has attempted to begin a new way of life, as there are several other needles and cookers in the bottom of the can.

The thin man asks me to sit in a chair so he can take a Polaroid picture of my face. Its purpose is to remind the addict, upon discharge, of the progress he has made. Before the thin man takes the photo, I attempt to smile, and I say to myself, "What the fuck do I have to smile about?" The flash goes off.

The man says, "Well, that's it" in a monotonous demeanor I interpret as indifference toward his job.

He leads me through the hall, into the elevator, and presses "3," the men's floor. The second floor is where the women stay. In the Tuerk House, men and women are separated at all times. It is the philosophy of this institution that in order for addicts to fully engage themselves in the rehabilitation process, they should take all precautions to avoid diversions. One powerful distraction addicts use to replace their dependency on drugs is the preoccupation with the opposite sex.

As the thin man and I step off the elevator and enter the hallway, I am faced with an element of rehab I have dreaded since my decision to admit myself: a line of approximately thirty men, waiting to be escorted to group therapy. The presence of other addicts in this multitude, brought to order, forces me into a submissive state. Each individual possesses a certain quality, whether in a facial expression, a story, or a mannerism, that reflects a different facet of my sickness. Cumulatively, these men represent my disease, addiction. I fix my eyes on the floor as I feel the gaze of the other addicts. Stripped of pride and self-esteem, I make my way behind the thin man.

This institution resembles, in many ways, an elementary school. The ceiling is white and houses fluorescent light fixtures down its center. The pigmentation of the walls and floor resemble the color of piss. Lining the hallway are the doors to the rooms; every room holds three beds and each bed has a dresser. There is one window per room. A rule of the Tuerk House dictates that the blinds are to remain shut, because as previously stated, this rehab is situated in a neighborhood where there are many Dope shops and we addicts need no more temptations than the ones we are currently facing.

As the thin man leads me down the hall, I look into a room and see several addicts seated at a table. They break out in laughter at the punch line of a joke. I am struck with jealousy, having not had a sincere laugh for as long as I can remember.

The slim man stops at my room, number 361. The man says, "Here we go, this is your room. Your bed is that one in the corner." There are items on the dressers of the other beds. A framed photo of a cute little black girl of approximately seven catches my eye. I suppose she is a relative of one of the occupants.

Before leaving, the slender man stops and says something that completely catches me off guard. "Good luck, I will pray for you." The sincerity in his eyes causes me to realize I had misjudged him. He turns and walks away.

I feel so sick right now that all I want to do is get in bed, curl up in a ball, and not move until the withdrawal is over. But first, I need a shower.

My bed has already been made; on it lie two standard white towels, a toothbrush, soap, deodorant, and a letter stating that if I need a razor, I must consult my counselor. Obviously, thoughts of suicide are common among recovering addicts.

The hallways are empty. Perfect. I cross to the bathroom, approach the shower, strip down, peel the clothes from my skin, and step into the stall. Most people, in considering a hot shower, envision a peaceful, relaxing moment of reflection and solitude. In my state, however, in the grip of withdrawal, and having not properly bathed for months, the sensation of the water on my skin will be almost unbearable. Just to imagine being clean leaves me feeling awkwardly uncomfortable. I turn on the water, adjusting the temperature.

I step toward the shower head, take a deep breath, and submerge my body under the running water, which beats on my skin like hard rain. Soon my body is acclimated to the water, and I feel comfortable enough to apply soap. As I wash, I note that around the drain, the suds rinsed from my body are black, similar to the soap scum produced by an auto mechanic's hands after a day's work. I scrub my body several times, each pass yielding lather lighter in shade, until the layers of dirt have finally been removed.

I step from the shower and grab my towel, and as I dry off, I amuse myself with the thought that the last time I showered I had dried myself with my dirty shirt. With the towel around my waist, I gather my toothbrush and toothpaste and make my way to the sink. I cannot remember the last time I brushed my teeth, and my gums are so sensitive that the cold water will sting like an abrasion. I wait until the water runs warm and begin brushing, and soon the blood gushing from my gums overpowers the taste of toothpaste.

I lift my head to look into the mirror for the first time in perhaps six months. *Damn, I'm not as ugly as I feel.* I stare into my eyes. I am looking at a stranger.

I cross the hall to my room. The light shining through the doorjamb tells me it's time to meet my roommates. I open the door and see a kid of approximately twenty, skin dark black and ashy, sitting on his bed and writing what seems to be a treatment plan. On the next bed, lying face up with legs elevated on his pillow, is a black man in his late fifties. His arms and hands are swollen, pitted and pock marked, and on his legs are the noticeable protrusions of abscesses.

The young man looks my way. "Yo, what's up? I'm Toby, and that over there is Dane."

"What's up, I'm Brandon," I say as I proceed to shake both of their hands.

Toby continues, "What brings you here, kid?"

"Dope."

He laughs. "Wait, let me guess, you one of those rich white boys who probably ran their mother's credit card up and was threatened to be kicked out, so you realized you had a problem and it's time to fix it, right?"

I reply, "No, actually I'm from an abandoned garage by Fayette and Patterson Park." Dane turns his eyes to Toby. He seems to understand that I have been set apart from the white stereotypes commonly known to them: BMW-driving rich kids who haunt black neighborhoods in search of drugs or prostitutes. Toby returns Dane's glance with a nod, and a personal connection, now established, sets us at ease.

As I prepare to put on the same clothes I have been wearing for the past few weeks, Toby asks, "Yo, where's the rest of your stuff?"

I reply, "You're looking at it."

Dane shoots Toby a look. Toby then turns to me and says, "Yo, I'm not a real smart black man but I'm guessing your family is done with you, and your friends are done with you too. The way I look at it, you ain't got shit and need all the help you can get."

I nod. "Yes."

Toby opens his dresser and tosses me a fresh pair of boxers, T-shirt, jeans, and socks. "Here, take this shit and there's plenty more where that came from." Dane then stands and throws me a sweatshirt. I thank them and again we shake hands.

Even though we are not the same color and our backgrounds are diverse, we have a mutual understanding through our common bond called Dope.

Dane relaxes with his feet propped on his pillow. Toby, on the other hand, has focused his attention on me. Although I respect and appreciate his kindness, I am Dope-sick and tired, so I keep the answers to his questions very short. The conversation feels like an interrogation.

TOBY: Yo, cuz, how old are you?
ME: Twenty-five.
TOBY: What you fuck with?
ME: Dope and coke.
TOBY: You pump or sniff?
ME: Pump.
TOBY: Damn! You was goin'!
ME: Yeah, pretty much. What's your deal?
TOBY: Well for me, I grew up aroun' the shit. The local boys would sell right on the corner down my street. I took a job here and there when I was a kid, you know what I mean, lookout for the squad cars for the corner shops on my bike at the age of thirteen. They let me start selling once I was old enough, like fifteen, sixteen. I started sniffin' every now and then, on Friday nights when me and my boys would go out to clubs. Soon it became an "every-other-day thing," and then, an "every-day-thing." But then I let it get me. I was droppin' weight, not goin' out with my boys, they could tell what was up, but we was cool, cuz I didn't let it get me too bad. But then it really got me. Soon, I was sellin' just to cover the habit, and I started shortin' the bags I was sellin', and my people finally came down, told me to clean up. No big thing. So here I am, I'll get through it and get back easy enough! I'm good like that. I always end up on my feet. So, what's your story, cuz?

Toby is interrupted by Dane. "Nigga, you remember what you felt like your first day here?!"

Toby answers, as if to a father figure, "Yeah, Dane."

"You know you wasn't up for no fucking conversation. Let the man sleep, Lord knows he probably needs the shit."

Toby replies, "You're right," and turning to me, sympathizes. "Yo, I holler at you later when you're up to it."

I curl my body into the bed and pull the covers over myself. Dane bids me goodnight. "Sleep well, nephew, I'll wake you when it's time to eat, and don't feel too bad; life ain't as bad as you think! Remember this, and never forget it, things could always be worse!"

"You're right. Thank you for everything, Dane. Thanks, Toby."

As I try to fall asleep, I think about my two new roommates, and how together, the three of us in this room represent the full circle of the Dope game. Toby is how we all started out. He thinks he has all life's answers and swears he will never end up a junkie. Next, there is me, on the next level of Dope addiction, yet still possessing enough youth and sense to escape a life of pain. Then there is Dane, representing those whose days of addiction outnumber those clean. At one point, Dane made the decision to sell his soul to the devil. Then, at almost sixty years of age, he woke up, wondering if there might be any hope for his future.

I am somehow intrigued by Dane, this original gangster, a powerful father figure who seems to have enough respect and street credibility to issue orders to whomever he wishes. His scars and abscesses attest to the fact that he has been to hell and back, several times over. What brings him here? Is rehab a part of a plea bargain through which he is avoiding a jail sentence? Perhaps he is sincere in his attempt for recovery, but why now, at his age? But then I see it. At the foot of his bed, on the dresser, sits the picture of a little black girl with a few baby teeth missing and one of the cutest smiles I have ever seen. She's so innocent, hasn't discovered that the world can be cruel. But, the more I think about it, she probably already has experienced the world's cruelty to some degree. By watching Dane go through hell, he, unintentionally, took her right along with him. As I drift off to sleep, my mind continues to contemplate Dane and his experiences on this earth.

chapter twelve
Physically Sick

Slowly, I drift into a carefree world. My body has shape, yet no density or consistency. It floats, curving, bending over and over like a piece of paper dropped from the sky.

And I land, delicately back in that abandoned garage, on the three wet cushions I call my bed. In the fantasy of my mind, I have just drawn up a sizable fix of coke and Dope. I hit a vein, and my eyes roll upward in utter ecstasy as the blood shoots into the syringe. I apply pressure on the plunger and let this wonderful drug take hold of my body and mind.

A warm sensation flows outward from my brain stem, like rippling water splashing over my body. A bittersweet scent fills my nostrils and my expanding lungs, forcing the delicious air into my bloodstream as I surrender to all present stimulus.

A shot of Dope. Freedom. Responsibilities disintegrate. Burdens dispel. The only thing that now has relevance is another shot of Dope. Neither morals, nor character, nor principles. Thirty ccs on the hypodermic will disperse life's petty obligations in all directions.

My eyes snap open and dart from side to side. Yes, the room is my own, the bed is my own, number 361-B. My nightmare is over, but I am not relieved. I wish it had been real.

It is normal for recoving addicts to, in a sleeping state, experience a succession of vivid images and sensations reminiscent of their drug experiences. This is because the dreamer is mourning the loss of something equivalent to the relationship one shares with a best friend, family member, lover, or mistress.

Withdrawal. The body, in adapting to continued drug abuse, undergoes defensive chemical alterations in order to lessen the drug's effects. This phenomenon, "tolerance," requires the addict to administer increased doses of the drug in order to achieve the level of high he once experienced. This progression develops into a matured state—"physical dependence." The body's chemical adaptations that once had occurred to oppose the drug now happen *in expectation* of the drug, and if unopposed, cause the addict to suffer depression, anxiety, and physical pain, or "withdrawal." Withdrawal may take up to several days, which is why addicts refer to the first week of rehab as "Hell Week."

With tearing eyes, mucus in continuous flow from my nose, I lie under the blankets, covered head to toe in a fetal position. I have a fever, yet I am shivering and cold. Although I am physically and mentally exhausted, comfort is an impossibility and sleep is futile.

The only thing keeping me together is the thought of my mother. I find comfort in imagining her calm, soothing voice, telling me, "Hang in there, baby, you can do it, you're strong. I have faith in you."

As I lie on the bed, I observe some markings that a former resident, who has slept on this very bed, has drawn on the ceiling. Above me are two groups of lines, which I recognize as a countdown chart to keep track of his days remaining in this place. But as I count them I realize there are only nine, and I come to a sad realization that this patient had not completed his fourteen days of detox and had gone back to the streets. A.M.A., against medical advice. He could be dead by now. I wonder. . . .

Nausea causes me to jump from my bed and run to the bathroom. My mouth, full of throw up, explodes warm vomit all over the bathroom tiles. I slump over the toilet, spitting my guts up. Since it's been quite some time since I've eaten, the throw up consists of bile and the lining of my stomach, mixed with a little bit of blood. It hurts so bad, but I'm somewhat happy because I know the toxins are leaving my body.

I stand up to wipe my mouth with toilet paper. I flush the toilet and stare at the vomit all over the floor. I don't want to clean it up, but I know it's the right thing to do. I'm starting to understand that this whole process of change begins with doing things I don't want to do. Discomfort. So I retrieve cleaning supplies from the closet, and mop, rinse, and clean the vomit from the floor. Now finished, I put the supplies away and return to my room where my warm bed awaits my arrival.

Now in bed, with wrenching pain throughout my body, I fade in and out. My reality exists in moments of awareness, separated by moments of non-awareness. . . .

FADE IN:

"Yo! Yo, white boy! White boy!" My eyes open, and I see Toby standing above my bed. "You ain't dead are you?" he asks with a smile on his face.

I reply, "No, but right now that might be my best option."

"Stop trippin', white boy we got you!"

Dane says, "You missed breakfast. It's time for lunch, you coming?"

I shut my eyes and shake my head. "No."

"You sure?" he asks.

I shake my head. "Yes."

Dane replies, "Nephew! You got to eat; you need as much strength as you can get to make it through that motha fuckin' jungle. My cousin works in the kitchen. I'm gonna get him to hit me off with some extra shit and bring it back up for you."

I whisper a feeble, "Thank you."

BLACKNESS.

FADE IN:

I awake and notice that Dane has procured extra food from the cafeteria. A sandwich and fries. This is no easy feat, because servings are limited to one meal a person. This gesture proves to me that Dane is a man of his word, but unfortunately, I'm so sick that the mere thought of eating makes me want to throw up.

BLACKNESS.

FADE IN:

My eyes open as I hear Dane's voice. "Nephew, you need to eat. Take a few bites of this." Dane holds a sandwich to my mouth and begins feeding me. "I know it probably makes you sick to think of, but it's another one of those things you just have to do."

As I take each bite, I grow more and more nauseous, but I need all the strength I can get. The faster I recuperate, the faster I can feel like I'm worth anything at all. Then and only then I can rebuild my life and most important, my mind.

BLACKNESS.

FADE IN:

The lights are out. Toby is asleep. Dane is on his knees praying.

BLACKNESS.

chapter thirteen
Dane

My eyes open. Toby stands over me. "Yo! It's time for the first smoke of the day, you coming, cuz?"

"What time is it?" I squint.

"Five. You coming?"

"I just can't . . ."

Things are bad, I think, when a cigarette, the one thing that will take the edge off, will require too much energy to smoke.

My two roommates scuttle about to make roll call. As they get dressed, Toby acts as though he's getting ready for a social event, changing several times until he finds the right outfit. Dane, on the other hand, preferring to let his reputation speak for him, throws on a pair of sweat clothes. As they leave, they extend their offer one more time, but again I decline.

I lay back in a spell of self-pity. Overtaken by the overwhelming urge to shit, I jump from my bed and hurry to the bathroom, but the exertion overwhelms my body so much that I can't hold back. Diarrhea runs down my legs. "Damn," I scold myself. "Look at me. Twenty-five years old and shitting myself like a baby." As I sit on the toilet to finish what I have already started, I wipe the shit from my leg. Physically and emotionally, I have been reduced to an infant. I stand and flush the toilet, humiliated and worthless.

As I exit the stall, I see a young white kid washing his hands and face. I size him up: a hundred percent Irish, red hair combed with a sharp part, an expensive-looking gold necklace, button-up oxford blue shirt, freshly ironed khaki shorts, new pair of summer sandals, clean shaven. All of these features lead me to believe that he is either a paid employee or a college intern, save one remarkable quality: upon his face is a smile.

"What's your name?" the white kid asks.

"Brandon. What are you, my counselor or something?"

"No, man, I'm a patient. I'm Sean Williams. Good to meet you."

I think, Fucking liar! What's so good about meeting me?! But I reply, "Yeah, good to meet you, too."

As I attempt to make my way to my room, he continues. "How long you been here?"

I stop, turning halfway to him. "I got here yesterday."

"So you're in your second day without drugs?" Obviously.

I roll my eyes. "Yup, my second day in here, my second day without drugs. Got any more questions for me?"

He replies, "No."

As I walk away, he calls out, "Hang in there, you can do it"— a comment I do not acknowledge. Why does everyone here seem to have such confidence in me? Don't they know I always fuck up?

Again in the room. Dane enters, followed by Toby, who storms through the door, rapping. Once inside, Dane assumes his usual position on his bed, propping his legs on a pillow, folding his hands behind his head.

Toby pulls a picture from his drawer and stares into the photo. He looks at me, looking at him. "You want to sneak a peek?"

I say, "Sure."

Toby shows me a picture of a beautiful black girl in sexy lingerie.

He says, "You like that shit, don't you, white boy?!"

"Yeah."

Dane, possessing only a fraction of Toby's energy, breaks his silence. "Nephew, how you holdin' up?"

I reply, "Fucking horrible, but I'm doin' it somehow."

"Just hold on, son. Lemme tell you, if I would have cleaned up at your age, I would look and feel like a completely different person now. I might look pretty bad at fifty-eight, but, at one point, I had it goin' on. Say, you ain't eat breakfast, you coming to lunch?"

"No thanks, not yet."

Toby tells Dane, "Come on, man. Let's hit lunch. White boy just needs sleep."

Dane looks at me, troubled. "Nah, son, I'll meet you down there."

Toby, uncertain, replies, "Yo, I'll just wait."

But Dane refuses. "Nah, go ahead, nephew. I'll meet you there."

Toby shrugs in an insecure manner. "All right I guess." He gathers up his nerve and leaves.

Dane knows I'm not holding up too well. I place my hand over my face in hope that he'll believe I'm just too exhausted to talk.

"Cuz, what's wrong?" he asks.

I answer, "Nothing, Dane, why?" I'm not fooling him. He knows the exact problem. He senses my self-doubt. He's fifty-eight; he's been here before.

Dane swings his feet off the bed and to the floor. He pulls a chair from the corner of the room, places it by the side of my bed, and in sitting, touches his right hand to mine. "Nephew, check this out."

Dane's voice alters in tone, from forceful and stern to caring and compassionate. "You're twenty-five, and by the looks of you, you've been to hell and back several times. I know this isn't your first time in detox so you know this feeling. But listen . . ."

I take a good look at Dane, and I can tell that he's having a difficult time with what he's about to say. In my condition, I don't have the energy for concentration. But, seeing that what he was about to tell me was so painful for him, I found myself clinging onto every word.

Dane continues. "When I was seventeen years old, my mother was a maid for some white folks and my father was a street hustler who made very good money by catering to the upper-class whites. By this point in my life I was a full-blown Heroin addict who got his fix by skimming off the top of each package I delivered for my father, usually to some white man in a big limo. It was a cold January morning. I'm up in my room throwing up due to lack of Dope in my system. When I heard footsteps on the way to my door, I felt better because I knew what was about to go down. After a knock on my door I yell, 'Come in.'

"My father entered. He says, 'Look here, son, I need you to go to North Broadway and East Preston. You'll see a white limo. Hop in and give this package to the man.' I act like I don't want to, just to make him believe he can fully trust me. When he leaves me with the package, I grab my needle, cooker, and some clean water. I stop at the convenience store bathroom one block from my house to fix up and skim some for later. I guess I skimmed a little too much, because I was so high by the time I got home, my father saw the condition I was in and took me straight to rehab."

Dane swallows and continues the story. "The second day into it I'm woken up by my counselor who tells me we must speak immediately. She takes me to her office, where my father sits in a pool of tears. He tells me the man I delivered to the day before kicked in the door that morning and stabbed my mother to death, and left a note that read, 'I bet you won't short any more of my packages.' "

I stare at him, sorry for the horrible experience he is still trying to recover from more than forty years later.

"Nephew, I tell you that story for a reason. Always remember: Yesterday's history, tomorrow is a mystery. Everything that has happened, or ever will happen, is somehow a part of a larger plan. You may not understand why you have to go through some experiences, but you have to trust and believe in the process. Because that process is your life, and that's all you got."

After a moment of silence, Dane says, "Enough of this deep intimate shit. You need some new food; that stuff I brought you yesterday is stale. I'll bring you a sandwich and something to drink." As he exits, he leaves me with one more statement. "I got your back, nephew, I'm here for you."

I don't know what I did to deserve his kindness, but I gladly accept it.

As I lie in the bed, I am overcome by a cramp so violent that it seems to contract my every muscle, ligament, and organ. The pain of being alive is almost too much to bear. My body involuntarily lifts my head and projects a mouthful of vomit directly to the floor, my dresser, and my shoes. In an attempt to clean the mess, I force myself to stand, and the room gets foggy. . . .

My eyes open. Toby is frantically shaking me. "White boy, white boy, please don't die on me! Come on, cuz, wake up, please!"

I look from side to side and realize that I am lying on the floor in the pool of vomit. "Sorry about the throw up, I'm gonna clean it up right now," I tell him.

I hear Dane's voice. "Like hell you are! I'll tell you what you're gonna do, you're gonna drink this water. Me and Toby will clean this up."

As Dane hands me a cup of water, Toby screams, "What? I don't even clean my own room, why should I clean that shit?"

Dane shoots Toby a very serious look. " 'Cause you should! Now get some towels, and a bucket and a mop." Toby doesn't question Dane's authority; he immediately heads to the hall closet to retrieve the supplies.

"I'm sorry, Dane. I meant to clean it up."

"Yo, I know you meant well. Don't worry about Toby, he just don't know any better."

Dane helps wipe the vomit off me as he gives Toby instructions on how to use a mop. I take a moment to grasp the significance of this situation, that two people I've just met are taking care of me in my worst condition.

After they finish wiping up my bile, Toby complains until Dane tells him to "Quit acting like a fucking baby. You got to understand something, son. Discipline. Lemme tell you, there's a difference between a grown man and a real man. And that difference is, a real man knows how to take personal responsibility for things, and to do the things in life that ought to be done. And this begins with doing the little things that you don't want to do, which give you the courage to face the bigger things. You'll come to see that as time goes on."

Turning to me, Dane says, "Okay, it's time to get to group. I know you ain't making this session, white boy. Toby, let's go."

Before Toby exits, he kneels down beside my bed. "Look, cuz, we're two different people from two different places who come off a little different. But at the end of it all, I'm here for you. If you need anything, just ask."

"Thank you, Toby, I appreciate that. I don't think you know how much that means to me."

He replies, "Yeah, I do," winks and exits.

Again I fade out. Dusk falls. As I lie in the pitch-black room, the door opens and I'm blinded by the hallway light.

"Brandon? Brandon, are you in here? Is that you?"

I reply with, "Who the fuck is that?"

"It's me, Sean Williams."

Christ! I forgot all about this kid and was hoping to keep it that way. What does he want?

chapter fourteen
Sean Williams

"Brandon? Can I come in?" asks Sean Williams.

I really wanted to say, "Fuck, no, you can't come in! I don't have the energy to be around someone displaying your level of happiness and joy!" But I take into consideration that Sean Williams is, after all, a good kid who probably needs to get some things off his chest to the only person in rehab he could identify with. After all, we are the only white guys there. I reply, "Sure, come on in."

Sean Williams grabs a chair, pulls it up to my bed, a bit too close, and sits, staring into my face. His air of intense enthusiasm is, to put it bluntly, uncomfortable. I break the silence. "What's going on, Sean Williams?"

"Nothing much. I was worried. I didn't see you at lunch or dinner today. I'm so glad you didn't leave, even though I thought you did."

"Your caring for me is a nice gesture, but the reality of the situation is I'm too sick to even make it to the bathroom. If I wanted to leave, I have nowhere to go, not to mention I don't even have ten cents to my name, let alone ten dollars for a fix. So at this point my only option is to remain in this bed. You don't have to worry about me going anywhere anytime soon. I can't afford it and I don't have it in me."

"I was just in the lounge watching TV with Toby, Dane, and some other fellows you haven't met yet."

Who the fuck gives a shit? Jesus, doesn't this guy take a fucking hint?

I say, "That's great and all, Sean Williams, but the way I feel right now I could care less if an atomic bomb was about to blow this whole world up. Actually, I might get excited if that were the case."

Sean Williams continues. "Man, your roommate Toby is hilarious. He's back there putting on a rap concert while his buddy supplies the beats with his mouth, while he uses the table for a drum."

I am taken back, amazed at this kid, this eternal optimist. No matter how hard I try to blow him off, no matter how little interest I show, he keeps trying to get to know me. This is pretty strange. I sit up to take in a clear picture of this guy named Sean Williams.

"Yeah, Toby is a handful," I reply.

"I hope you don't mind, but Dane told me about you, and he told me I could find you here. He said that I should come and talk to you, about stuff," Sean Williams said.

This guy is a friend of Dane's? I become more receptive to the conversation.

"What brings you here, Sean Williams?"

"Coke," he tells me. "Where you from, Brandon?"

"East Baltimore, and yourself?"

"I'm from Harford County. As you probably know, it's real nice there. My parents have a nice house, and I had a good childhood and a lot of great opportunities. Well, anyway, a few years ago, I started smoking weed and drinking on the weekends. I had one group of friends who were using coke. One night I was out with them and got curious and did my first line before the wine was served. I really liked it! It started out as a social thing, but then I got into it really bad. First I did a bump or two when I was up late studying or trying to complete a term paper in time for a tight deadline. Then I was doing a bump before class to stay awake, then lines in the bathroom at parties. Part of the problem was that I had the money to pay for it, so, I kind of dug quite a deep hole for myself before things fell apart. By the end, I was at a point where I would barricade myself in my room and do like two eight-balls a day by myself. I would start puking out my windows and calling the police saying people were after me. It got totally out of hand."

I figured as much. Sometimes I used to spot rich cokeheads from Harford County driving around in their BMWs in the shadier parts of Baltimore City looking for a score when their usual connections were dry. These were rare occasions, ones I thanked God for, because rich whites are afraid of black people, so they would inevitably see me and ask if I could score for them. They're naïve, paranoid of getting busted, and scared of the neighborhood, so they're easy to take advantage of. In addition to a cash fee for making the score, I'd burn them as well. If they wanted dime bags, I'd get them nickels. If they wanted eight-balls, I'd pinch off half. But if I was having a horrible day, they were shit out of luck because I would just disappear with their cash. And the beauty of pulling a scam on one of these punks is they always have too much to lose and are frightened to take retribution.

I never cared for these Harford County brats, but something about this Sean Williams kid shows character. I like him for some reason. I'm curious, and now I'm the one asking the questions. "How old are you, Sean Williams?"

"Eighteen."

"Is this your first time in rehab?" I ask.

"Yup. That's why I really wanted to come here. My parents wanted me to go to some really rich-kid rehab that's more like a vacation than a lesson. I thought about going there, but to me, going someplace nice seemed more like a reward than a wakeup call. I don't want to stay isolated in a rich-kid world. I don't think that would help me understand what I can lose in life if I go back to using. I decided I need to gain a little . . . worldliness, I guess is a good way to say it. I wanted to be with guys who have way worse backgrounds than me, so I can understand what addiction really means, how bad things might get, and what I might turn into if I don't shape up."

"Do you still live at home with your parents?"

"Yeah," he replies. "They're really cool and super supportive of what I'm doing. I'm going back home instead of a halfway house when I get out of here, but I'm gonna make it. I don't want to get high anymore," he says with determination.

I figure I should share some of my experiences with Sean Williams. Hell, it might help the kid. After all, everyone else here is trying to help me. What was that Mrs. Evans said? The "therapeutic value of one addict helping another." I guess it's my turn to help.

I perk up, as much as my body would allow without vomiting. "Check this out. At one time I was exactly like you. I was eighteen, in rehab. You like coke, well I like Dope; that's the only difference. My mother was very supportive; everyone still trusted me. I hadn't really lost anything yet due to drugs and I still had a good bit of cash put away for when I was released. All the old-timers would approach me with the same comment: 'Young man, I wish I had the chance to try to get clean at your age. Take advantage of this opportunity. Stop while you have the chance.'

"As you can see, Sean Williams, I didn't heed their warning, because I'm offering you the same advice right now. What they said was true. Now I'm passing the word. If you don't stop, you'll end up just like me, if you don't die first. I have no one in my life because I didn't learn during my first trip to rehab. I've betrayed, robbed, and lied to everyone who cared about me. You still have a home to go to. You still have hope to salvage your relationships. I have no one and nowhere to go when I leave here. It's a very sad and lonely road, but you don't have to travel it. You still have a chance, I swear to you, Sean Williams." As our conversation winds down, I feel that I might be developing a friendship with this kid.

We are interrupted by an announcement over the loudspeaker. "Okay, it's that time, gentlemen. Return to your room; lights out in ten minutes. Congratulations on another day clean."

chapter fifteen
Mentally Sick

I get some more sleep. When I awake, I stare into the darkness around me. Toby is sleeping quietly. Dane bellows out loud snores. I've given up on trying to keep track of the time; withdrawal has made the concept irrelevant. Life now consists of two times: day and night.

I am burning hot and my sheets are drenched. I relocate to the cold cement floor. The cold hard tiles feel so good on my body, but I am still unable to find relief. My head is pounding. Pounding with pain, but also questions.

Along with the physical pain, withdrawal brings emotional pain. The pain of ignorance. The realization that there are so many things to understand.

Self-doubt plagues me. Can I really do this?

A thousand daggers stab at my mind: my childhood, my mother, my brother and sister. All the friends I've lost. All the pain I've caused. This is what makes detox so difficult—facing reality. I'm full of shame and guilt, with no one to lean on because I've torn apart every relationship I have.

I've mistreated everyone in my life. When people loved me, I saw opportunity to take. When they showed me kindness, I saw it as weakness. I stomped out the good intentions and feelings of the beautiful people God had blessed me with.

How could I be so selfish?

All I have ever done with those who have loved me is betrayed their trust. I was a dreamseller, a medium through which my loved ones could project what they wanted to believe, what they dared to dream—that I would be well. I sold them a dream, something that never existed in the first place, their own idealistic vision of me. The dream that I was a recovering addict who just needed a few dollars so I could get something to eat, or I needed money to buy new clothes for a job interview, or I needed a security deposit for an apartment. I told them anything they wanted to hear, anything to get my precious next fix.

My mind was clouded for so long, all I could see was that fucking drug.

I must learn to re-create the way my mind thinks and reacts.

My brain needs to change. A real chemical and emotional change, not a drug-induced stupor.

I pace like a caged lion.

What's this? I spot a familiar-looking blue-covered book on Dane's desk that is titled, *The Basic Text,* which addicts call "The Big Book." This paperback is equivalent to a recovering addict's Bible, because it outlines the AA and NA Twelve-Step program. I'm familiar with this book because I was given a copy during a former trip to rehab. I took it home and would act as if I was reading it whenever I wanted to scam my mother for drug money. Occasionally, in an act of defiance, I would cut up dope on the cover. I never even thought about really reading and understanding it until tonight. I grab the book and walk out into the hallway with a blanket wrapped around me, looking somewhat like a monk.

I hear the washer and dryer running in the laundry room at the end of the hall. When I arrive, the small, warm room seems perfect for me to do some reading without being distracted. The vibration and heat of the dryer feel good on my back as I open the Blue Book and begin my journey.

The book teaches me that in order to recover, addicts must put to rest our current behaviors, responses, and reactions that had set us up for failure in life. We must recondition ourselves and learn to create a new lifestyle centered around priorities, positivity, morals, and values. It outlines techniques to transform old habits into a new, productive, fresh way of living. The book breaks recovery down into a format. If the addict really desires to recover, and has the will to follow the steps, this book can pave the way to a successful recovery.

I lose track of the time until I hear voices as everyone is waking up. Morning. Before the hallways become full of people lining up to go to breakfast, I hightail it back to my room to avoid any conversations.

As I enter the room, Dane and Toby are waking up. Toby says, "Where you comin' from? What, you have a date last night?"

I look at my bed to find that it has been made. Dane says, "I know you must have had a rough night and you could use a little help."

"You didn't have to do that, Dane."

"Man, shut up, nephew. I've been in your situation and someone was there to help me."

I grab my towel and toothbrush and proceed to the showers, feeling relaxed, comfortable. The heat from the water is absorbed through my skin, into my bones, and provides relief from the withdrawal.

As I brush my teeth, I glimpse myself in the mirror again. As

I mentioned before, for the past few years I have avoided my reflection because it evokes feelings of depression. But this time, the outcome is positive. Now I see hope, progress, a future. I see someone I recognize. Brandon?

I leave the bathroom feeling much better. I'm physically clean, mentally clean, and I'm prepared to make improvements.

I enter my room to find that someone has left a bag of clothes on my bed and a note that reads:

> Brandon,
> I thought I'd stop by this morning. I asked how you were and he said you had a pretty rough night. Way to hang in there! You give me hope, and our conversation gave me a lot of inspiration. I thought you could use some extra clothes. They're all brand new. I seemed to have over-packed, so help yourself. I'll see you later.
>
> Your friend,
> Sean Williams

It's so unusual for people to show me gratitude. I search my feelings for the appropriate response and realize I don't really know how to react.

A strange, unfamiliar sensation scratches at the pit of my stomach . . .

What's this? Hunger? I'm actually starved; it's a fucking miracle. My body is showing signs of life. I'm coming around. I make a dent in the pile of food that has been accumulating on my dresser by the grace of Dane's street cred: donuts, sandwiches, French fries—I eat it all, and top it off with a vitamin that Toby gives me.

Toby shouts out, "He's alive. Maybe you're not going to die on me after all, white boy."

"I'm not going out that easy!"

Knock, knock, knock!

Dane says, "Come in."

The door opens. It's a thin black man of average height. He has a fresh haircut and is sharply dressed.

"Are you Mr. Novak?" he asks.

"Yeah, what's going on?"

"Mr. Novak, I'm Guy Leeper, your counselor."

I shake his hand.

"We have an appointment this morning," Mr. Leeper says.

"Oh, yeah, I completely forgot. Sorry, man."

"Don't worry about it. Get yourself together and meet me in the office in a few minutes," my counselor says.

"I can be ready in one minute. If you just wait a second, I'll go with you."

Guy Leeper replies, "Seriously?"

"Yeah. Let me throw some pants and a shirt on; I'm pretty much ready to go."

"Don't forget to brush your teeth," Mr. Leeper says.

"Already did!"

"I like your motivation," Guy says.

"Motivation for what?"

He replies, "Motivation to change your life. Let's go to my office. Today is the day we start airing out your old life and bringing you into the new one, Mr. Novak."

chapter sixteen
The First Step of a Long Journey

It is 8:30 A.M. I am cradled in the deep cushions of a soft, velvety chair, the purpose of which is to comfort those who employ it. It is not working for me.

It is the counselor's job to assess client strengths, problem areas, severity of dependence, and readiness to change. He must develop strategies that assist clients to set goals and to effect change. Since I am here for only a two-week rehab, Mr. Leeper has less than 14 days to achieve these goals.

Mr. Leeper sits quietly, shuffling papers and writing notes. My anticipation makes me feel as if he's doing this just to agitate me.

Finally, Mr. Leeper looks up. "Mr. Novak?"

"Right, yeah, you got it," I reply.

He gives me the standard introduction: "My name is Mr. Leeper. I am a certified counselor, and I'll be helping you out with your drug problem. I can answer any questions you have. Hopefully we can form some kind of relationship, because what it all comes down to is that the more you trust me and let me in, the more I can help."

He blinks, as if to accent the importance of his following statement. "But ultimately, Mr. Novak, I can only help you if you want it, and you and only you know if you're truly done with this drug problem of yours. You may be able to lie to me, but ultimately, you're only lying to yourself. I get my paycheck regardless, if you want help or not. But by the look of all your previous attempts to get clean, you could probably use my help."

I stare at him, waiting to hear the rest.

He proceeds. "Look, Mr. Novak, I know this isn't fun in here, a grown man constantly being told what to do, when to eat, when to smoke, when to go to bed, when to wake up, basically being treated like a little kid. I don't say that, Mr. Novak, to belittle you or make you feel like I'm better than you in any way. At one point in my life I sat on the other side of this table in that same chair you sit in at this very moment. I, too, was once a client of this treatment center. By no means was it easy, but it was absolutely worth every struggle and hard time I went through to obtain the life that I now live."

He looks at me to see if I'm with him. I'm listening.

"What's your drug of choice?" he asks in a calm, serious tone.

Still nervous and uncomfortable, I answer, "Dope."

"Have you been arrested for drugs or drug-related charges?"

"Yes," I reply.

"How many times have you been arrested?"

"Maybe fifteen or twenty."

"Well, I'm looking at your chart here. It says this is your third time at Tuerk House, and you have spent time in what looks to be seven other rehabs. Is that correct?"

"Something like that."

He continues. "Well, if it gives you any encouragement, I didn't get it on my first try either. Actually not on my second, third, or even fourth try. Sometimes the individual may need a drastic relapse to see clearly what it is that causes addiction: a disease. Mr.

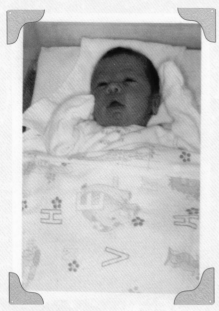

Me, just born: December 10,
1977, 11:25 a.m., 6 pounds,
11 ounces.

Here I am, just a little kid,
with my German shepherd,
either Jake or Sunshine (we
had two).

Was I a cute
kid, or what?

I guess I was 5 here.
For some reason, I don't
look too happy with my
He-Man sword and shield!

Me, at about 7,
the age when I
really took to the
skateboard.

I am about 10 or so in this photo.

Okay, here I am at about 12 or 13. I had begun smoking pot and having a few beers here and there.

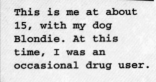

This is me at about 15, with my dog Blondie. At this time, I was an occasional drug user.

Me, at about 17 or 18, with my dog Blondie. At this point, I was committed to my drug abuse and traveling down the road of addiction.

Photos courtesy
Pat Novak

NAME: *Novak Brandon*

RT-14 TUERK HOUSE   C

BED # *361B*   H

ADMIT DATE: *8/11/03*   DOB: *12-10-78*

Here is the famous photo that was taken on the
day I arrived at the Tuerk House. I weighed
115 pounds or so at the time. I was about
to smile and thought, "What the fuck do I have to
smile about?" Then, *snap*, the Polaroid was taken.
The year of my birth shown is incorrect. (I was
actually born in 1977, as I mentioned.) I lied
about this whenever I got arrested. That way, the
computers at police stations wouldn't pull up all
my prior rap sheets. I had gotten so used to
lying about my birth date that I had forgotten
the real one!

Photo courtesy Brandon Novak

April and Phil Margera with Jess and Bam,
circa 1986, when Bam began skating. I met
Bam about two years later.
Photo courtesy April and Phil Margera

A 180 stale fish. I was about 7 or 8.
Photo courtesy Pat Novak

Photos by Geoff Graham

I am the little kid in blue. Here, Bucky Lasek is pulling an ollie to fakie on a ramp in Dundalk, Maryland, Bucky's hometown. You can tell by my face how much I looked up to him.

Now I am watching in awe as Bucky Lasek pulls off an indy grab.

That's me pulling an ollie, one foot. As a kid, I was an apt skater, prior to the discovery of drugs.

Here I am in my early teens pulling a frontside 180 nose blunt.
Photo by Geoff Graham

This photo was taken in 1996 on my last
tour with the Powell Peralta team, right
before Mike Vallely gave me the ultimatum
that made me quit the team. *Left to
right:* Charlie Wilkins, Mike Vallely, me
(obviously stoned), and Danny Wainwright.
Photo courtesy Mike Vallely

Here are some of the
awards I won for
skateboarding in my
youth. There were a
lot more, but many
have been lost or
demolished over the
years. Photo courtesy
Mandy Novak

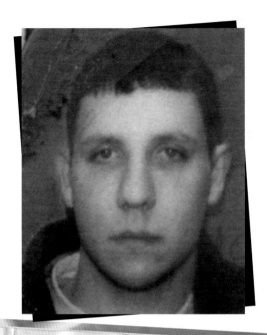

DATE: 06/28/01
TRICT 01

INDEX OF CRIMINAL CASES CLOSED FROM 01/01/81 THROUGH 12/31/00
(INCLUDES CRIMINAL AND HOUSING AUTHORITY CITATIONS AND FUGITIVE WARRANTS)

PAGE B092
JOB CODE A70CA201

DIST/ LOC	CASE NO.	TRACKING NO.	DEFENDANT NAME	CASE DISP DISP DATE	WRITTEN CHARGE	CHARGE VERDICT	DATE
01 01	6B00142596	966005604480	NOVACK, BRADLEY T JR MRE				
01 01	3B00151196	966005610500	NOVAK, BRANDON T	TRL 10/25/96	CDS:POSSESSION	6412	10/25/96
01 01	3B00151196	966005610500	NOVAK, BRANDON T	TRL 10/25/96	CDS:POSSESSION	6412	10/25/96
01 01	3B00151329	966002348334	NOVAK, THOMAS J JR	TRL 10/25/96	CDS:POSSESSION	6412	10/25/96
				TRL 03/26/99	CDS:POSS PARAPHERNALIA	NP	12/31/96
					CDS:POSSESSION	G	12/31/96
					CDS:POSSESSION	NP	12/31/96
01 03	2B00399905	996004158774	NOVAK, BRANDEN T		LOITERING	NP	12/31/96
01 03	3B01349435	016004110345	NOVAK, BRANDEN T	TRL 11/24/99	THEFT:LESS $300 VALUE	NP	11/24/99
01 03	5B01516765	036004122615	NOVAK, BRANDEN T	TRL 03/05/01	CDS: POSSESSION-MARIHUANA	NP	03/05/01
04 03	6B01518404	992002565536	NOVAK, BRANDEN THOMAS	JTP 08/01/03	CDS:POSSESS-NOT MARIHUANA		
					CDS:POSSESS-NOT MARIHUANA		
01 03	3B01445594	021001701991	NOVAK, BRANDON THOMAS	TRL 06/17/03	LOITERING	NP	06/17/03
				TRL 03/11/03	BURGLARY-FIRST DEGREE	NP	02/04/03
					BURGLARY-THIRD DEGREE	STET	03/11/03
					BURGLARY-FOURTH DEGREE	STET	03/11/03
					THEFT: $500 PLUS VALUE	STET	03/11/03

3B01349435	Novak, Branden T	12/1977	Defendant	Baltimore City District Court 1400 North Ave.	CR	Closed	
5B01516765	Novak, Branden T	12/1978	Defendant	Baltimore City District Court 1400 North Ave.	CR	Closed	05/29/2003
803216006	Novak, Branden T	12/1978	Defendant	Baltimore City Circuit Court	Criminal	Closed	08/04/2003
808064011	Novak, Branden T	12/1978	Defendant	Baltimore City Circuit Court	Criminal	ACTIVE	03/04/2008
000000CH16839	Novak, Branden Thomas	12/1978	Defendant	Baltimore County District Court	Traffic	Closed	02/02/2004
000000CH16840	Novak, Branden Thomas	12/1978	Defendant	Baltimore County District Court	Traffic	Closed	02/02/2004
000000CH16842	Novak, Branden Thomas	12/1978	Defendant	Baltimore County District Court	Traffic	Closed	02/02/2004
000000CH16843	Novak, Branden Thomas	12/1978	Defendant	Baltimore County District Court	Traffic	Closed	02/02/2004
000000CH16844	Novak, Branden Thomas	12/1978	Defendant	Baltimore County District Court	Traffic	Closed	02/02/2004
4C00111598	Novak, Branden Thomas	12/1977	Defendant	Towson District Court	CR	Closed	10/11/1999

These are a few of my arrest records. The rest have been lost in the paperwork shuffle. Photos/records courtesy Brandon Novak

DEFENDANT TRIAL SUMMARY

The above case was POSTPONED today, 06/12/2003.
    REASON: NO OFFER.
YOUR NEXT COURT APPEARANCE IS SCHEDULED FOR TRIAL on 08/01/2003 at 08:30 a.m. in Room 3 at
the District Court of Maryland for BALTIMORE CITY located at 1400 E. NORTH AVE, BALTIMORE, MD
21213-1400.

(NOVAK, BRANDEN T)

6/12/2003   Defendant

Tracking No.

DPSCS-DPP-ADM 19 (REV. 6/00)

STATE OF MARYLAND
DEPARTMENT OF PUBLIC SAFETY AND CORRECTIONAL SERVICES
DIVISION OF PAROLE AND PROBATION
2100 GUILFORD AVENUE ❖ BALTIMORE, MARYLAND 21218
V/TTY FOR THE DEAF 1-800-735-2258 (MARYLAND RELAY SERVICE)
VOICE: 410-333-6270, EXT. 346
FAX: 410-333-2874

ROBERT L. EHRLICH JR.
GOVERNOR

MICHAEL S. STEELE
LT. GOVERNOR

MARY ANN SAAR
ACTING SECRETARY

JUDITH SACHWALD
DIRECTOR

Date: AUGUST 8, 2003

BRANDEN NOVAK

Dear MR NOVAK:

You have been placed under probation, parole, o
Division of Parole and Probation (DPP) and were ins
Our records indicate that you failed to report to the Int
your conditions of supervision. Accordingly, you a
following receipt of this letter to:

Agent	Office Location
#31 A SMITH #2982114	3027 E MADISON STR... BALTIMORE, MD 21...

Please understand that if you fail to report as instr...
violation of your supervision, and a warrant for your...
bring a copy of this letter with you when you report.

If you have questions, please contact your agent.

Sincerely,

DEPARTMENT OF PUBLIC SAFETY AND CORRECTIONAL SERVICES
DIVISION OF PAROLE AND PROBATION
INSTRUCTIONS TO PAYOR

Case Name: Novak

Agent/Monitor: Horsey

Telephone Number: (4...)

On 12/14/99 you were placed on parole/probation/mandatory supervision. As a condition of that
supervision, you were ordered to pay as follows:

$ Restitution			
$ Court Cost	$ Fines		Additional Fees
$ Alcohol Testing Fee	$ Attorney's Fee		
$ LET	Monthly Supv. Fee	$ 25.00 Monthly Supv.
	$ 120.00 DPP LAP Testing Fee	$ Per Drug Test
	TOTALS $ 570.00		

If any of the above monies owed are to be determined at a later date, your payments will be adjusted
accordingly.

Your payment plan is as follows:

First payment is due on 12/14/99 in the amount of $ 65.03
Thereafter, monthly payments are due in the amount of $ 35.00 for
_____ months. Additional payments as follows:
+35.00 per month

Unpaid debt will be forwarded to the Central Collection Unit A 17% collection fee will be added to the unpaid
debt. Failure to pay as directed could result in you supervision being revoked.

Money order or certified check only – do no send cash. Make money orders or certified checks payable to the
Division of Parole and Probation. Mail to:

Division of Parole and probation Collection and Accounting Unit
P.O. Box 2356
Baltimore, Maryland 21203

1. Always include your Parole & Probation case # 446934 on both your envelope and certified
   check/money order.
2. Any correspondence or questions should be directed to your agent/monitor.
3. Always notify your agent/monitor in the event that you change addresses. Also,
   let your agent/monitor know of any changes that affect your ability to pay as ordered
4. Overpayments in the amount of $3.00 or less will not be routinely refunded. To
   receive a refund of $3.00 or less you must request same in writing.

I understand and accept the above conditions.

Signature of Payor: X Branden Novak   Date: 12/14/98
Federal law provides that you do not have to disclose your social security number. ☑ I do or ☐ I do not authorize
Division of Parole and Probation rto release my social security number to the Central Collection Unit to collect any
unpaid monies. ☐ I do, ☐ I do not authorize release of my social security number for use in the HIDTA Automated
Treatment and tracking System (H.A.T.T.S).

Signature of Payor: X Branden Novak   Date: 12/14/9...

Anne Arundel County Crime Lab - CDS

Controlled Dangerous Substance Violation
Report Date 1/16/2003   Report # 1

Offense Description : Controlled Dangerous Substance Violation
Laboratory Case # : L03-0042
Complaint Number   : 0173, SCHAUMAN   Page 1 of 1
Case Officer   : Charles L. Johnson, Forensic Chemist II - CDS
Analyzed By   : 1/7/2003   Case Names:
Offense Date   :   NOVAK, BRANDON T - Suspect

Reference : 2B1 POST

Agency   : MTA - Light Rail
Attention : Submitting Officer

Results of Examination/Analysis:

Item 1   One heat-sealed plastic bag containing:
            4 glass vial(s) containing: white powder described as IN A
            CELLOPHANE WRAPPER

    Conclusion: Chemical and instrumental analysis revealed the presence of
            Diacetylmorphine, commonly referred to as Heroin, which is a
            Schedule I Controlled Dangerous Substance.
            TOTAL WT. = 4.11 g
            CDS WT. = 0.31 gr

I hereby certify that I am employed by the Anne Arundel C
the Maryland State Department of Health and Mental Hygi
tested by me utilizing analytical and quality control proced
Hygiene

The evidence is being retained in the CDS Evidence Roo

Reviewed By _____

OF SHOW CAUSE

...NED TO APPEAR ON NOVEMBER 26, 2001
..., AT 120 E. CHESAPEAKE AVENUE,
..O SHOW CAUSE WHY YOU SHOULD NOT BE
..D PROBATION ON THE CASE NUMBER SHOWN.

ANNE ARUNDEL COUNTY POLICE DEPARTMENT
REQUEST FOR LABORATORY CDS EXAMINATION
CHAIN OF CUSTODY LOG

Request for Laboratory Analysis

Crime L03-0042   Page __ of 01

Suspect : BRANDON T. NOVAK   ☐ Juvenile
Suspect :   ☐ Juvenile   MTA - Light Rail
Suspect :   ☐ Juvenile   03-700933
Suspect :   ☐ Juvenile   Anne Arundel County Crime Lab - CDS
Suspect :   ☐ Juvenile
Suspect :   ☐ Juvenile   Officer's Name/ID WILLIAM SCHAUMAN 0173   MTA
Suspect :   ☐ Juvenile   Date of Offense   PD
Suspect :   ☐ Juvenile   01/07/03   Police Case No./Narcotics No.
                                 ☐ Juvenile   District/Squad/Unit   03-700933
                                 ☐ Juvenile   MTA/SEAMAN NARC PD 2B1   Court Tracking No.

Item #   Count   ☑ Seizure   ☐ Search Warrant   ☐ Purchase   ☐ Recovery

1   4   PINK TOP VIALS W/ WHITISH POWDER IN PLASTIC BAG.

Officer's count/amount verified by   Sgt. D. Bong # 636

I the undersigned, hereby certify that the evidence submitted in this case, as listed above, while in my custody, remained and was delivered in essentially the same condition as when I received it, except
that material or portion thereof consumed in the analytical process at the Crime Laboratory, and that I received and delivered it as indicated on this date and time stated.   Date: 1-07-03

EVIDENCE RECEIVED FROM | DATE | TIME | EVIDENCE RECEIVED BY | | DATE | TIME | EVIDENCE RELEASED TO | DATE | TIME
BRANDON T. NOVAK NORTH Jay | 1/7/03 | 1314 | P.O. W/ SCHAUMAN 0173 | | 1/7/03 | 0950 | DROP BOX | 1/7/03 | 1630
Evd Run Guy | 1/10/03 | 1355 | Chas Johnson | | | | Evd Run Guy | 1/9/03 | 108
 | | | | | | | Evd Run Guy | 1/21/03 | 08:10

TO: NOVAK, BRANDON THOMAS

MD 21224

STATE OF MARYLAND VS. NOVAK, BRANDON THOMAS

N O T I C E

YOU ARE HEREBY NOTIFIED THAT, ON MARCH 11, 2003, IN
ACCORDANCE WITH MARYLAND RULE 4-248, THE COURT, ON THE MOTION OF
THE STATE'S ATTORNEY, INDEFINITELY POSTPONED TRIAL IN THE ABOVE
CASE BY MARKING THE CASE STET ON THE DOCKET. A STETTED CASE MAY
BE RESCHEDULED FOR TRIAL AT THE REQUEST OF EITHER THE STATE OR
THE DEFENDANT WITHIN ONE YEAR AND THEREAFTER ONLY BY COURT ORDER
FOR GOOD CAUSE SHOWN. A CASE MAY NOT BE STETTED OVER THE OBJECTION
OF THE DEFENDANT AND IF YOU WISH TO HAVE THE CASE RESCHEDULED FOR
TRIAL, YOU SHOULD NOTIFY THE COURT IN WRITING OF YOUR REQUEST.

Photo by Adam
Wallacavage;
cover courtesy
Bam Margera.

This photo was taken
during the filming
of *CKY3*. I threw up
right afterward.
Photo by Adam
Wallacavage

My cameo in *CKY3*.
This skit lasted
all of 30 seconds.
Photo by Adam
Wallacavage

This is a photo of what Bam calls a "shopping cart slam."
Here, Bam videotapes Art Webb 1986 (yes, his nickname is 1986)
pushing, and Jess Margera takes one for the team.
Sequence by Adam Wallacavage

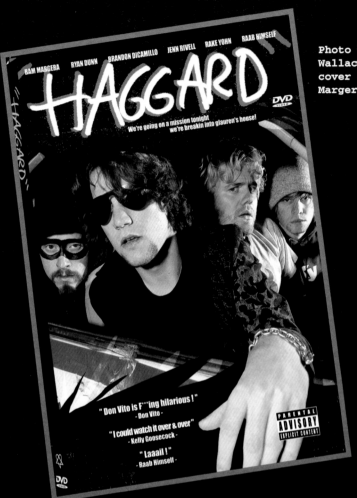

BAM MARGERA   RYAN DUNN   BRANDON DICAMILLO   JENN RIVELL   RAKE YOHN   RAAB HIMSELF

HAGGARD

DVD VIDEO

We're going on a mission tonight
we're breakin into glauren's house!

"Don Vito is F***ing hilarious!"
- Don Vito -

"I could watch it over & over"
- Kelly Goosecock -

"Laaail!"
- Raab Himself -

PARENTAL ADVISORY
EXPLICIT CONTENT

DVD VIDEO

Photo by Adam
Wallacavage;
cover courtesy of
Margera/Frantz.

Next two pages: These pics are from the documentary *The Making of
"Haggard,"* a behind-the-scenes look at the production of the film
as well as a documentary about how Bam and all his friends dealt
with my addiction. This sequence follows my argument with Ryan
Dunn (of the *CKY* videos and *Jackass*). He ends up frisking me and
finding a cooker in my pocket. He pushes me and leaves, furious.
Later, we hug. Shortly thereafter, I have a big talk with April,
Bam's mother, and we hug. By the night's end, I had once again
conned everyone into believing I was recovering.

Video stills courtesy Margera/Frantz

This photo of Bam's parents, Phil and April, was taken in 2003, right around the release of *Haggard*, the movie.
Photo by Pat Cavanaugh

Tony Hawk arrives on the set of the film *Haggard*. His presence plagued me with sadness, reminding me how I destroyed my skating career. There I am, seated between Hawk and Bam. It was supposed to be a happy occasion, but I might have cried at any second.
Photo by Adam Wallacavage

No sooner had Tony Hawk arrived at
Bam's house for his cameo role in
Haggard than he started shredding
Bam's half pipe.
Photos by Adam Wallacavage

Bucky Lasek had a cameo role in
Haggard. Here he is shredding the
ramp—ollie to fakie—in Bam's backyard
during production.

The guys shooting *Haggard*. *Left to right:* Ryan Dunn, Tony Hawk,
Bam Margera, and Joe Frantz.

This is the classic Bam Margera look that he rocked
during the production of *CKY3* and *Haggard*.
Photo by Adam Wallacavage

Bam and I wreaking havoc in his backyard in 2006.
Photos by Ryan Gee

Here, Bam and I drink a toast to my completion of my
manuscript for the book *Dreamseller*.

Here is a photo taken on March 8, 2008, after Scott's recent release from prison. If it were not for Scott, I would not be alive today. Photo by David Stuck

This is Joe Frantz; he coauthored this book. When I met Frantz, I hated him because he always called me out on my drug abuse. Needless to say, we became great friends. Frantz used to work in big advertising and when he met Bam, he took on various producing, writing, shooting, and cameo roles on Bam's TV shows and films—to name a few: Bam's TV shows *Viva La Bam* and *Bam's Unholy Union*, the films *Haggard*, *Minghags*, the *CKY* series, *Jackass 2* and *2.5*, etc. Frantz was producer and director of photography on all of Bam's music videos for CKY, HIM, 69 Eyes, Clutch, etc. He has also directed videos for The Bloodhound Gang, Jedi Mind Tricks, All Else Failed, Punishment, etc. *Why* the hell does this guy *always* wear flannel? Photo by Adam Wallacavage

Me and Frantz are good friends, although we fight a lot. Here he is about to tape my mouth shut. Photo by Joe DeVito

Below is a photo taken from Bam Margera's film *Minghags*. I play a character called Gay Biker. Next to me is Bam's aunt (Phil's sister), Ruthie "Boof," who plays my wife in the film. Photo by Ryan Gee

Guy Leeper has been one of my drug addiction counselors for years. His advice and guidance have helped me and many others through some of the most difficult times in our lives. Photo courtesy Guy Leeper

A recent photo of Mandy and me. Photo by Ryan Gee

A few tattoos: "Killing Loneliness" is a song that the Finnish band HIM wrote about me. "Carpe Diem" is a phrase from a Latin poem: it means "Seize the day." And "No More Fucking Heroin" is the tattoo that will live in infamy. Bam Margera made me get this when we made the film *Haggard*. Of course, it turned out to be one big heartbreaking betrayed promise!
Photo by David Stuck

As fans know, Bam put me on his hit MTV show, *Viva La Bam*. Here I am on the Metal Mulisha episode. Yes, that is Gwar rocking in the background.
Photo by Ryan Gee

4/25/99

Mom   How's it going? It felt really good to see you guy's on saturday it was very special for me to see you guy's when I was sober and doing well for my self. I cant begin to thank you two enough for helping me through the roughest time in my life, I have never experienced anything like that befor in my life. And I must admit you guy's were the last people I thought would be there for me like that! you two showed me what the meaning of true love is. I'll never forget what you did for me, you all saved my life. Today I have 50 day's clean and feel great. Staying here was honestly one of the best decisions I could have ever made. this program was a blessing sent from god. It saved my life. I should be starting work on tuesday makeing 9 to 10 an hour. I'm really eager to start working, I've Also been becoming very interested in joining culinary school. Now that I have a little clean time, my dreams and Ambitions are starting to come back to me And I cant wait to get started on them. When I leave here I'll have About 4½ month clean + that's A blessing. I pray for you two and mom + kelly and the rest of my true family every nite. Well guy's I have to go and get ready for an N.A meeting.

P.S. I'll call you about going
to A meeting either on sat. or sun.

I love you guy's
Browden

This is obviously a letter I had written to my mother while in rehab years ago.

Novak, one of the first things you are going to have to change, if you have the desire to cure your disease, is your thinking, attitude, and behavior, in every aspect of your life.

"Mr. Novak, I'm only scratching the surface with you right now, and I think you're doing pretty good because you seem quite receptive to my theory on how to fight your problem. And I plan to go much deeper with you. However, we can't do that until we develop a more trusting and comfortable relationship with each other."

He stares at me again. Am I supposed to respond?

He breaks the silence. "I feel like I've asked enough questions for the time being. Do you have any for me, Mr. Novak?"

One came to mind: "Yeah. If you don't mind me asking. How long have you been clean? What was your drug of choice?" Now I was curious.

"I liked to shoot Dope and coke all day every day. I was addicted to drugs from the age of fourteen to forty-four. In 1993, I began methadone treatment in order to stop taking heroin, but I still shot coke until 1998. On this November twentieth of 2003, I will have four years clean."

"Did you ever question yourself on being able to stay clean?"

"Of course." Mr. Leeper looked upward. "You see, Mr. Novak, we as human beings condition ourselves to a certain way of living. In your case, and in my case, too, it was the lowest state of poverty possible. We addicts set our standards on a much lower level than let's say a 'normal person' does. So we live on this animalistic level so long we can't even fathom living as a functioning productive member of society. It seems unobtainable. And so, as a result, we settle for a life full of failure and pain, and that becomes what's normal. Abnormal equals comfort to junkies. Creating this situation is a way to avoid reality and ourselves."

We sit in silence until Mr. Leeper says, "Mr. Novak, I'm fairly confident in your desire to put that needle down and keep it out of your arm. There are three things you must remember during your recovery process. They are honesty, open-mindedness, and willingness. If you practice them, and accept my help, you can do it."

He closes my file and stands, drawing our session to a close. "Well, Mr. Novak, I think that about does it for today. You have morning lecture right now so you go on to that and we'll continue tomorrow, okay?"

"Yeah, that's fine with me." A strange excitement washes over my mind, the anticipation of healing.

Minutes later, I stand in the doorway of the lecture hall. The instructor is in mid speech, delivering the lesson to the room full of addicts I have successfully avoided for the past two days. The addicts, craving distraction, focus on me. I make my way in.

In scanning the rows of seats, I manage to avoid eye contact with those who are sizing me up. I notice the only other white person in the room, Sean Williams, who smiles at me. Next to him is Toby, giving me the finger. Dane, sitting beside Toby, slaps Toby's head as if to tell him he needs to take this lecture seriously. Dane gives a wink and a nod of his head, indicating to me and the others in the room that he is inviting me to sit with him. I return his nod and proceed to my appointed chair.

The others return their attention to the instructor, and Toby wings a penny at my head. It just misses and hits a landscape painting behind me. *Bap!* The instructor glances at the back row to find the culprit, but Toby plays it off, acting as if he is taking notes. The instructor shrugs it off and continues his speech.

As I sit, Dane leans close to my ear and says, "How you feel, nephew?"

"Different!"

"Different in a good way or different in a bad way?"

"A good way." I grin.

The lecture is on the concept of "self acceptance." On the dry erase board are written four words which I recite over and over: Acceptance Leads to Recovery.

I look to Sean Williams who seems to be jotting down the information in the lecture verbatim. Meanwhile, Toby occupies himself with trying to get the attention of a girl who sits a few rows in front of him.

As I mentioned before, the Tuerk House upholds a no fraternization policy, and violation of this rule is grounds for immediate dismissal. Consequently, in group lecture, the women are seated in the first few rows and the men are seated far behind. A big burly monitor sits between them, to oversee all activity.

The mentality of the addict is to develop a method to achieve what an authority figure forbids. This is called "getting over." We junkies are fixated on risky situations, cheating other people, having a secret, breaking the law right under the noses of the casual observer. This pacifies the addict with a feeling of superiority, as well as floods their body full of endorphins and adrenaline, therefore producing a slight "high."

An example of what one might consider getting over in the Tuerk House is what is called "flying a kite," a system of breaking the anti-fraternization rule by passing notes to women right under the watchful eye of the monitor. Toby has devised such a system. He rolls a penny on the floor toward the far end of the room. This distracts the monitor's attention, as his reaction is to look in the direction of the noise. At that moment, Toby slides the folded note across the floor, under the rows of chairs, directly to the woman. To my amusement, the woman catches on and picks up the note.

In a half hour, class is dismissed. The monitor watches as the women exit first, one row at a time in single file, followed by the men, who exit in the same manner. The last to leave the room are Dane, Toby, Sean Williams, and me, who are seated in the back row. In rehab the back row is nicknamed "Death Row," because it is logical that anyone eager to learn will sit as close to the front as possible.

As we are about to leave, Dane, Toby, Sean Williams, and I are stopped by Mr. Tworek, the instructor. Mr. Tworek is in his midfifties, white, with a receding hairline, skinny as a stick. "May I speak to you gentlemen?" he asks.

Everyone honors his request and steps to the side. Except Toby who says, "Man, we ain't done shit!"

Toby walks away from Mr. Tworek, who steps after him. "Get back here! I am talking to you!"

Toby turns to Mr. Tworek and yells, "Get the fuck out of my face!" Mr. Tworek, a frail man, is intimidated. He shrinks back and Toby storms off, slamming the door behind him, startling Mr. Tworek and causing him to jump.

Straightening his tie and regaining his composure, Mr. Tworek directs his speech toward the rest of us. "You gentlemen better start taking this class more seriously. You're playing with your lives here, literally, and from the looks of your cards, I don't think any of you have a winning hand. I worry about you three, and your friend. I sincerely hope that you straighten out and fly right. You need to understand the severity of this situation. Think of this class as the difference between life and death, literally, your life and death. Hopefully you can convince your friend of this before it's too late."

Dane tells Mr. Tworek, "Don't worry 'bout Toby. We'll talk to him."

Mr. Tworek hugs all three of us in order to let us know there are no hard feelings.

Once in the hallway, as I head back to the room, Dane calls after me. "Come on, white boy, we're going out for a smoke break and you are, too. "

"Nah, Dane, I feel like shit. I'm gonna go lay down."

Dane asks, "What's the problem, nephew?"

I reply, "Nothing. I'm just gonna go back to my room and crash out for a bit."

"Get the fuck out of here!" he says. "You need to start socializing. You know what they say, 'Idle time is the devil's workshop.' You need to start communicatin' with other people so you can stay out of your head! It's a dangerous place to be, all by yourself, so here's what you're gonna do. You're gonna turn your white ass around and come smoke with us!"

Sean Williams steps out from behind Dane and chimes in, "And we're not taking 'no' for an answer!"

This vision of a rich white kid, smartly dressed, backing up the order of an old-school gangster like Dane, causes a strange sensation in my head. . . . What *is* this? The feeling begins in my temples, creates tension in the back of my neck . . . and so, for the first time in as long as I can remember, I am laughing.

Outside, in the "smoking area," a fenced-in back lot of the Tuerk House, there is a line of men standing against the wall. A monitor passes cigarettes to them, one at a time. The ritual smoke break, to me, resembles a Dope line, with one difference: after everyone cops, instead of going separate ways to get high, they split off into groups to discuss issues relevant to their lives—feelings, families, relationships, plans for recovery, what chick they are going to fuck, or what kind of dope they are going to shoot upon their discharge.

As Dane, Sean Williams, and I listen to Toby recollect his sex exploits, we hear a voice call out, "Brandon!"

The four of us stop talking, our attention diverted to an old, short, dark-skinned man who is approaching.

chapter seventeen
A Ghost from the Past

"Brandon!" the stranger calls out. He has a thick-bearded mustache, which connects to his hair and resembles a gray lion's mane. His clothes hang from his frame, accentuating his wiry musculature, which has worn its shape into the deterioration of the fabric.

The stranger makes his way past the rest of the addicts and over to us. I still don't recognize this man. My mind is racing. Who the fuck is this? Did I rip him off? Did I steal one of his packages?

Finally upon us, the stranger says, "Brandon! What's up? White boy, I haven't seen you in years! I figured you were in one of three places: prison, rehab, or six feet under!"

"Well, you got one of them right," I say, and he senses that I don't recognize him. Now the situation turns into a game, *his* game, a test to see how long it takes me to remember.

Through my peripheral I can see Dane, Toby, and Sean Williams looking back and forth to each other. I understand Dane and Toby well enough to know exactly what they are thinking, because I am thinking it, too, a possibility of violence. Sean Williams, who is not experienced in this type of situation, I am sure is planning the fastest way to notify a monitor if any trouble should arise. With my friends at my back I take a deep drag of my cigarette, trying to remember who this old man is. Finally, he smiles and gives a hint. "Remember the bank on St. Paul?"

"Get the fuck out of here! Isaac? Is that you?"

"Yeah, white boy, it's me!"

"Oh, shit!" In the presence of an old friend, the situation has changed. In a way, I feel more at home.

I smile, noting the deeper lines in his face, the gray hair, the whites of his eyes a bit yellow.

I introduce Isaac to my new friends. "Sean Williams, this is a good friend of mine, Isaac." Sean Williams, as usual, demonstrating his politeness, smiles and extends a respectful handshake.

Dane then nods, and Isaac nods back, confirming the mutual acknowledgment that they are two of the same.

Toby smirks. "What's up, Grandpop? Where the fuck did you get those busted-ass shoes? Ha-ha-ha-ha!"

The silence that followed was an indication of what was about to happen. When Isaac senses danger or vulnerability, his dark wide eyes fall into a blank stare, and I have always dreaded the moments that follow. It's been about three years since I've seen him and this is the exact type of enraged fit he was in when we parted ways. We're right back where we left off; the only thing that's changed is the date and time. Before I can stop it, Isaac has Toby by his neck, slamming him against the wall. Toby's facial expression changes from a smug grin that says, *"Yeah, I told that old junkie,"* to *"Uh-oh, I just fucked with the wrong person!"*

Dane and I grab Isaac and attempt to pry his fingers from around Toby's neck. We are used to this type of shit. By jumping in and not taking sides, we are affording both men a way out of a full-on fight and allowing them to save face. Sean Williams, on the other hand, reacts by frantically running for a monitor.

Two monitors charge in and split us apart. Toby screams in

the most threatening voice possible, "It's not over yet, bitch! I got yours! You hear me? It's not over yet!" Obviously, he would not be talking so tough had it not been for the fact that two enormous monitors held Isaac back.

The monitors push Toby inside the building to cool off. He storms up the stairs, yelling, "It's not over yet, you old mother-fucker!" Contrary to what Toby says, we know it's over and done with.

The monitor says with authority, "Smoke break's over!" Patients curse under their breath. Cigarettes are the only drug we have access to and we only get six a day. We all take our time walking back inside; some of the guys stop to make small talk with the monitor, just a ploy to buy more smoke time. I tell Dane and Sean Williams to go on without me; Isaac and I need to catch up.

On our way back upstairs, Isaac and I go back and forth with questions.

I ask, "How's your grandmother?"

"She passed away," he says in an unsettling voice.

"Fuck, I'm sorry to hear that, Isaac." Isaac's mother was an old-school free-baser, or "basehead," as they used to call the coke smokers prior to the advent of crack. One night, when Isaac was eight years old, she left him alone and never returned. Eventually, when the authorities found him living alone, they were shocked to learn that he had been taking care of himself for several months. But the reality was that Isaac had really not depended on his mother anyway. He was so used to being without her and knew how to survive in her absence. Child Welfare Services took custody, and after some research, discovered his one living relative, a grandmother. Isaac had heard stories about his grandmother from his mom, about how he had his grandmother's eyes, nose, and personality. When he met her for the first time, he recognized her because they did look very similar. After that, Isaac and his grand-mother took care of each other.

The two of us end up in a quiet conference room where we can speak privately.

I take a good, hard look at my old friend. "Damn, Isaac, last time we were together, remember that shit?"

"Do I remember?" he says. "How can I forget? That bank was tighter than a virgin's pussy!"

"Well, I heard you got knocked off for that shit and caught eight years."

"Nah," Isaac says. "The bank was no big deal. Later I caught the eight and did five."

"What for?"

Isaac replies, "Armed robbery."

"What the fuck did you rob?"

"I'd been watchin' this bank for two months. It was the perfect hit. As I went in to take care of business and get the money, there was an undercover cop depositin' his check. Before I knew it, I had one of those cop-issued nine-millimeters pointed at the back of my head. But they only gave me eight because it was a fake gun I used, and I convinced the jury that I didn't have the heart for pullin' a trigger. So, as you can see by the looks of me, during my vacation, I lost it all. When I was released, I had nothing but the clothes on my back. I couldn't pay any bills or take care of any responsibilities while I was down. Lost my grandmother's house, too."

This made me feel even worse. Hell, I used to live there.

When I first met Isaac, I had been getting high for about two years and had already started with petty street scams. One day, I heard about a new grade of Dope circulating, rumored to be the best in Baltimore City. One catch: it was only sold in one Dope shop, which did not serve whites. This had nothing to do with racism, but a code of streets ethics, because if cops see a white person in an all-black neighborhood, all they have to do is follow him and he will lead them directly to the Dope shop. But being the Dope fiend that I am, and hearing that the best Dope in town existed in West Baltimore, I set out on a mission to see for myself if this rumor was really true.

After hours of searching the streets, I spot a forty-year-old lady who is obviously a junkie like me. "Sweetheart, where you hittin' up here?" I ask.

"You police, white boy?"

"Nah, baby, just hard up. I'll hit you off with a ten spot if you tell me."

"Come on, white boy." She brings me to a corner entrance of the shadiest alley in West Baltimore and points. "There you go, baby, now kick me down ten before I'm seen with you. You on your own now." I hand her the ten bucks, pull my hood over my head, and turn the corner.

I have never seen so many customers in a Dope shop line. Kids, adults, teenagers, men, women. Parents with children. One is carrying a baby. One is in a wheelchair. Some are homeless, some are in three-piece suits. Some are beautiful, some are covered in open sores. But what these people do have in common is one distinguishing feature: they are all black. With my hood drawn to obscure my face, I join them hoping to score the best Dope in the city.

I study the operation and appreciate its efficiency. The dealers have a four-man team: the first takes the cash, the second hands out the bags, the third re-ups (is responsible for holding the quantities of both cash and Dope), and the fourth stands watch. In this way, they are able to serve one customer approximately every five seconds, and it takes me less than six minutes to reach the front of the line.

The Dope is sold in fifteen-dollar bags. With my sweatshirt sleeve pulled over my hand, I hand the first man sixty bucks and request four. He is so busy examining and counting the money that he does not even lift his head to see the color of my skin. I open my palm, and the second dealer is about to place this precious Dope in my hand, which he notices is white. He pulls back. "White boy, are you out of your mind? Get the fuck out of line! And you ain't getting your money back, neither!" Now to a dope fiend like me, sixty bucks is equivalent to a million dollars, so there's no way I'm stepping out of line without one of two things, my money or my four bags. I worked way too hard for this reward and I deserved it. At this point I'll take a bullet over this. Sad, I know.

The dealers insist I leave; I insist I am not going anywhere empty-handed. As we argue back and forth, the people in the line are growing anxious, in fear of two possibilities. First, the dealers will have to resort to shooting or stabbing me. Not that anyone gives a shit, but this will mean that the Dope dealers will have to close shop. Second, the dealers will close shop and the customers of the Dope line will beat me down. Either way, this would mean that the remaining junkies would have to walk away without a score. So, after almost twenty seconds of my arguing with the dealers, a homeless woman at the end of the line screams, "Get the fuck out of line, white boy!"

A man in a business suit behind me yells, "Get out the neighborhood, white boy!"

The situation escalates, and there are now sixty people in an alley all against me. The Dope man repeats the same sentence over and over again. "You're beat, white boy. You're beat, white boy." I continue to stand there like I'm deaf, hoping they just give me my bags to get me out of there.

Just as the situation is about to take a violent turn, this guy Isaac—then in his mid-40s, with black hair and a sparkle in his eyes—steps out of line and vouches for me. "Look, I brought him. He's with me, he's cool. Just hit him up this once, he won't be back again." This shows that Isaac has a lot of character and individuality, because a Dope fiend with the promise of a fix never steps out of line. But by this time, he was too late.

The dealer yells, "Then you both get the fuck out of line! You can come back tomorrow, but take this white piece of shit with you right now before he gets fucked up!" As we leave the rat-infested, piss-smelling alley, I thank him for his help, and tell him how much it meant to me.

Junkies usually do not express their feelings, but surprisingly Isaac did. He told me he had thirty bucks for Dope and was willing to split a score. My immediate reaction was "Hey, look, I'm no fucking faggot. Don't expect no shit from me."

Isaac says, "Look, white boy, I ain't for that shit neither. You just look ill and I know what that shit feels like, so you can come with me if you want, you stubborn motherfucker, or you can go back there and try to get your sixty bucks back."

Isaac and I continued on to another Dope shop, copped, and ended up at his grandmother's house. Isaac's grandmother was the sweetest, kindest lady. She fixed a meal, and Isaac allowed me to take a shower. From then on Isaac and I were running partners. We stole, pulled scams, and hustled together, and he and his grandmother graciously let me live at their house. My new living conditions were ideal: I now had a friend, and that friend had Dope dealers right outside his front door. The perfect relationship, sealed in Dope.

As the months passed, our friendship deepened. We had something rare among addicts, a relationship based on trust. Since we had lost almost everything else in our lives, we cherished this bond we had together, in our little end of the world, cooking up Junk in his grandmother's basement.

At one time we ran a scam that entailed filling bank dime wrappers with sand and pebbles, leaving a few dimes on each end. When packed correctly and taped shut, behold, eight dimes appeared to be five dollars. In the beginning the scam worked well, but as time went on, other junkies started running with it. Soon banks were on the lookout for junkies trying to cash in dime wraps.

On the morning our relationship ended, we sat in his dark, damp basement, surrounded by old broken needles, ties, empty bags, vials, old lighters, and assorted cookers. We were sick that morning and sat in silence as we packed our dime wraps and listened to the call of the Dope boys out front. Their voices rang out like church bells on Sunday: "Red and white out! Black and white here! John Gotti hittin' in the hole!" These are the local brand names of Dope, which insure standards of quality and promote brand loyalty, just like Coca-Cola and Pepsi do for soda. Normally those were the words I prayed to hear, but on this particular morning, each time those voices echoed through the streets I grew sicker.

We pack six dime wraps and make our way to the business district, arriving at the bank just as it opens. Usually we were more prepared for this scam. We would shave, put on clean clothes, brush our teeth and hair, and get Celia, a twenty-one-year-old junkie who cleaned up nice enough to pass for a college girl, to do

the exchange. But this morning we were too sick to take any precautions and looked to be exactly what we were, two dirty Dope-
sick junkies trying to pull a scam.

As we enter the bank, Isaac walks to the desk to fill out paperwork, as if he wants to open an account. It is his job to hang in the
back in case there's a problem. I stand in the line trying to time
the situation so that I could get the young female teller instead of
the bald white man of sixty wearing thick bifocals. No such luck.
"Next!" he calls to me.

This man looks like the typical crabby old son of a bitch who
hates rap music, rock and roll, blacks, and kids who wear their
baseball caps backwards. He thinks the moral fabric of society has
deteriorated since he was a kid, which was probably the 1930s. My
senses tell me to turn around and walk away, but all I can see is a
bag of Dope. Not police, not jail, not the armed security guard at
the door. Just a bag of Dope. The hope of a fix overrides the ability
to make a rational decision.

The old man looks at me with disgust. "Can I help you sir?"

Trying to emulate the verbal skills of a Yale graduate, I reply,
"Hello-Sir.-How-are-you-doing-today?" Did that sound too stiff?

"Fine." He stares.

I reply, "Good. My grandmother gave me these rolls of dimes
for my birthday so I figured instead of just letting them collect
dust in the corner I might as well just trade them in on the way to
class this morning." Who the hell would ever say that?

He asks, "Do you have an account here?"

"No, sir, but my mother does."

"Okay. Can you write her account number and name on each
roll?"

This is an indication that things are going wrong, because they
never ask this question. Obviously, he is suspicious and I feel as if

he is stalling me, but again, I somehow manage to convince my-self that this still might work. "Sure, no problem, sir."

The elderly man hands me a pen and stares as I write a ficti-tious number on each roll. I begin to panic. Hell, I have no idea how many numerals are in an account number. Are there dashes? Are there *letters*? I just write as sloppily as possible so that the num-bers cannot be read at all and cling to the hope that this will not make a difference.

By the time I finish scribbling on the dime wraps, my hand is shaking nervously. The teller takes the wraps directly to his boss, who is shuffling a stack of papers. The boss, in his early fifties, with a fresh haircut, shave, and manicure, has not so much as a wrinkle on his suit.

The old man, careful not to let me see his lips or facial expres-sions, speaks quietly into his manager's ear. The boss's eyes drift over to me. At this moment I finally realize this scam is not going to work, no way. And now I have something else to consider: how the fuck am I gonna get out of this bank without going to jail? I look over to make sure Isaac is aware of the situation. I catch his eye; he looks at me, then glances at the armed security guard. That lets me know he has got the guard.

As the teller makes his way back over to me, the manager picks up a phone and dials rapidly. I turn and walk away. The teller calls after me, "Excuse me, sir . . . excuse me, sir! *Excuse me, sir!*"

With the attention of every customer and employee fixed on me, the bloated armed security guard, who resembles the Pills-bury Dough Boy, steps in between me and the exit. "Excuse me, sir, could you step to the side? We would like to speak to you."

"Sure, no problem," I reply in a compliant tone. "Is there a problem, sir?" *Of course there is, dipshit!*

"No, sir. We just need to speak to you for a moment." I feign subservience, as if I am stepping to the side as per his order. . . . Suddenly, I break into a sprint toward the exit, but the back of my sweatshirt is grabbed by the hand of this lard-ass security guard.

"Get off me, fat boy!" I yell, grabbing my sweatshirt and pulling. The situation resembles a tug-of-war over my sweatshirt. As someone pulls the bank alarm, Isaac dashes across the bank and tackles the security guard, allowing me to dash out of the bank and make my escape. As I run down the street, looking to my sides, I realize that Isaac is not with me. I stop on the street, wondering if I should turn back. Suddenly a police siren kicks on in the distance. The fear takes hold and I run. I want to help my best friend, but there is nothing I can do.

Isaac and I, in the Tuerk House, sit in silence. Isaac plays with his beard and I rub my fingers through my hair.

The intercom clicks on. "Okay, ten minutes to lights out. Congratulations, gentlemen, on another day clean."

"Well, I guess it's that time," I say.

Isaac replies, "Good night, Brandon."

"Good night, Isaac." We go our separate ways.

chapter eighteen
From the Beginning

I am in Mr. Leeper's office, cradled in the softness of the armchair that was designed to comfort and relax those who sit in it. Why am I nervous?

Mr. Leeper is well dressed: a thin-striped tie, freshly ironed light blue shirt, brand-new navy-blue slacks, and a white pair of shoes, which appear to be worn for the first time. He even smells great. Recovered addicts take pride in their appearance, a symbol of an improved state of being.

"How you holding up, Mr. Novak?" Mr. Leeper asks.

"Okay I guess, given the circumstances."

"It could always be worse," Mr. Leeper replies.

"That's what Dane told me," I say to myself.

"I believe we got off to a great start yesterday. You exhibited several signs of your willingness to change. You know, Brandon, I have a lot of clients, some are willing, some aren't. It is my job to treat each one in the same way. It's up to you to accept or deny the advice and guidance I'm offering. Now, before we really start to get to the root of your problem," Mr. Leeper says, "ask yourself: Are you ready?"

"Yes," I reply.

"So, Mr. Novak, I've read over your files. I know a bit about your past, your family life, and how it wasn't the best. Unfortunately, paperwork is only face value so we're gonna have to go over all that stuff."

He continues with this bombshell: "After we talked yesterday, I called and spoke with your mother."

A moment ago I felt excitement about this session. Now I'm angry, no longer receptive to his help. I don't believe he had any right to call my mother without consulting me first. How could he tell me he is trying to build a trusting relationship, only to betray me?

"Don't you want to know how it went?" asks Mr. Leeper.

I shake my head with a look of disgust on my face.

"Mr. Novak, we're going to do this thing now, and truthfully, if you really want to go get better, there's no need to sugarcoat anything."

All my past decisions have left me in prisons or abandoned houses. So, at this point, I am pretty fucking vulnerable, and looking for guidance. Although Mr. Leeper is not perfect, he has achieved what seems to be impossible: quitting drugs, and right now he's the only person in my life willing and able to guide me in that direction. So, I decide to give him my trust. You might call it a "leap of faith."

"Okay, how'd it go?" I whisper.

"Well, Mr. Novak, I can tell you she's ecstatic, but at the same time terrified."

I open up. "I knew that before you said it. This is *exactly* why I didn't even want to tell her I'm here. I'm infamous for building up her hopes and dreams only to shoot them down at the first chance I get to act on free will. Do you know how many times I've done that to her? Do you know how many times I've made her cry?"

"Well, what do you intend to do about it?"

"I don't know, all right?! I *want* to get better, I *want* to stop doing drugs, but at the same time, not fifteen minutes goes by in this place that I don't think of getting the fuck out of here so I can shoot up again!"

"Good," Mr. Leeper says.

"What the fuck's good about that?"

Mr. Leeper tells me. "Your honesty. Your truthfulness with facing yourself. And because you've been honest with yourself, you can begin to become realistic in your assessment of your future decisions."

"I don't know what decisions to make. I look at my life as a junkie, and I weigh it against a life where I have a house, a wife, a bank account . . . a toothbrush. . . . I get so fucking overwhelmed. . . . Can I really do this? When I recover, what will I do? Where will I go? How will I pay rent? How will I get an apartment with no money or credit? I don't even have a bank account. I don't even have a driver's license. When the rehab process is complete, what will I *be?* I don't even know who I am now!"

"These are things you will have to face. But you need to do this slowly. Like sobriety, your problems must be faced as they come, they must be taken, as the saying goes, 'one day at a time.' The decision is entirely yours. You can either face your problem, or run away from it and continue your life as an addict. Let me ask you, what is your problem, today, right now, at this very moment?"

"My problem is, that every time I go to a rehab, the withdrawal is the easy part. The pissing my pants, the throwing up, the diarrhea; it's a passive process and I let it happen to me. It's *easy* for me. After the physical pain leaves me, I have to examine my life and then the physical pain is replaced with an emotional pain. An emptiness."

"Describe the 'emptiness,' Mr. Novak."

"I look at my life, and all I see is a trail of ruined relationships. People who loved me and don't trust me. Look at me. I'm a disgrace. My mother has spent over forty thousand dollars of her hard-earned money for a dozen inpatient rehabs, outpatient houses, and three-day detoxes, only for me to end up in this position."

As the tears overpower my ability to speak, Mr. Leeper gives me a few minutes to gain control. Then he continues. "Your mother is quite impressed with your ability to take action by seeking out help. She said a few other things, as well. For one, she told me she has always served as the enabler. She knows it's not the right thing to do, but her heart breaks to see you in pain and the only remedy that seems to make you better is a couple of dollars, which she knows you probably spend on drugs. But she feels powerless in the situation. Although she seemed very determined to make sure she doesn't act as your crutch anymore.

"You're twenty-five, right, Mr. Novak?"

"Yes."

"At what age did you experiment with your first drink or drug?"

"I was about eleven years old. Me and a few friends smoked some weed in the woods.

"Well, what were your hobbies? Where did your interests lie before you found heroin?"

"Before I got wrapped up in drugs I was a skateboarder."

"You did what?" Mr. Leeper asks.

"I rode a skateboard. For a living."

"Tell me about this."

I search my Heroin-infested brain for the proper way to begin the story, mentally turning back the clock to my childhood. . . .

chapter nineteen
Bucky Lasek

Saturday morning. My mom is buzzing about the house like a whirlwind, simultaneously doing yard work, laundry, dusting, sweeping, mopping, and vacuuming, cleaning the house from top to bottom.

In less than one hour after I wake, I arrive at the crowded parking lot of the local shopping mall and skate toward the action: the Powell Peralta skate demo. A voice booms through a loudspeaker, announcing the names of the skaters; each trick they perform is met by a thunderous applause. Here were hundreds of kids paying homage to the living legends who brought inspiration: Tony Hawk, Mike Vallely, Steve Caballero, Tommy Guerrero, and of course, Bucky Lasek.

Bucky Lasek, then fifteen or so, was our hometown hero, born and raised in Dundalk, Maryland. In my eyes he was God, he could do no wrong. I studied him; I dressed like him and imitated his skating style. And around my neck, I wore a gold rope with the letter B, the closest I could find to the one I saw him wearing in a photo. My friends made fun of me, but I didn't care because he was my idol. I wanted to be just like him.

The demo draws to a close. The professionals are bombarded by fans who line up for autographs. This was an opportune time for me to skate the street course, which was now open to the general public.

As I am about to make my run, from behind me I hear a voice ask, "You're Brandon, right?" I turn and I am struck with an emotion somewhere between honor and horror. Bucky Lasek!

My first instinct was, actually, to run! I stand there for a moment, until I finally muster the courage to reply, nervously, "Yeah?"

Bucky smiles. "What's up, man? What did you think of the demo?"

"It . . . it was awesome," I reply shakily. "How did you know my name?"

"I've seen you around; I know who you are. I've been watching you skate today, and you definitely have a lot of talent. You're really good, especially for your age. I can tell."

I am unable to contain my excitement. "Really?!"

"Really," he assures me. "Hey, I'll tell you what, after the demo I'm headed over to Sport Elite to hit the miniramp, you're more than welcome to come if you want."

"Hell, yeah!" In an instant, I make a decision: I am going to rise to this occasion, prove myself, and befriend Bucky Lasek, my hero. I push my foot to the asphalt with all my might and zip across the parking lot. I hit the quarterpipe, and in midair I grab my board backside, closer to the front of my front truck, and begin to spin 360. A quarter of the way through, I karate-kick my right foot out and tuck it back; then when I'm about to land, I let go of the backside, grab right before I place my foot back on the board, and ride away from the three-sixty Judo Air like it was just a warm-up trick.

The announcer yells over the P.A., "Wow! And it looks like our Baltimore crowd needs to extend fifteen minutes of fame for a young hometown hero! Let's hear it for the little guy . . . whatever his name is!" Everyone at the demo claps, and as I turn around, Bucky shoots me a big smile.

On the way to Sports Elite, I think about Bucky at the demo. He saw something special in me. He recognized that I had talent and skill, and not only that, he seemed to like me. Is this a dream?

As we enter Sports Elite, I am greeted by Pat Alban, the owner, who speaks with a thick Cuban accent. "What's up, slim?"

"Not much, Pat."

"I hear Bucky invited you back to skate," he says. "The pressure is on, slim. Everyone is already in the back. Follow me."

Pat walks me through the shop and through the legendary back door, which leads us to the ramp area where a session is in full force. Bucky sees me. "Well! Looks like you made it!"

I climb to the top of the ramp and await my turn to drop in. Somehow, the stress acts on my mind as a motivator. I edge my foot over the coping, my whole body quaking with nervous energy. Well, here it goes, do or die! Somehow I pull off a flawless run: A drop in, pivot-to-fakie, Caballero-to-fakie, chink-chink brought back forward, a blunt-to-fakie, and as I pull out of the ramp, everyone in the place is cheering!

At the end of the session, Pat Alban approaches. "Slim, do you ride for anybody?"

I answer, "No."

Pat says, "Well, you do now!" He walks away, and in a minute he returns with a box full of team shirts, stickers, a skateboard, trucks, wheels, and accessories. Everyone watches as he hands me this gift and pats me on the back, saying, "Welcome to the Sports Elite team, Brandon!" As the skaters applaud, I turn to look at Bucky, and the world seems to slow down, as in a slow-motion movie sequence. This was all for me. The applause, the cheers, the smiles. I had earned them. In one day, my life had completely changed.

As the months passed, Bucky took me under his wing. I watched him closely and carefully; I analyzed his skating, emulated his lifestyle, and listened to his advice in personal matters. What he did, I did; what he said, I said. I was in *awe*.

Bucky had become my father figure. In time, Bucky spoke on my behalf with Todd Hastings, the team manager at Powell, and he allowed me to start traveling with the Powell Peralta team. To me, this was by far the greatest opportunity I could attain. At times I needed to remind myself that I was actually living, not dreaming, this experience. I was skating, living, and eating at the very same table as all my childhood heroes—the greatest skateboard ensemble in the history of the sport!

The highlight of my excursions was a cross-country trip to Tony Hawk's house in California. Tony had the ultimate backyard setup that was every skater's dream: a vert ramp with spine to miniramp, then spine to a bowl. When I saw it for the first time, I stood motionless. I was speechless to think that even the possibility of such a lifestyle existed in the universe. There, for several days, I shared in Tony's backyard paradise, pushing the boundaries of my physical stamina.

Tony was gracious and made me feel at home. He awoke every morning in tremendous spirit, skated with tenacity, and encouraged other skaters. He held daily barbecues for his guests and straggling visitors. His business matters were conducted quietly and with patience, and any stress he may have felt was well managed and not apparent. If our stay in his home was an imposition, he did not show it in the slightest way. Tony allowed me and Bucky to use one of his cars so that I might fully enjoy the experience of seeing California for the first time.

Another vivid memory I have from my stay is Tony's cat. For some strange reason, it loved to shit in the bathtub. During one stretch, all the guests went without showers because no one wanted to clean it up. The situation was discussed among us and somehow emerged as an endurance contest, to see who could stand to go without showering the longest. After four days the tub was full of cat turds, and finally, Bucky, not being able to tolerate the situation any longer, lost. He cleaned out the tub and showered. Even though he lost the contest he was revered as the hero of the situation as the rest of us celebrated and took showers.

In the following years, I traveled the country to skate with the Powell Peralta team for audiences at demos and contests and signed autographs for fans and little kids. I owe it all to Bucky Lasek.

In telling this story to Mr. Leeper, I stop to take a deep breath and to assure myself that he is still following. The counselor is staring at me in complete silence, looking lost. I laugh.

"What's so funny?" Mr. Leeper asks.

"Nah, it's nothing," I reply.

"No, sir, Mr. Novak, if we're working on building an honest relationship, I want to know what's so funny."

"It just seems that the table has turned for us."

"What do you mean?" Mr. Leeper asks.

"The look on your face. You look exactly as I felt when I first stepped in your office this morning."

Until this point, Mr. Leeper had a pen in his hand, taking notes. He places the pen in his folder, which he closes and lays on the table beside him. We stare at each other and I understand that, as experienced as he is in his profession, he is at a loss for words. The fact that my case has presented a challenge to this man fills me with satisfaction. Mr. Leeper is an authority figure, and I have stumped him.

"Well, I'm not going to lie to you, Brandon. That wasn't the type of background story I'm used to hearing. So, you really know what it's like to have some things going on in life. You had a great career, only to give it up for a ten-dollar pill of Dope."

"Yes. I went from skating in front of thousands of people and signing autographs to begging for spare change on the corner."

"Okay, Mr. Novak."

"Call me Brandon. If we're gonna get personal, I prefer we're on a first-name basis."

"I got you, Brandon. From now on, call me Guy then." Guy then tells me, "I have a question for you."

"Go ahead, Guy, shoot!"

"Up till this point, your role model was the professional skater Bucky Lasek. At what point did that change?"

"I'd say at around the age of seventeen. As my skateboarding abilities progressed and my talents increased, I became somewhat of a celebrity. Whatever I did, I had fans behind me. As the cliché goes, the world was in the palm of my hand." Then I told him the following story.

One afternoon, I was at the skatepark reviewing some footage I had just shot for a skate video. My eyes were accustomed to peering into the luminescent viewfinder of the hi-8 camera, so my retinas were a little burned out. Suddenly, almost mysteriously, a metallic-blue Mercedes pulled up. Through my affected vision, it seemed to cast a radiant sapphire glow. I squint as two figures, washed out in the bright sunlight, step out of the car. I'm curious.

My eyes regain their sight and focus on the girl. Twenty-something, dark hair, red lipstick, gorgeous. The man is white, in his late twenties, a bit overweight, receding hairline, long hair in a ponytail. He is dressed casually—sweatpants, old T-shirt, new sneakers. On his wrist dangles an expensive diamond-studded gold Rolex.

The two of them approach. I can't imagine what they might want.

"What's going on?" the guy calls out.

"Not much."

He reaches out and we shake hands. "I'm Dwight. Pleased to meet you."

"I'm Brandon."

"I know all about you," Dwight tells me in a laid-back manner. "As a matter of fact, I think we might we be quite valuable to each other."

"What do you mean?" I ask.

"Let's just say that we should get together and talk sometime. Here's my number; give me a call when you think the time is right." He hands me a plain white business card that reads "Dwight," and lists a phone number.

"Cool man, I'll give you a call."

He gives a knowing look, expressing a deep implication. "You definitely should. It'll be worth your while." Then, in the same blue aura in which his Mercedes arrived, it made its departure.

chapter twenty

A Conflict of Interests

In the next week I found myself thinking about this mysterious man named Dwight. The picture of him was still clear in my memory. His Mercedes, his Rolex, his beautiful girlfriend. I had lost his business card, and in a way I was glad. If I didn't have a way of calling him, I wouldn't give into any temptations that I might not be able to resist.

In the folds of the bottom layer of clothes were the objects that had not been taken from my pockets prior to the wash: a pen, a dime and pennies, a piece of plastic unrecognizable, and last, Dwight's business card.

The card. I examine it: plain and white, warped but legible, the name "Dwight," followed by a phone number and no indictaion as to what business it represented.

Guy Leeper breaks into the story. "So, I take it you called Dwight."

"Yeah, I called him. I don't know why. I mean, here I was doing great in my skating career. I had it all. But for some reason, I thought I needed more."

I knew that whatever business Dwight was in, it wasn't legal or positive. But in my lifestyle, the risks and the danger had always secretly appealed to me. Beating the odds, and doing what most consider impossible, the psychology that had driven me to become a skater, was also calling me to engage in other risky behavior. Every time I ask myself, "What might I gain? What might I lose? What might I become? How might this affect future events?" I find a way to reassure myself that in the end things will be all right.

I make the call to Dwight.

"Hello?" the voice answers.

"Is this Dwight?" I ask.

"Who's this?"

"Brandon."

"Right on, bro, I been waiting for you to get back to me. You around today?"

"I'm headed to Highland and Eastern Avenue to the skate shop."

"What's the name of the shop?"

"Sports Elite."

"I'll be there in twenty-five minutes. Wait for me," he says.

An hour later, outside Sports Elite, I climb into Dwight's metallic-blue Mercedes.

"Pop the trunk?" I ask.

"Why?"

"For my skateboard. I don't want it to fuck your seats up."

"I don't give a fuck about this car! Just put it on the floor in the back!"

"Okay, if you say so."

"You hungry?" Dwight asks.

"A little."

"Good, we'll go to Ruth's Chris," Dwight smiles.

"Ruth's Chris? That costs like sixty bucks!" I tell him.

"Don't worry about cash," Dwight replies. "When you're with me you won't ever spend a dollar."

"Well fuck, yeah, let's go to Ruth's Chris!"

Upon our arrival Dwight is, and therefore we are, given VIP treatment. After an hour or so of conversation, I make several observations about Dwight:

- His behavior does not reveal the signs of stress exhibited by most men.
- He makes no references to having any deadlines or people to answer to and he seems to be his own boss.
- He has plenty of money and does not give a damn about spending it. He has ordered me the most expensive cut of meat on the menu, seemingly out of principle.

As I examine his character and lifestyle, I find myself intrigued.

"Anyway, there's a point to this lunch," he tells me.

"Right on. What's the deal?"

"I have an offer for you and I think you'll be interested. I think you know as well as I do, you're at a great point in your career. You're well known and have respect. I know you do a bit of traveling. Unlike myself, at airports you probably have it pretty relaxed through security. Every time I'm at the airport I get harrassed, searched, questioned. It's just a fucking hassle. In cars, or in a tour bus, I'm sure you rarely get pulled over. You look innocent. Not me. Cops pull my ass over all the time. That's why I never travel with anything on me. That's why I pay other people to help me out. That's why I found you."

He answers the next question before I ask it. "I'm willing to pay you to transport cash for me. I'll schedule the deliveries around your trips so nothing looks out of the ordinary. At the most, the amounts will be around a hundred thousand or so. For any trip you take, I'll give you ten percent of whatever you transport for me. It's basically risk free, because the last thing anyone would associate you with is drug money."

This proposition is far too complicated to consider right away. "I'm not really sure, man."

Dwight assures me in a relaxed voice. "I'm not expecting you to make a decision right now. There's no pressure here at all. No rush. You have my number. Think about it and give me a call."

Before leaving me in front of my mother's house, Dwight shakes my hand, palming me off some cash, which I count after he drives away. Five hundred dollars, in fifties, just for listening to the proposition.

Less than a week later, I am again on the phone to Dwight.

"Yo, it's Brandon."

"Hey, what's goin' on?"

"Not much. I was calling to let you know I'm going to California next week."

"Right on," he replies. "Well, why don't we meet up in about twenty minutes?"

A few hours later, we are seated in a five-star restaurant with his girlfriend. He orders a round of after-dinner drinks for her and himself, and, telling her we will soon return, leads me to the parking lot.

In the comfort of the metallic-blue Mercedes, Dwight hands me a piece of paper with a phone number written on it. "This is the number of the guy who will come to pick the money up from you once you're in L.A. Call him *as soon as you touch down*. This is very important. They will be positioned next to your hotel and will come as soon as you call. They will be waiting. If you stall, it will cause problems."

Referring to a bag in his backseat, Dwight tells me, "There is one hundred ten thousand dollars in there. Ten is yours for transporting the rest. But there's one thing I need to say. I don't say it to insult you, or imply that we don't have confidence in each other, but it has to be said. I'm trusting you with a lot of my money, so it would be in your best interest to make sure it finds its way to the proper owner." As he says this he lifts the bottom of his sweatshirt, revealing a handgun in a belt holster.

My defenses take over. "Look Dwight, I'm not out for any of your cash! Remember, you found me. You're the one who came to me. I never asked you for anything. Don't go accusing me of trying to steal from you."

Dwight holds up his hand silencing me. "Those are strong words you just threw out. Now look, Brandon, let's back up and relax a second. One thing we don't need is for us, this partnership, to get off on the wrong foot. I'm not trying to insult you or make accusations, but those are things that just have to be acknowledged. It's just business. Okay? You cool?"

"Yeah, I'm cool. I understand." I sigh, letting go of my emotions.

"Cool," he replies.

It is at this point that Dwight becomes my hero.

chapter twenty-one

The Initiation

Guy Leeper asks, "So that's when your role model changed from Bucky Lasek to Dwight. When you traded in your skateboard for drug money."

"I guess you could say it like that. It's sad. I knew it was wrong, but I did it anyway."

"Just curious," my counselor says. "How did it feel for you to smuggle the money on the plane, knowing you were jeopardizing your skateboarding career?"

"Well, it was hard work, and it made me so stressed that I almost threw up a few times, but somehow I enjoyed it. I actually got a satisfaction from it."

The airport. I approach the security line and wait my turn to go through the metal detectors, trying to project the appearance of someone who's not nervous or paranoid, which is difficult because I have a hundred thousand dollards of drug money strapped to my body. Is a guard going to ask me questions? When I reply, am I going to stutter or swallow? Can they tell I am nervous? Do they suspect? Am I blushing? Will I be chosen for a random pat down?

In my head, I review the meticulous preparation I had performed less than three hours ago, prior to my ride to the airport,

I stood in my room naked, fresh out of the shower. On a table before me were the following items:

- Ten bundles of ten thousand dollars, all in hundreds, wrapped in cellophane plastic wrap
- Five rolls of black electrical tape
- Two boxes of kitchen plastic wrap

As I prepared for the trip, I repeated Dwight's instructions in my head, as if I were reciting a newly learned prayer: "Brandon, now I want you to listen to me very, very carefully. The instructions I am about to give you are more important than any test you took in high scool, more significant than the fine print written on your skateboarding contract, more crucial than making your first Holy Communion. Okay?"

"Okay," I told him, giving my utmost attention.

He continued. "To successfully smuggle this money through the airport, you will have to fasten it to your body with electrical tape and plastic wrap. So, before you pack for your trip, go to Kmart and buy a few boxes of plastic wrap, the kind that your mom wraps food in before putting it in the freezer. Not the waxed kind, the cellophane, the kind that is impossible to tear in a straight line even though there is a serrated metal strip on the box. You'll also need a few rolls of electrical tape, the black kind that stretches. Get ten rolls so you don't run out, just to make sure.

"Now, when you get home, first, wash your hands. They need to be clean for what you are about to do. This has nothing to do with fingerprints. It has to do with dirt and sweat from your hands, which will cause the tape and cellophane not to stick. Now, wrap each ten-thousand dollar bundle in plastic wrap. Not too tight. They should be flimsy and able to bend to the shape of your body.

Then shower. Get real clean, make sure all the dirt is off your body, and use deodorant soap, because you don't want to sweat too much. Moisture will make the tape and plastic wrap not stick to you. When you get out of the shower, dry off real thoroughly, and don't use powder. Powder will also make the tape and plastic wrap not stick to your body. Again, I can't stress enough how important this is. You don't want to find yourself in a position where a ten-thousand-dollar bundle of cash falls out of your pants leg, while a bunch of security guards are staring at you. Got it so far?"

"Yes," I reply.

"Okay, now that you're clean and dry, the idea here is to use the electrical tape to fasten the wrapped ten-thousand-dollar bundles to your body. You have ten of them. Tape one on each calf, one on each inner thigh, and one on each back of your upper arms. As you fasten the bundles to your arms and legs, wrap the tape around each limb three times, so that the money is strapped to you by each end and the middle. Then, tape the remaining four bundles onto your stomach, long ways, wrapping the electrical tape around each bundle separately, all the way around your trunk, just above the hip bone. Then, when all four bundles are fastened, wrap a piece of electrical tape three times around all four bundles, again all the way around your trunk. Once the tape is secure, pull the plastic wrap around those parts of your body where the money is so that it is firmly in place. Three times should do it. Remember, when you secure the money to your body with the plastic wrap, the end result should not leave the money feeling stiff, it must bend to your body shape, just in case a guard pats you down. If the money feels too stiff, undo the whole thing and start over, rewrapping the original bundle in the plastic wrap so it feels a bit looser. After you're done, put on baggy clothes. A long-sleeved T-shirt and an oversized sweatshirt. Baggy "home-boy" pants.

Make sure they're too long so you have to cuff the bottoms. This will make sure they don't show any shape except the fat wrinkles in the denim. You're thin, so it will appear as if it's all a part of your body frame. And the baggy clothes will appear as if they are part of your dress style."

I snap back to reality as I near the front of the security line. It is almost my turn to pass through the metal detector. I hope to God I don't set this thing off. I should be okay; I followed Dwight's advice to a T: "Wear no metal. Make sure of this. No belt buckle, no boots, no watch, no necklace, no pocket change, no pens. Make sure the pants and shirt have no metal snaps or buttons. Wear sneakers without metal lace holes. Your objective is to pass right through the metal detector without setting it off, without a security guard looking at you twice."

The guy in front of me steps through the detector, sets it off, and it emits a series of beeps. He is pulled to the side and frisked, and it is discovered that he has forgotten to remove his watch.

My turn to walk through the metal detector. I wait for the guard to wave me through. He looks at me. I feel the urge to swallow, but I cannot let myself. The guard waves for me to walk through. Here I go. I step through the machine. No beep. Thank God! But wait, are they suspicious because I was the only one in line who did not set the damn thing off?

As I walk to my gate, the rest of Dwight's advice rings in my head: "Undercovers never wear business suits. Look out for people in windbreakers, jogging gear, or sweat outfits. Undercover cops love wearing any kind of sportswear because it enables them to move fast for a takedown. And especially, above all, watch out for guys with hip packs. This is where undercovers keep their cuffs and shield. There's nothing cops love more than to tackle someone, cuff them, and shove that badge right in their face."

As I recall this advice, I notice three guys sitting at my gate dressed in sweat suits. One wears a hip pack. Are these undercovers? Are they waiting for me? Am I paranoid? They might be a group of gym equipment reps. I *think* they might be observing me, but if I look at them again, they might notice me looking and I might appear suspicious. My instinct is to go to the bathroom to calm down, but if they see me going there, they might construe it as suspicious behavior, especially right after seeing them.

My mind is flying in circles.

I decide to do something that will make me look like the most average passenger at the airport. I head to the airport McDonald's and wait in line. I take my time eating to minimize the time I'll have to wait at the gate. I am too nervous to have an appetite and feel as if I am not eating this cheeseburger and fries, but rather pushing them into my stomach. I become nauseous.

As I board the flight and head toward my seat, I hear a male voice behind me. "Sir, excuse me. Hey. You there!" I keep walking to my seat, praying to God that he is talking to someone else. "Sir!" I feel a forceful hand on my shoulder. Is this it? Am I caught? I turn around to face a flight attendant with his hand gripping my shirt. "May I please see your ticket, sir?"

I search my pockets for my ticket. Shit, where is it? He is tapping his foot. I find the ticket in my back pocket. As he examines it, I try to plan a getaway. But how? I'm on a plane on the middle of an airport runway, and there's nowhere to go. I am trapped. I feel defeated. I mentally prepare myself to go to jail.

The flight attendant looks at the ticket, then to me. "Okay," he says, "you're in seat twenty-three-D. All the way towards the back."

No shit, asswipe! You put your hands on me and yelled at me in front of everyone just to tell me that the seats are in numerical order? I am so pissed off at how he just spoke to me that I wish to God I wasn't transporting illegal drug money, so I could scream at him for treating customers in such a poor manner. I look at him and manage to smile meagerly. "Thanks," I reply. The fuck-face does not even say "you're welcome."

Once airborne, I feel a strong urge to piss, but because I want to avoid drawing attention to myself, I hold it in. For six long hours my bladder is killing me.

As the plane soars through the clouds, I view the world from this new perspective. I can almost see the curvature of the Earth. Here I am, a sponsored skater, living the dream of a million kids on the planet beneath me. How could I be such a fool, to jeopardize everything I've worked for since I was old enough to ride a skateboard? I wish to God I could take this all back.

I try to clear my mind as I stare into the clouds. The clouds transform, and somehow I clearly see a vision of my sweet mother's face. Comfort. She is smiling, proud of me and my accomplishments in life. All my fear subsides. In this state of heightened emotion, I return to an experience I had forgotten, yet, I could recollect this particular day as if it were the present.

For my sixth or seventh birthday, my brother and sister had gotten me my first skateboard. I have never, before this day or since, been so excited about a gift. That was the day I realized that skateboarding was my calling. I skated until the sun had set and the moon had risen, and my mother told me it was time for bed. I remember the anticipation I felt for the next morning, so I could skate all day once again.

That night, as my mom tucked me into bed, after we said my prayers, I remember asking, "Mom, can I sleep with my skateboard tonight?"

She replied, "Sure, Brandon. Why?"

My answer was sincere. "In case I die in my sleep tonight, I want to die with my skateboard."

My mind returns to this flight, which seems to last an eternity.

So this is where my priorities have changed.

chapter twenty-two

A Change of Priorities

I touch down at LAX.

Within twenty minutes I climb into a van with Todd Hastings, the team manager for Powell Peralta.

Todd says, "Good to see you, Brandon. How was the flight? Everything okay?"

"Yeah, it was great. Had trouble sleeping, though." If he only knew.

"Ha ha," he replies, glancing at his watch. I can tell that he is pressed for time. "Okay, we have this team dinner; it officially starts at six o'clock. Some of the guys are already there now, so, let's head over there and join the rest of the team."

What? No! I have to make the call to the rightful owners of the cash, which is still wrapped tightly around my body. I scramble for the right words to buy time. . . . "Whoa, whoa, Todd. Let's slow down. I just got here, man. I need to go to the hotel, check in, and take a shower real quick."

Todd tries to blow me off. "Oh, yeah, there will be plenty of time for that later. Right now we need to go to the team dinner."

No way! Dwight's connection is standing by and waiting for my call. I can't screw this up. I call Todd out. "No, listen, the flight sucked, and I need just a minute in my room. Let's go to the hotel, so I can get situated."

But Todd is steadfast in his convictions. "Ah, no, right now we're going to the company dinner, that's where the team is. Got to."

I consider Todd's position as team manager, reviewing all I know about him.

His job is one of prestige, but also diplomacy. It is his duty to maintain a pleasant relationship and rapport with the team members—not only to deal with the gracious, seasoned pro athletes who set the example for the others to follow, but also to appease the pushy little prima donna skate punks who are testing the boundaries of their newfound power and sense of self-importance. I had always strived to be one of the sportsmen who are amicable and appreciative. But now, as much as I hate to be a pain in his ass, the drive for self-preservation compels me to push the issue.

I insist, "Come on, Todd! The hotel is right by the dinner! What's the big deal?"

As Todd sighs, I realize I am victorious, although I now have a new black mark in Todd's personal ledger.

"Okay, okay. Fine. Do you have a watch?" he asks.

Out loud I tell him, "No, I didn't wear one." In my head, I continue, *"Because I didn't want to set off the airport metal detector and alert security to the fact that I have a hundred thousand dollars strapped to my body!"*

Todd replies, "Okay, I'll give you twenty minutes, from the time you get to the lobby, to the time you get back downstairs. Can you do that?"

"Cool, Todd, no problem."

Todd looks at his watch. "Remember, we're on a schedule, and you're holding us up!"

We arrive at the hotel. Once in my room, I am on the phone,

dialing. After it rings four times, a Spanish-accented man answers. "Hello?"

"This is Brandon, Dwight's friend. He said you would be waiting for my call."

"How was your trip, was everything smooth?"

"Yeah, we're all good. You want to get together?"

"We'll be there soon." Click. He hangs up.

We'll be there?! Who the fuck is *"we"*?!

After twenty minutes, the phone rings. I pick up. "Hello?"

"Hey, it's Todd. I'm down in the lobby waiting."

"Oh, okay, I'll be down in a minute."

"Make it quick, we have to get going, *now!*"

"Okay, just one minute." I hang up.

I sit on the bed, my head in my hands, unable to think clearly.

Five more minutes go by. Man. Skateboarding is my career. I mean, really, what am I doing, risking it all? What is this urge inside me that is so influenced by the sense of danger and risk?

Knock! Knock! Knock! My heart is pounding so hard, it feels as if it is going to burst out of my chest. I feel like I'm about to have a nervous breakdown.

I walk to the door, wrap my hand around the doorknob, and inhale.

I open the door and find myself face to face with two characters: a seventy-year-old Hispanic hunchback woman and what appears to be her fourteen-year-old grandson. Of all the drug-dealing stereotypes I had expected to see at this moment, these two were not on the list. What the fuck have I gotten myself into?

The young boy grabs my hand and shakes.

"Are you Brandon?" he asks.

"Yes."

The boy says, "I'm Javier, this is my grandmother, Esmeralda."

Esmeralda says not a word. I invite them in and shut the door.

Esmeralda grabs Javier's shirt and pulls him closer, whispering Spanish into his ear. The boy does not take his eyes off me. My mind is spinning. Am I safe? Who are these people? Are they wired? Is this a setup? Are the police going to break in and arrest us? Is someone else going to come in and kill me? Why did I think this was a good idea?

Javier asks, "My grandmother wants to know how you know Dwight."

I begin to feel a great sense of urgency to complete this transaction. "Dwight is my boss. Javier, do you want what I brought for you?"

"Yeah," he says.

As I turn and start to step into the bathroom, Esmeralda yells something in Spanish. Javier rushes across the room and blocks my path.

"Where are you going?" Javier asks.

"To get the money," I tell him.

"Where is it?"

"It's on me. Strapped to my body," I say.

Javier, speaking Spanish, interprets my words to Esmeralda, who barks a series of orders. It is clear that she is in charge, and I wonder what kind of gun she is hiding in her purse—which is unzipped right next to her hand.

Javier says, "My grandmother prefers that you stay in the room. We should all stay together."

I reply, "Fine. If that's what you prefer."

I strip down to my boxers, and as I unwrap and untape each bundle, I hand them to Javier, who passes them to his grandmother. She counts them with speed and efficiency, three times per bundle. During this process I develop a great respect for these two and their operation. This comforts me because dealers who practice smooth business transactions rarely do anything to foul things up.

Javier opens up his book bag and places the money in a school project binder. He closes the bag and extends his hand for me to shake. His grandmother turns and walks out the door. Javier follows, leaving me standing alone in my boxers. Done.

Two minutes later, I'm in the elevator, staring at the illuminated floor numbers.

In the lobby, there is no sign of Todd. I run to the parking lot and find him in the van, pulling away. He sees me and stops for me to climb in. There was no need to tell me that he was leaving without me.

"Todd, I'm real sorry. Me and my girlfriend are going through some rough shit right now, and we got into a major bitch match on the phone. So, which skate shop is sponsoring tomorrow's demo?" I change the subject and keep the conversation going, feeling smug that I had beaten the odds.

At this point, my patterns are starting to change. When I used to fly into a Powell tour, the first thing I'd do is call up my homeboys and go skate. Now my priority was a drug-money transaction. What's happening to me? I am, for some reason, going against all better judgment, defeating my lifelong aspirations, reversing all the hard work I've put into my career. But inside, I felt invincible. In my distorted mind I could conquer skating, as well as become an entrepreneur in the drug trade.

Guy chimes in, "So, you got away scot-free?"

"No I didn't get away with it scot-free. Not at all."

That single event had an effect on my lifestyle and would forever alter my relationships, my attitude, my life.

chapter twenty-three
The Calm Before
the Storm

In the next few months I made several more cash runs for Dwight, usually by bus, successfully smuggling several hundred thousand dollars throughout the country and delivering it where requested.

Dwight and I are cruising in his Mercedes, discussing our business relationship. Dwight drives, keeping his eyes on the road ahead. "You know, I like you, Brandon. Not once have you skimmed, not even so much as one thin dollar. I put my trust in you, and you pulled through for me. You're loyal. And in our business, that's rare, man. Very rare. I think it's time to take things to the next level."

"What do you have in mind?"

"Future prospects."

We go to Dwight's apartment. On the wall is a numerical security panel. Dwight types in a code, then four beeps ring out and the door unlocks. The door is painted to look like wood, but I notice it is cool to the touch: metal, burglarproof, fireproof. Dwight leads me through the doorway, flips on the light.

Inside, past several paintings and pieces of antique furniture, against the far wall, sit several large rectangular objects, covered in tan cloths. Dwight pulls off one of the covers, revealing a large footlocker fastened with a sturdy combination lock.

He opens the footlocker. Its contents: four twenty-five-pound bricks of marijuana, compressed and vacuum sealed in several plastic layers. Between each layer is a thick coating of petroleum jelly, which is used to contain the pungent scent of the weed during transport. Also inside is a triple beam scale, the kind used in high school science classes to measure exact weight down to the gram.

As Dwight's eyes give a keen and speculative look, I know that the conversation to come will seal my fate as the distributor of large amounts of this product.

That night, we dine in a five-star restaurant. I have become quite accustomed to this ritual. In front of me sits an enormous white plate; its rim meticulously decorated with an intricate design painted by hand in sauce and accented with green leaves. In the center of the plate an immense shrimp tail is surrounded by lump crab meat. Next to the plate rests three different forks, which I suppose are to be used for specific courses. A glass of freshly opened Perrier, slightly chilled, is in my hand.

Four of us are seated at the table. I take a moment to analyze Dwight, the man to whom everyone present pays full attention. Dwight is the least respectable looking person in the group. He is overweight, out of shape, and to an outsider might appear low class—until they glance at his wrist and see the Presidential Rolex.

Dwight does not need to position himself at the head of the table in order to impose his authority. His status in the drug game grants him the right to speak whenever he wishes. The first word of his every sentence commands silence from anyone who might be in mid-conversation.

Next to Dwight is the most beautiful woman in the restaurant, his girlfriend. She represents class and elegance, resembling a woman in a famous painting in which the technique and time period become secondary to the striking beauty of the subject.

Last at the table is a six-foot, two-hundred-fifty-pound guy named Leo. He has the biggest fucking ears I've ever seen, and he wears a black baseball cap in which he tucks the upper third of each. Unfortunately, the lower two-thirds are so large that it makes no difference if the upper ears are tucked or not. In an attempt to hide his fat, he wears large, baggy clothes that draw attention to his obesity rather than obscure it.

This is the first time I have met Leo, but I am starting to figure out the role he plays in Dwight's organization. Dwight has a few of these kinds of guys working for him, as does every drug dealer with any clout. He is what is referred to on the streets as Dwight's bitch boy. He takes all the big risks Dwight refuses to take and probably does not receive nearly the amount of money that he deserves to compensate him for the consequences of getting caught.

Leo is involved in this game, not for the cash, but for the sake of his reputation. He was picked on in high school and developed a poor self-esteem. Although he is intelligent and got good grades, he lacks something that meant much more to him than a good report card. He needs to belong, and the drug trade is always taking job résumés for those who want to be paid off in social acceptance. So, for him, the risk of the job is worth it.

Until this point I felt superior to Leo, but now, I realize that we are really the same. He could make great money as a businessman, and I could do just as well as a pro skateboarder. But, in the end, we both need something more to satisfy us: love and acceptance. All the positive morals, values, family, and friendship my mother had given me fade into the shadow of this desire. I sip my Perrier, choosing not to consider the matter any further.

The waiter visits our table. Dwight gives him a slight nod and the waiter presents him with the check. Dwight glances at it, reaches his hand in his raggedy pants pocket, and produces a big wad of cash. All hundreds. He flips out four of them, throws them on the table, and stands.

Dwight looks at me. "Are you ready, young'un?"

I say, "Sure, but don't you need to wait for your change?"

He chuckles. "You have a lot to learn, don't you, kid? That's all right, we got time. We got plenty of time. Come on, let's go."

Dwight pulls me into his web, and I don't mind. Like Leo, I'm now in Dwight's pocketful of bitch boys. He's got me.

chapter twenty-four
The Cage

There is a logical and natural progression of substance abuse that leads users down the road of addiction. In my early high school years, I began to fulfill this stereotype. First, it was drinking beer and liquor at parties. Next I was smoking pot on weekends. Soon, I was smoking after school, then before school. Then I graduated to hash, acid, mushrooms, whatever was available.

My life was going downhill, ironically, because I had respect. I was more popular than the high school jocks: the football and basketball players who were lucky if they got a quarter scholarship for their hard work. I was a skateboarder on the Powell Peralta team; I had already made it! Everyone wanted to talk to me in school and invite me to their parties. I did as I pleased, and could do no wrong. I was perfect. No one dared to tell me I was messing up my life.

I surrounded myself with yes-men who wanted desperately to be my pal. And they were willing to score me drugs to be accepted. Valium, Vicodin, codeine, Percocet, Xanax, Zoloft. These are a few of the socially accepted drugs to which many parents are addicted. And as Mom and Dad's medicine cabinets were more accessible than street drugs, soon I was scoring handfuls of pills from my friends.

My main source was the largest drug network in the world, the pharmaceutical companies. Through them, the most powerful psychoactive drugs known to man are legally and liberally dispensed to kids: lithium, Ritalin, and Prozac, to name a few. "Meds," they are called. The abbreviated name washes away the stigma of child drug use. After all, if adults considered the possibility that their child's poor academic and behavioral performance might be an indication of inadequate parenting, they would have to accept the responsibility to guide, teach, and help their kid improve. And so, these meds, seen as quick fixes to so many child "chemical imbalances," were gladly handed over to me by students who wanted to fit into my world.

One day when I was about sixteen, a friend gave me a bottle of his Ritalin, which I didn't really like. So I traded it for some cocaine that another friend had stolen from his brother. Two small bags of coke. He also threw in a third bag of a light brown powder. When I asked him what it was, he told me it was Heroin. I stashed it under my bed and forgot about it.

About a month later, I came across the bag again. At first, I couldn't remember what it was. Then I remembered. Heroin. Well, I'll try anything once, I thought. I sniffed a bit of the powder, and immediately fell to my knees. In the next moment, I ran to the bathroom as puke forced its way up my throat.

And then I felt it. I had heard others refer to it as "euphoria" for years. It was a feeling like no other. Even though this drug had brought me to my knees and caused me to vomit, it also brought indescribable joy. I had found the ultimate high.

I was afraid to use Heroin again after this. What would happen if I liked it *too* much?

But when I met Dwight the following year, my attitude was to change. As my dealings with him increased, I noticed that his moods were sometimes dramatically altered. I knew he must have been doing something. Coke, perhaps.

One night before going out to a restaurant, I saw him perform a ritual I would soon grow accustomed to witnessing. First, he placed two crisp hundred-dollar bills on his coffee table. One bill he folded, and into it dumped a bit of brown powder. The other hundred-dollar bill was rolled and used to snort the contents of the folded bill. "Do you know what this is?" he asked.

"What is it?"

"This is heroin," Dwight informed me, in the voice of a chemistry teacher presenting a classroom lesson. "Do you want some?"

"No, thanks," I told him.

After Dwight became comfortable doing this in my presence, I realized he needed to have this drug before we cut up brick weed, before we counted money, before he went out of the house, before he did anything. He brought a small bag of it wherever we went, and if we were in public, he would dip a key into it and snort a little bit every so often. Every time he did this, he would ask, "Do you want any of this? Are you sure?"

On one hand, I really wanted to use this drug with Dwight. To my impressionable high school mind, he made the Heroin lifestyle look cool. He had a nice car and a beautiful girlfriend. He was his own boss and he had plenty of money. Then I would look at the burn holes in his shirts caused by the many cigarettes that had fallen from his mouth as he nodded out. I don't want to become like that, I thought.

Soon his invitations to partake in his drug of choice became strong suggestions:

- "Come on, Brand. Just try a little."
- "I'm telling you, this is the shit!"

- "Come on, just try some! Just once! This is the best drug in the world, Brand, believe me!"
- "Brand, I gotta say, I'm disappointed in you. I thought you would have been down by now."

And so, one day, when he asked if I'd try a little of his Dope, instead of saying, "No," I said, "Yes." He smiled. I had impressed him, and he now had a partner to do his drug with.

A month or so later, Dwight and I are seated on a Greyhound bus. We are headed for New York City to visit his girlfriend, who is now a model. We took the bus because Dwight has Heroin and does not want to risk being pulled over by police on the road.

We arrive at Dwight's girlfriend's loft apartment, which was financed by Dwight. The building security guard informs us that regulations require guests to produce a form of identification in order to gain entrance. I grit my teeth and look to Dwight, who says, "What, you don't have ID on you? You serious?" I am nervous. The last thing in the world I want to do is inconvenience Dwight, my boss.

"All right, come on!" Dwight sighs.

"Where are we going?" I ask.

"To get your ass an ID!" Dwight leaves the apartment building, walking at top speed through the cold New York air, in a display of anger for this inconvenience. I follow in silence behind him, hiding from his line of sight to avoid reminding him that we are walking the streets of New York City in sub-zero temperature because of me. I am left with the feeling of sickness at the thought that he might be upset with me.

Dwight leads me to a corner bodega in which there is a photo booth featuring options for several laminated ID cards on which your picture can be printed. Three minutes later, I look at my new photo ID that reads, "Medical Alert Card." The photo of me is so out of focus, I can hardly recognize myself. A ten-year-old could tell you that this ID card is bullshit, but Dwight assures me it is fine.

We walk away, and Dwight leads me in the opposite direction from his girlfriend's apartment. "Hey, Dwight, it's this way," I point.

"We got a stop to make. It's this way." Outside a deli, several Puerto Rican men are standing. These guys are intimidating, to say the least. The leader is two hundred and forty pounds, dark, with medium-length slicked-back hair, several lines shaved into his eyebrows, and precisely pointed sideburns. He wears a blue and black Gore-Tex jacket, Timberland boots, a gold watch, a gold rope necklace, and a small gold-hoop earring. As Dwight scores from them, I go into the deli and buy a pack of smokes.

Back at Dwight's girlfriend's apartment, the same security guard glances at the fake ID and lets me sign in.

As Dwight and I sit with his girlfriend in her apartment, a television news report announces that a snowstorm is approaching the area, which they are already referring to as the Blizzard of 1996, the storm would eventually leave over a hundred people dead. Dwight realizes we need to leave now or run the risk of getting snowed in. So, Dwight and I snort another bag of Heroin and hop a cab back to the Greyhound station.

As we wait for our bus, we are approached by two Port Authority officers.

"What are you, a runaway?" asks Officer Jenkins.

"No," I reply.

"Why are your eyes so pink?" asks Officer Farnan.

"I'm tired," I say.

"Let's see some ID," demands Officer Jenkins. Dwight produces his driver's license. The officers glance at it and hand it back. I hand them my brand new ID, my fake fucking "Medical Alert Card."

"This isn't a legal form of identification," says Officer Farnan, handing it back. "Do you have anything else?"

I swallow. "No, that's all I have with me. I left my driver's license at home."

The officer looks at Dwight. "We're going to have to ask your friend here some questions. Are you related to him?"

"No, we're not related," Dwight replies. The police release Dwight, and he takes a cab to Baltimore.

In the Port Authority office, the officers force me to empty my pockets, and find four bags of Heroin.

I start to cry. Deep down I knew that, by virtue of the life I had been leading, jail was inevitable and a debt overdue. The most disheartening part of this ordeal occurred when I was being transported to Central Booking. From the backseat of the squad car, I had a clear view of the "Brooklyn Banks," a famous skate spot I had been shredding since I was eight years old. I could almost see a young version of myself, laughing with my friends, learning new tricks, skating under the warm evening sun.

Inside Central Booking, I am fingerprinted and led through my first booking process, a procedure to which I would soon grow accustomed.

The cop behind this desk obviously hates his job, hates his life, and hates me. A few days prior, I had gotten my tongue pierced, and seeing the metal stud sparks his anger. "What's that in your mouth?" he snaps.

"I got my tongue pierced the other day," I say.

I can tell this is the type of cop who gets off on verbal abuse of those charged with criminal offenses, so I accept the fact that I can do no right in this angry, frustrated man's eyes. I am sure he feels he has been overlooked for promotions, has a failing marriage, and is a closet alcoholic, and he is going to take it all out on me, the living depiction of the ills of society and the manifestation of all his problems. "You got your what?" he asks in a malicious tone.

"My tongue pierced."

"Jesus fucking Christ! Hey, would you look at this fucking kid?" He draws the attention of the other officers and continues, "A fucking pierced tongue! Well, your momma must be proud! What a goddamn fucking faggot!" The other cops chuckle. "Well, let's see what your cell mates think of your little tongue piercing. Get up, little faggot. We're going to the Cage."

The Cage. A holding tank in which the criminally charged await their arraignment, an ordeal that can take over twenty-four hours. The exact length of time of this paperwork process is determined by several factors, the most relevant being the officer's interest in completing the work. There are many reasons why, if the police so desire, the length of your stay in the holding cell might increase. For example, your paperwork might "get lost," they may be forced to "do it over," their computer system may temporarily "be down," or they might simply be "too busy." These dissatisfied cops, who deal with the scum of the earth on a daily basis, are anything but enthusiastic about helping a junkie like me get home. In short, if they decide they do not like you, "your ass is going to sit in the slammer for a long time."

The Cage. A small cell, crammed with approximately twenty people. A set of locker room–type benches allow some people to sit. Floor space is precious. The toughest, most hardened criminals claim the most space by lying down. The first-timers either sit with folded legs or stand in this oppressive environment.

In the corner is a small stainless steel toilet. The seat is covered with piss and reeks of shit. Of course, there is not a single piece of toilet paper in sight.

The cell is freezing cold. I'm not sure if the holding tank is under renovation, or just designed this way, but a narrow gap in the ceiling is open to the outdoors. Through this hole, snow is falling into the cell, accumulating on the floor and creating a stream of melt water. The water drips into a hole between the floor and the wall forcing several rodents out to scurry among us. The cops have taken the inmates' clothes, except for our pants, T-shirts, and shoes, which have had the laces removed. We have been told this is for our own protection because we might use the shoestrings and other articles of clothing to hang ourselves or suffocate each other. However, they offer nothing to prevent us from contracting pneumonia.

"Hey, you!" I hear someone call out. I don't turn around, hoping he's not talking to me. "Hey, you!" Oh no, he *is* talking to me! I turn to see the Puerto Rican guy from whom Dwight had bought the dope. He's with his crew of dealers, and I pray that they don't have a problem with me.

"Hey, you remember me, right?" he demands as his friends stare me down. Am I supposed to say yes or no?

"Ah, yeah, from the deli, right?" I ask.

"Yeah! What's you in for?"

"I got shaken down and they found some bags on me. How 'bout you?"

The Puerto Rican man spits, "Tsss! Dude who runs the deli called the cops on us and we had to make a split. Motherfucker always does it to us, we know it's him. We didn't get caught, but we came back later, rolled up on the motherfucker. Beat his pussy ass, and shoved some sticks in his eyes. Before you know it, the cops roll up on us. So here we are."

They shoved *sticks* in the guy's eyes? Jesus Christ! Luckily, the Puerto Ricans weren't interested in giving me a hard time. They were more interested in asking about my Jason Lee prototype skate shoes that I got at a trade show, which hadn't yet been released in stores.

After hours on the wet, freezing cement floor next to the piss-covered toilet, I can no longer feel my fingers or toes.

Finally, I am presented to a judge for arraignment, who issues a time and date on which I must appear before another judge and grants my release. I jump a cab to the Greyhound station, which was in the process of closing down because of the blizzard, but still hoped I could catch a bus.

Ten hours later, a voice booms through the loudspeaker, "Attention, attention. We are sorry to inform you that Greyhound is officially closing down all routes due to current weather conditions." *No!* Here I am, stranded in New York City with no friends, no recollection of where Dwight's girlfriend lived, in the middle of a major blizzard, wearing only a fleece jacket and a T-shirt. What the hell am I going to do?

Outside, freezing in the snow, I beg a police officer for help. He informs me that only three blocks away is a shelter for kids, and I run as fast as I can to make it before I freeze to death.

I get to the shelter and am let in by an elderly woman who listens to my story and invites me to stay for the night. Within minutes I am surrounded by thirty Dominican kids, ages twelve to seventeen, who insist that I part ways with my Patagonia fleece jacket:

"Yo, that's a sweet-ass jacket, Holmes. It'd fit me real nice."

"Hey, man, why don't you kick down that jacket, man?"

"Tell you what, you need to let me wear your jacket for a while."

"You want to come into here, you gotta learn to share. And you can start with your jacket."

Scared out of my mind, I phone my mother, who is able to find Dwight's phone number in my room. I call Dwight repeatedly, begging God for him to answer. At two in the morning, I am able to reach him. He gives me his girlfriend's address and I have a cab bring me to her apartment. Here I again present my fake-fucking "Medical Alert Card" to security. I enter her loft and collapse from exhaustion for two days until Greyhound is up and running. When I get back to Baltimore, I am sick for a week with the flu.

For most people, this experience would be a deterrent against breaking the law again. But the addict learns quickly to lower his standards of living in order to adapt to this lifestyle. A filthy way of life becomes normal. Sad but true, this episode has altered my mind, and I have now taken a one-hundred-eighty-degree turn for the worse. I see nothing wrong with this. Sometimes, the simplest things in life are the hardest to grasp . . . at least, when your perception is clouded by the disease of addiction.

chapter twenty-five
Downward Spiral

Guy Leeper says, "I can guess where this story is going. This sounds like where things are about to fall apart."

"You'd think that I would have learned my lesson," I tell him. "Anybody else would have. But, no, not me. I still had a fighting chance to gain back everything I had let slip away, but I had lost sight of what I was losing."

In the months that passed, my business relationship with Dwight deepened with our mutual appreciation for Heroin. A snort of several small lines of brown powder through a hundred-dollar bill would give me a euphoric complacency, accompanied by the illusion of success and social rank. In the same way skateboarding had filled the void in my life, now the profits of a substantial drug deal made me feel like a productive member of society.

Heroin was one of the most accessible drugs in Baltimore City. Fifteen dollars at any corner Dope shop and I was holding. A score at the Dope shop instilled in me a sense of accomplishment. My mind was now gone, and my vision was too clouded to see it. The small bag of powder erased all my responsibilities, self-discipline, and aspirations.

One morning after smoking pot with some friends, I went to school reeking of marijuana. This fact, compounded by my reputation as the school druggie, got me expelled, only a few weeks prior to graduation. My poor mother met with the principal in order to try to prevent this. However, this issue was only one of several dozen she was dealing with in my descending lifestyle.

At this point, I began doing drugs, any drugs, all the drugs I could, nonstop.

My last tour with Powell Peralta was a struggle.

On the first day of the tour, we load into the bus. Old friends shake hands and catch up with each other, discuss professional progress, and look over the itinerary.

The mainstays of the Powell Peralta team at the time are Steve Caballero, Danny Wainwright, Charlie Wilkins, Jayme Fortune, Jeff Taylor, Rachman Chung, Gershon Mosley, and Bucky Lasek, whom I have not seen for several months.

Bucky approaches and says, "Brandon. It's been a long time. What have you been doing to yourself? You look like shit."

I meet his statement with humorous sarcasm. "Thanks, buddy!" But Bucky's face does not change, and I realize he wasn't joking.

Todd Hastings has now moved on, and Mike Vallely is in his place as team manager. Mike is not much taller than me, but he is twice as wide. Huge chest, broad shoulders, thick neck. His style of skating is so aggressive that you can hear him skate from two blocks away; every land cracks like thunder. Mike has a reputation as an ultimate professional, a tell-it-like-it-is, clean-cut, straight-edge, no-nonsense white boy who will not hesitate to confront anyone who makes apparent disrespect for him, or what he stands for. And as far as managing the team, he is making sweeping changes. He approaches; we shake hands. "Hey, Novak. You doin' all right?"

"Yeah, I'm doin' great, Mike."

"That's good. Because I've been hearing some things." Mike shoots me a smile that expresses his insinuation. "I'm keeping my eye on you, Novak!"

The tour is strange. I feel like an outsider, as if I am no longer a part of the team. However, a degree of comfort lies in my pocket, in a small cloth sack containing pills and several baggies of Heroin powder.

The first demo. I am not landing anything. I'm dizzy. A few fans ask me if I am okay. The other skaters don't seem very concerned about my condition. They probably understand it's self-induced.

A child of perhaps six or seven approaches, hand outstretched, offering a bottle of water. "Here, Brandon, you look like you need this." I recognize in his voice a familiar innocence of youth, which my lifestyle has strangled from me. I thank the boy, a vision of my former self. The water does not quench my thirst. It weighs heavily in my stomach, making me sick.

As I cross the course toward the shade of a tree, I vomit uncontrollably on the middle of the street course, in front of all the fans and my fellow professional skaters.

As vomit drips from my chin to chest, I lift my head to see Bucky, my onetime hero, who had done everything in his power to perpetuate my success, shaking his head. His former enthusiasm has transformed into disgust. How did I let myself get like this?

Humiliated, I skate to the sideline, leaving my team members to skate around the pool of my vomit for the remainder of the demo. I have, in effect, regurgitated on the Powell Peralta team name.

After Vallely's next run, he skates my way and calls, "Sitting this one out, Novak?"

"Yeah, I'm pretty sick today. I think I have food poisoning."

Mike hears me but doesn't acknowledge my answer.

After the demo and autograph signing, as we load into the bus, Vallely approaches me with a confrontational look. I try to climb on board before he has a chance to speak with me, but his booming voice can be heard by the entire team. "Brandon, I'd like a word with you."

"Yeah? What?"

"Look, I don't know why you came on this trip, but this is a skate tour. I don't think you take it too seriously, but the rest of us do, and we worked hard to be here."

"Uh-huh." I roll my eyes. Mike steps closer, three inches from my face making it physically impossible to ignore him.

"Now, I know, and you know, that you have some pot on you, and probably a few other things that aren't legal. These kids who come to our demos aren't blind, and they aren't stupid. They can tell you're on drugs, and they can spot you sneaking off to get high all the time. Like it or not, we're role models to these kids. I know you don't care about that, but I won't let you set a bad example for them while you're a part of this team, my team, understand?"

I am very uncomfortable with this guy barking in my face. I step back and he steps forward, this time placing his hand on my chest. I want to tell him not to touch me, but I know he will keep pushing until his point has been made. His hazel-green eyes stare at me as he presses the issue. "As long as you have drugs on you, this tour is in jeopardy. When we skate together, you are compromising your own safety and everyone else's. If we get pulled over and the cops find drugs on you, we'll all be in trouble, and the bad publicity will reflect on the rest of us. So here's what's going to happen." Mike points to a street gutter. "You're going to take all your drugs and you're gonna throw them where they belong, down this gutter, and you and I are going to stand right here until you do!"

Sometimes, when being called out, it is easiest to leave your opponent with the false sense that he has won. "You're right, Mike. Fuck, I don't need this shit. I'm not even into drugs anyway. I only had this stuff because some fan gave it to me. I'll definitely throw this stuff out, it makes no difference to me." Mike, of course, knows this is a lie, but he is willing to tolerate the charade as long as I do as he told me. He watches me empty my pockets and throw my bag of stash down the gutter as I hold back my pain.

Later that night, at a party, I convinced some fans to drive me back to that gutter. With a tire iron, I lifted the sewer grate so I could reclaim possession of my drugs.

After the tour Mike Vallely phoned me. "Look, Brandon, you have to understand that there's a real big problem here."

"What, are you telling me you're pissed or something?"

"Brandon, pissed happened months ago. Here we are, your team, and you disrespect us. When was the last time you even practiced?"

"What do you want from me? Where's this going?" I demand. "Sounds like you're beating around the bush to me."

"Well, I'll tell you, and only because you leave me no choice. I'm putting an ultimatum on the table, and I'm leaving the decision up to you. Okay, here it is: one, either you check yourself into a rehab and you clean up and start making improvements, or two, you'll just have to quit the team. You make the choice!"

Now, for something which I have worked so hard for since I was a kid, I do not even allow a full breath of air to enter my lungs before I answer. "Well, Mike, thanks for everything, but I quit."

Mike pauses. "Okay, then, I guess you and I have nothing more to talk about."

"I guess not."

"I'll see you around, Brandon."

"Later."

Click. The phone disconnects in my ear.

That night, I went out with Alexia and my drug friends and celebrated the fact that I had quit my lifelong dream. At this point, the drugs were deteriorating my morals, my value system, and all that was positive in my life.

Everything I once created for myself was now gone.

Guys interrupts. "So, then with your skateboarding career out of the way, you allowed yourself to reject any responsibility in your life."

"Yeah," I respond. "And the sad part is, I thought I didn't care. I actually convinced myself that it didn't matter to me that I had just given up on all my aspirations."

"Well, Brandon, the important thing is that you realize *why* you did this. You were creating an environment for yourself in which your addiction would be possible. You had, essentially, cleared your schedule of all other activities, and your defenses forced you to suppress your feelings so you could believe that you no longer cared about things that once mattered. Like your family, your friends, your skateboarding team. And at this point, you *needed* the drugs to ignore your emotions."

I stare at Guy Leeper. He is exactly right.

Guy prompts me, "What ended up happening with Dwight?"

It's the universal story of every junkie who has ever been on top. Eventually, the weight of Heroin pulls him to the bottom. Like so many other addicts throughout history, and like me, the world he had spent his life to build crumbled down around him.

After Dwight's appetite for Heroin grew and he began using all day, every day, he neglected his business. At first, he was late with payments to his suppliers. Soon he was making fewer deals because he was too high to pull them off. One time, his connections in Mexico sent him a hundred pounds of weed, which he sold but failed to pay for. They couldn't understand why Dwight had fallen short on payments—after all, they had a history with Dwight, and he had always been reliable. When they realized he had become a drug addict, it made sense. So, in reconciliation, they flew him another hundred pounds of marijuana and sent two men to stay with him until he sold it and worked off his debt. This kept him alive and bought him amnesty, but after that, his Mexican connection would never do business with him again.

Two months later we drove to our pick-up neighborhood and he handed off his Rolex for about a grand's worth of Heroin. When I visited his apartment, I noticed that his possessions were sparser. I concluded that he had been pawning them.

One afternoon, he picked me up in his metallic-blue Mercedes. He was upset because his girlfriend had broken up with him and it was strange to see him in this condition, because, if he had experienced emotions of unhappiness during the course of our relationship, he must have gone through great lengths to suppress them. When he asked me if I was holding, and I said no, he drove his Mercedes to the dealership and sold it back to them. He then phoned a cab that took us to our pick-up neighborhood to score.

In time, the items missing in his house went beyond decorative knickknacks to include the centerpieces of his lifestyle: his surround-sound stereo system, his rear-projection television set, his furniture.

"When was the last time you saw Dwight?" Guy asks.

I remember I had just scored some Dope and went directly to Dwight's place to shoot up. He wasn't home, and I had to piss, so I went in the alley next to his house. Some cops spotted me and pulled their car up to the mouth of the alley, blocking me in. Quickly, I stuffed my two fifteen-dollar bags in my asshole. Uncomfortable, yes, but also impossible to find in a frisk search. They ran me in and stuck me in jail for loitering, just to give me a hard time. After I got out, I went back to Dwight's apartment to use the Dope I had hidden so well.

As we prepared to shoot up, Dwight told me, "I'll give you anything I have for one of those bags. You can take anything in this apartment." How about that? The man who was once my hero, was offering me anything in his possession for a fifteen-dollar bag of Dope that had been in my asshole. I looked around his apartment, which was once filled with the expensive furnishings of a lavish lifestyle. Now it was almost empty, except for a bed, a dresser, and some dirty clothes. I told him I couldn't accept anything from him, and shared my Dope as kind of a sick farewell party. I left Dwight's house that night and never returned.

Guy takes a breath, regrouping his thoughts. "It sounds like things must have gone downhill from here."

"Actually, Guy, no. For a while after that, I still managed to keep shit together enough to . . . well, actually, screw up some pretty major opportunities for myself. I swear, I don't know what it is about me, but I make the worst decisions known to man. I think it's time for me to go now. I'm done for the day."

Guy says, "No, sir, you are not done for the day. As I have indicated before, your life is now dominated by guilt and remorse for what you have done, which makes it easy for you to reject any sort of help. It is important for you to understand that you must now face these things in order to begin to accept yourself. This is the only way you can gain freedom from the isolation brought on by your guilt, anger, fear, and self-pity."

I sit in silence.

Guy takes a hard look at me. "Now, Brandon, we are going to do this. I am going to ask you, and you need to answer. What were you just about to tell me?"

I give an ironic smile. "Well, it might be hard to believe, but this junkie sitting in front of you was in a movie and had a documentary made about him."

"You what?" Guy asks.

"Well, I should start off by telling you that a friend of mine, Bam Margera, was in a TV show and a movie titled *Jackass*. He put out a few skateboard films, and then he made an independent movie called *Haggard*. He put me in the film and made a "making of" documentary about how they made the movie. But *The Making of Haggard* ended up being a documentary about how my friends dealt with me and my addiction."

"What was this fellow who made the film's name again?" Guy asks.

"Everyone calls him Bam. His dad gave him that nickname because he was so destructive when he was a little kid. Anyway, I met him when I was young; we knew each other from the skateboarding scene. Bucky and I used to hang out with him on a regular basis. . . ."

chapter twenty-six
Bam Margera

I was twelve years old, waiting outside my house with my skate-board and a bag of clothes. Judging by the decibel level of the music emitted by the eighteen-inch speakers that took up the entire trunk of Bucky Lasek's pale blue custom-built Honda Civic CRX, I knew he was less than two blocks away. Excited, I stepped to the curb. Bucky whipped around the corner, picked me up, and we sped away on the Civic's sixteen-inch chrome rims, which caused the custom body to ride so low that it seemed to bump the ground with every pothole, ditch, and speed bump. This began our weekend ritual, the journey to West Chester, Pennsylvania, the home of our skateboarding pal, ten-year-old Brandon "Bam" Margera.

Bam lived in a small rancher, situated across the street from the town sewer plant. The yard smelled like shit, especially after a rain, but the odor mattered little to us because Bam had a back-yard miniramp. He also had access to a bunch of great suburban skate spots, which were rarities in Baltimore.

Bam's mom, who allowed us to call her by her first name, April, was a real-life version of June Cleaver, the mother on television's *Leave It to Beaver*. Between our arrival and the time we headed back to Baltimore, she provided a nonstop supply of homemade pies, cookies, cakes, cobbler, turnovers, pastries, and my favorite, Rice Krispie Treats.

The itinerary at Bam's house was set in stone. First, we would skate all day. Afterward, we would take showers, watch the video footage we had taken, and discuss our progress. April would wash our clothes and prepare our dinner, and while we ate we would discuss the tricks we were going to learn the following day. In our world there were no girls, no bars, no drugs. They were the best days of my life.

I was always amazed by Bam's powers of concentration. He forced those around him to focus. Each moment spent with him was centered around skating and staying productive.

In the time I spent with Bam, I began to sense that he felt a degree of jealousy toward me because of my association with the Powell Peralta team. Bam had always dreamed of skating for the Powell Peralta Bones Brigade. These elite skaters seemed to have been chosen by the very hand of skateboarding itself for the purpose of sculpting its future through their talent and personalities. Bam was considered the young, promising "little guy that could," the skating prodigy who would be the next big name in skateboarding . . . until I came around.

Not only was Bam envious of me, but I was equally, if not more, envious of him. This was for one simple reason: Phil Margera, Bam's father.

Phil was everything a father could be. He was strong in mind and body, attentive, understanding, generous, and committed to his family. He was everything that every kid wished his father was.

Phil's work ethic would make most men exhausted just to consider. Although he awoke at sunrise and reported to his shift at the grocery store bakery by seven, and did side jobs to make ends

meet, when Bam and his brother Jess got home from school, however, Phil considered it his duty, privilege, and pleasure to spend
the rest of his waking hours with them. While other fathers spent
their weekends pursuing their own interests, Phil simply had no
other interests to pursue. From the second he awoke, until his
head touched the pillow at night, Phil devoted every precious second to his family.

Phil was supportive of Bam's decisions and committed to help
his son in every way. Unlike most parents who discouraged their
sons from pursuing a career in skateboarding, Phil drove Bam
to whatever skate spot his son wished and would videotape Bam
skateboarding with his friends and idols for hours or until the tape
ran out.

I recall hearing about an occasion when Phil was playing with
his young sons on the living room carpet. He looked at his sons
and then to God, saying a prayer, begging that if it was in the
Lord's divine plan to take one of his sons, or if either of them were
to experience a life of pain, to please take him in their place.

Phil extended his fatherly care to every child in the neighborhood. When other kids tried to gain autonomy from their parents by spending time away from home, they went to the Margera
house. Kids loved the Margeras because they knew if they were
with them, they would have fun—or rather, the kids were afraid
to *not* hang out with the Margeras because of the fun they might
miss. Take, for example, the story of the "Yellow Buick."

Phil drove a mid-70s Buick he had bought from his brother
Vince "Don Vito" for $200. The car was yellow, although you
could hardly see its color through the layers of stickers coating
the car from roof to hubcaps, promoting Bam's favorite bands
and skateboard companies. You couldn't miss this car in any parking lot.

Many of Bam's friends had parents who drove Mercedes and BMWs, but when there was a community event, the kids would beg their parents to let them ride with the Margeras in the Yellow Buick. The other parents couldn't understand why.

The Yellow Buick had a seat belt warning mechanism with an unusual malfunction: instead of sounding the *ding-ding-ding* made by other cars of its era, the Yellow Buick belched out a hideous, disturbingly loud buzz when the front seat belt was not connected.

On a trip, with the car piled full of twice as many kids as was legal, Phil would provide the setup. "Okay now, Bam, I just got the car fixed, but it could still explode at any second. But it *should* be okay, so I wouldn't worry about it."

The kids would exchange glances. "Wait, the car might . . . *explode??*"

"Yeah," continues Phil, in a tone of utmost sincerity. "But the mechanic just installed a special alarm, so when it sounds, we still have a good fifteen or twenty seconds—plenty of time to get out. We should be fine."

This speech was always met with dead silence as these kids faced the possibilities of their demise.

Soon, in mid-traffic, Phil would carefully disconnect his seat belt, triggering the alarm: *Zzzooowwwzzzzooowwwzzzooowww.*

The kids would look at each other in horror! Doom.

Phil then nailed the gas, screaming, "Oh, no! Bam, listen! It's the alarm! This thing is gonna blow! We have to get the heck out of here!"

Bam and anyone else in on the joke would have to hold their hands over their mouths to contain their laughter. Meanwhile, the other kids were terrified. "Pull over! Pull over! Let us out! We don't want to die!" they cried.

Phil would swerve the car all over the road, yelling, "I can't pull over! I can't! The traffic is too bad! We only have fifteen seconds! Bam, kids, get ready to run! We're almost out of time!"

Phil prolonged the charade of trying to pull over for almost twenty seconds, as each kid braced for the explosion that would consume them all.

After Phil pulled the car to a stop on the side of the road, the action would begin—the clawing, scratching, pulling, pushing, as each kid fought for his life to be the first to escape flaming red death. Outside, they scattered in all directions, leaving Bam, Phil, and whoever else in on the joke in a fit of laughter that wouldn't stop for an hour.

As time passed, our weekend excursions to Bam's house in West Chester became less frequent. Bam and his Pennsylvania crew came to visit us in Baltimore, but before long they grew tired of what few skate spots our city had to offer.

I was kind of relieved when Bam didn't show up for his weekend visits anymore. It wasn't that I didn't want his friendship, but we seemed to be growing apart. He would want to skate non-stop, all day, every day. When he would fall asleep at night, he would dream of the tricks he wanted to learn, and he'd wake up with an eagerness and determination which seemed to increase as each day passed. It was as if he had almost *too much* energy for me to keep up with. And another factor weighed in. I had discovered a companion more suitable to my life, Drugs.

A few months passed since I had seen Bam around. Then one hot summer day, I was skating with Bucky Lasek at the National Skateboarding Association contest in Bricktown, New Jersey. Suddenly, from the opposite side of the half pipe, a little guy of about twelve dropped in frontside ollie to late shuvit, came back to do a pop shuvit to nose stall, hit the other side with a nose blunt, came back to do a one-foot ollie to fakie, then ended with a chink chink

270 out! Every trick he landed had great speed and precision and a unique style.

Bucky laughed and applauded. I squinted at the figure.

"Wait, is that *Bam?*" I asked.

"Yep! He's been practicing, obviously," Bucky replied.

Later during the contest, Bam had a great run. The most memorable trick of the day was when Bam pulled off a one-footer in front of Bill Weiss, a skater of about six-foot-three, who reacted as if Bam had delivered the kick right to his face. The judges placed Bam in the top ten. As I watched the crowd cheer him, the smile on his face brought back vivid memories of our friendship. I truly understood that, regardless of how talented I was, Bam's drive to succeed would make his name endure through the future of skateboarding, while mine would fade away.

As the years passed, I watched as Bam's career took off and he became a celebrity, while my skateboarding career dwindled to nothing more than a memory.

It was springtime, and I was twenty-three when I got a phone call from Bam, out of nowhere.

ME: Hello?

BAM: Brandon Novak!

ME: Who's this?

BAM: It's Bam! Long time no see!

ME: Bam?

BAM: Yep! I saw Bucky the other day, and we got to talking, and I asked, "Whatever happened to Novak?"

ME: Cool! What's going on?

BAM: Well, for one, I hear you're addicted to heroin!

ME: Well, not anymore [lie]. I'm sixty days clean now [lie]. Other than that, everything's going great [lie]!

BAM: You still skate at all?

ME: Yeah, from time to time [lie]. Since I'm clean, I've been skating more and more [lie].

BAM: Cool. Well, I'm making *CKY 3* right now. You feel like coming by to make a cameo? I have a skate ramp in my backyard at my parents' new house. You should come by for a couple of days and lay the hammer down. I have a new house, you can stay there with me; it'll be just like old times.

CKY stands for Camp Kill Yourself. The *CKY* videos were top-selling films that Bam directed and produced. They were skateboard videos with a twist.

Before *CKY* skateboard videos consisted of skating segments with skits in between. Most people grew tired of the generic and formulaic skate videos that were being released. The videos lacked mass appeal; they were entertaining only to those who were heavily involved in the sport. Essentially, if you weren't a diehard skater, you would watch a skate video once or twice and shelve it forever.

Bam Margera, who fate had somehow thrown in the midst of this video/skateboarding zeitgeist, changed all that.

This was a time in history when broadcast quality video technology first became affordable to consumers. Three-chip mini-DV cameras had just been released to the public and were on sale at department stores and camera shops. Now, finally, independent filmmakers could shoot on a format that yielded beautiful color and resolution and would not degrade with each subsequent copy. One more advent of this period was central to the video revolution: digital nonlinear editing. For the first time, an edit in the middle of a program could be changed without causing the editor to redo all the edits that followed. The creative process was no longer secondary to the technology that once had restricted it. And the affordability of the equipment required for digital nonlinear editing made the concept even more appealing. Anyone with a few thousand dollars could buy a computer, be their own editor, and bypass large editing studios, saving thousands of dollars. In these new developments in the film medium, Bam saw opportunities to make his own videos. And now, Bam needed inspiration.

A few skate videos at the time featured "slam sections," consisting of rapidly edited tricks that were not landed, in which the skaters were hurt. These segments became many people's favorite part of skate videos. They appealed to people's strange infatuation with pain while reminding audiences what the sport was all about—the danger of landing the tricks. Bam decided to place himself and his friends in situations in which they could not win and pain was sure to follow. For example, he invented a sport in which a participant would ride in a grocery-store shopping cart that was pushed by a friend full speed into a curb. The impact would cause the person in the cart to fly through the air, and land on the concrete. Bam called these "shopping cart slams." Painful? Yes! Entertaining? Hell yes!

Bam incorporated skating, skits, slams, and his own sensibilities into his *CKY* videos. What he offered to the public wasn't just a series of skateboard films. He showed the world through the eyes of a suburban skate rat. Finally, the world had skate videos that were entertaining to skaters and nonskaters alike. Everyone could watch these films over and over.

No one could predict the social significance of these videos or their influence on pop culture. They were far removed from big Hollywood productions, they were never on the shelves of top retailers, and they were never advertised. Yet the fans sought them out and bought millions of copies worldwide. The *CKY* videos changed the way people videotaped, the way people watched movies, and the way filmmakers worked. Bam, his pal Ryan Dunn, and the rest of his crew would eventually join forces with the staff at *Big Brother* magazine, leading to the inception of a television show and a motion picture series called *Jackass*.

Even though I had no idea how important these films were to become, I was excited to be a part of the video project, and to see my old friend Bam as well. I stayed for a week at Bam's house and made an appearance in the video *CKY 3*.

When Bam picked me up from the West Chester bus station, we hadn't seen each other for years. But the moment we made eye contact, I knew the bond we had shared as kids still remained. Strangely, although he was on the verge of worldwide fame, he felt an allegiance to me because I was one of the friends he had prior to making it big. Even more strangely, he felt that he owed me. When we were younger, my presence had challenged him to be his best. I was the more popular skater. I was in the magazines. I was on the Powell Peralta team. In his mind, he felt that *I* was the one who should have been famous, not him. As a result, he felt the need to help me set my life straight.

In the time we spent together, the topic of conversation often turned to my addiction. Bam would always conclude the dialogue with the possibilities of my recovery and "comeback" to the sport of skateboarding. At that point I had never for one second entertained the notion of making a comeback, or stopping my drug use.

Recovery was something I had gotten into the habit of agreeing to when others would mention it. But Bam, in his naïveté, took the idea of recovery seriously.

I remember the first day of shooting *CKY 3*. The guy who filmed it was Joe Frantz, a Philly boy who used to work in big advertising and had dropped out of the game to become an indie filmmaker. Bam introduced us. "Hey, Frantz. I want you to meet a friend of mine. This is Novak. Novak used to be a skater on Powell Peralta. But then he became a heroin addict and threw it all away."

Frantz shook my hand, probably wondering if this strange introduction was some sort of joke. To please Bam, I confirmed it. "That's right! I used to be a skater, and I blew it all because I got addicted to heroin."

Frantz's eyes turned toward Bam, who said, "But now, he's skating every day and he's trying to make a comeback. Right, Brandon?"

"Yep!" I agreed.

Frantz said, "I've known a couple junkies in my time. How long you been clean?"

"A couple months," I told him.

"Then I'm sure you'll enjoy this joke: How can you tell when a junkie is lying?"

"How?" asks Bam.

Frantz delivered the punch line. "When his mouth is moving."

I didn't laugh.

Guy Leeper stops my story and asks, "Did Bam think this joke was funny?"

I run my fingers through my hair, staring at the ceiling of the counseling office. "Well, Guy, Bam was pretty young and naïve. He was only twenty, and other than seeing bums on the street in Philly, I was the first junkie he ever had contact with. So, to answer your question, Bam didn't laugh at Frantz's joke because he did not yet understand its full implications. But he soon would."

chapter twenty-seven
Haggard

After the production of *CKY 3*, Bam and Frantz discussed shooting a motion picture follow-up to the *CKY* series, a movie called *Haggard*. Bam wanted me to be a part of it.

I was living above a Laundromat in one of the worst sections of Baltimore City. For me, this neighborhood was perfect, as Dope shops were plentiful. Although I was the only white person for blocks in any direction, the locals began to accept me, which made it easy to score.

The owner of the house I lived in was Ida, a fifty-something heavyset black woman who wore glasses so thick that when talking to her, I couldn't tell which direction she was looking. Ida was the mother of one of my running partners, who had recently gone to jail. She treated me like a second son and allowed me to live in his room while he was away. I didn't have a job, but every so often I would pull a hustle or make a deal that allowed me to give her fifty bucks or so.

When I got Bam's call, I had just stolen Ida's VCR and sold it for a few bags of Dope. I hoped she wouldn't notice that the VCR was missing, since she never used it. I returned to her house, prepared to deny everything, to find a note by the phone listing Bam's name and number. I dialed him up, and in less than five minutes, he gave to me the opportunity of a lifetime.

BAM: So, me and Frantz and the guys are making a movie called *Haggard*. It's gonna be a legit indie film. There's a part in it for you, if you want. I'm paying for the movie out of my own pocket; it's not a huge Hollywood deal or anything, but I can pay you a few hundred bucks . . .

ME: Yeah, sounds great!

BAM: And guess what? Bucky Lasek and Tony Hawk are gonna be in it, too, in cameo roles. How's that for coincidence?

ME: Man, I haven't seen those guys in forever [nor did I want them see me in such pitiful condition].

BAM: And listen, I've been thinking, you should stay at my house, too. That way, whenever we're not shooting the movie, you can skate my miniramp and come with me to FDR skatepark. And you'll stay off drugs, because I'll be keeping an eye on you all the time. Who knows, with us skating all the time, and no drugs around, you could get good enough at skating to make that comeback we've been talking about!

And there it was, an opportunity presented to me that would eventually perpetuate my drug addiction!

The part I was supposed to play in *Haggard* was that of a computer tech-head named Shorty. But my lack of sobriety and inability to memorize lines led Bam to change my part to that of a drug dealer.

After a week in West Chester, Bam gave me my first payment, a check for three hundred dollars. I hightailed it back to Baltimore and bought two hundred dollars' worth of Heroin and a two-way pager, which I thought might be an easy way for me to communicate with my drug connection (cell phones were very expensive at the time). I was so high on Dope, I never did figure out how to get the goddamn pager to work. I became obsessed with it, fiddling with it for hours. On the production, Bam and the guys devised a way to get the pager out of my hands. They wrote an impromptu gag into the film in which Bam took the pager out of my hands and threw it across the room. I never saw the pager again.

In one shot, my character was supposed to be making a drug deal outside Fairman's, a landmark skateboard shop. The camera, positioned inside the shop, was filming me as I stood across the street, passing a conspicuous-looking package (supposed to be drugs) to a black guy. Now, keep in mind we were in West Chester, a white bread college town. These people were so afraid of black people, that they considered a block on which several blacks lived "the ghetto" and were afraid to drive past there at night in fear that they might be carjacked or murdered.

As soon as we were done with the shot I walked back into Fairman's. Suddenly, five cops ran around the corner with nightsticks drawn! Apparently, a concerned citizen had seen me and this black guy passing the shady-looking package back and forth and phoned in our descriptions. Bam and Frantz watched from Fairman's window, laughing their asses off. "Where's Novak?" Bam asked. "He should see this!" I'll tell you where I was, I was in the basement of Fairman's, hiding my Heroin in the inventory, in case the cops came in and started asking questions.

Later, we did a couple of takes inside Fairman's. I thought I was doing great but, apparently, I was not. Frantz was shooting the movie in super-16-millimeter film, which I had no idea was expensive as hell. I was expected to get all my lines right on the first or second take, but I was fucking them up, big time.

On a break, I went back to the basement to recover my Dope.

I stared at the wall of inventory, and to my horror, I realized that my precious Dope was shoved into a single sneaker in one of sixty boxes, and I couldn't remember which fucking one. As I was fighting my way through this wall of sneakers, I could hear Frantz and Bam upstairs, having an argument. This wasn't out of the ordinary, because the two were killing themselves to make this film, staying up for days at a time, and tensions ran high. But the subject of this particular argument was me.

FRANTZ: Dude, what the fuck is up with Novak? We did seven fucking takes and he still didn't get his lines right.

BAM: He's never made a movie before. I don't know, he's just nervous or something . . .

FRANTZ: *Nervous?* He's strung like a fucking violin! Look, I don't give a shit if he wants to kill himself, but he's wasting fucking film, which is expensive! Every time he screws up a line, it costs fifty bucks!

BAM: Well, I'm trying to help him out, okay? Novak is a friend of mine.

FRANTZ: Yeah, great! For our movie premiere, you and your "friend" can sit in your basement, eat popcorn, and watch half a movie, because we ran out of film during production.

BAM: All right, all right! I'll talk to him and see what's up.

FRANTZ: Oh, I'll tell you what's up, you gave a junkie a paycheck and guess what he spent it on?!

BAM: Let's just talk about this later.

I found my precious Heroin and entered the bathroom, ready to fix. As I closed the door, I felt it being forced open. I turned and was face to face with Frantz, who closed the door behind him. I knew right away that a speech was coming.

"Brandon. Listen and listen close, because I'm only gonna say this once. I'm older than Bam and the rest of these guys. I'm not taken in by this self-serving feel-good let's-all-jump-on-the-band-wagon-to-help-the-poor-junkie-joy-ride. I've known addicts. One of my best friends in college died of a heroin overdose."

I interrupt. "Frantz, I don't know what you believe about me, but look—"

"No, you look! This isn't a debate. This isn't even a conversation. It's a monologue. It's me telling you, if you're gonna scam everyone in West Chester, fine, but I know you're on dope and I'm here to tell you, if you do one thing to harm Bam, Phil, or April, I'll come down on you so fast that you'll wish you OD'd years ago!"

Jesus Christ, does this guy ever shut the fuck up?

He continues. "Look, Novak, I like you. I see the good in you but I also recognize the bad, and that's why I'm prepared to be your good friend as well as your worst enemy. Every time you're high, every time I catch you with drugs, every time you fuck up, I'll call you out in public and draw as much attention to you as possible. Understand?"

I decide that the easiest way to deal with Frantz is to comply with a nod of the head, looking down to the ground as if I have been humbled, to let him feel as if he has won the battle. "Yes, I understand."

My ploy works. He extends his arm in what seems to be an honest handshake of friendship. Ha-ha! We shake and Frantz pats me on the back. "Okay, Brand. The good news is, I consider you a friend, and I'm a pretty good friend to have. So, let's forget this bullshit and go make a movie." He opens the bathroom door and motions, as if to say, "After you, Novak."

I look back at the bathroom and again at Frantz. A strange grin has come over his face. Does he know I was about to shoot up prior to his entrance? If so, is this his sign of victory, to cut me off? Or is he so happy with himself after his little speech that he has forgotten that if I had actually come in here to take a piss, I still haven't? We go upstairs. I am irate that I am not as high as I really wanted to be.

A few days later, I had hidden my Heroin and needle in the bushes next to Bam's miniramp. Ryan Dunn, a short, stocky guy who was in the *CKY* videos and *Jackass,* is visiting the Margeras. They are all seated in the kitchen, where they have a clear view of both the miniramp and the bushes. All I have to do is wait an hour and retrieve my stash when no one is around. But I want to get high and can't wait.

I go out on the ramp and begin skating. Acting as if I am having an "off day," I purposefully mess up a few tricks, shooting the board into the bushes in order to create opportunities to find my bag. I realize how this looked to everyone inside the house when Ryan Dunn storms out to confront me. "Dude, it's so fucking obvious that you have something hidden in the bushes. I can't believe you think we're so goddamn dumb that we can't see what you're up to!" So fucking what? What the fuck do you care? As if my drug use has any consequence to you!

Dunn searches the bushes for my Dope, which he doesn't find, thank God. "I can't believe you, Brandon! You're supposed to be off this goddamn shit, and here you are, doing it right under the noses of all the people who care about you!"

I ask myself, "Why is Dunn, who doesn't even know me, who doesn't give a shit about me, who doesn't even talk to me when he sees me at the bar, suddenly interested in my well-being?" Then I see it: Bam is videotaping our argument through the kitchen window. Reality slows down for a moment, as I make several observations.

I think, If I was a black homeless guy, covered in piss and sleeping on the street, Dunn wouldn't give me a dollar to save my life. But now that the camera is rolling, and he sees an opportunity to use my addiction to be the center of attention, *now* he shows concern. I get it, he's acting for the fucking camera.

I look at Bam as he holds the video camera and films the entire scene with a shit-eating grin on his face. He's *enjoying* this. To him, videotaping the misfortune of my life is like watching a TV show. I am this kid's fucking entertainment.

I make a decision. If situations like this will make my free ride at this house last longer, and give me the means to remain an addict, I'll play the game. I make up my mind to be an actor in Bam's little world, and to let him be the director. The scene ends as Ryan and I embrace, with Dunn acting as if he is so worried about me that he sheds a tear. Now that Bam had seen the plot unfold, he devises a resolution. "Okay, Novak! Tomorrow, I'm taking you to get a tattoo that says, 'No More Fucking Heroin' right on your stomach, where you can see it every time you look in the mirror. And from now on, if you ever do heroin again, you'll see the tattoo and you'll feel like such a piece of shit." Gee, Bam, do you actually think this will work?

The next day, to Bam's satisfaction, I get the tattoo, as he films it. All this footage ended up in the documentary, *The Making of "Haggard."*

I tell Guy Leeper, "Now that I look back, I realize how much I misjudged things. I was so accustomed to using people, and being used by other people, that I forgot the human traits of kindness, generosity, charity, and tenderness. Of course Dunn could have cared about me without really knowing me. Of course Bam could have been concerned about me, even if he did videotape my argument with Dunn. Hell, maybe this was his way of dealing with his friend's addiction. But I was so caught up in my drug world, I could only see through a junkie's eyes. My rationale, that Bam was using me, allowed me to use him back."

I pull up my shirt, and show Guy my tattoo, which reads, "No More Fucking Heroin." "Getting this goddamn thing was a joke to me. In my mind, it was nothing more than Bam's bragging piece. He had just turned twenty-one and could now take me to the bar, command me to pull up my shirt, and show people his accomplishment. I began to feel like Brandon Novak, Bam's trained animal."

Guy stares, waiting to hear the rest.

"But, Guy, this really mattered little to me. I had learned to hide my real feelings years ago. I had the means to kill my negative feelings with Dope. And so, I was determined to make the most of West Chester for as long as I could."

Bam's friends and the people in town viewed me as "that guy who was addicted to heroin." My identity became that of the drug addict. But, oddly enough, I wasn't ashamed. I felt liberated. If I messed something up, I had an excuse: I was an addict. And if I did the normal things a person is expected to do, such as return a borrowed item, show up on time, or not steal, I was given praise. People were proud of me for doing nothing all day, as long as they believed I had stayed clean. I was in a no-lose situation.

Because I was constantly seen with Bam, and he was always talking about me, I became a local celebrity. I brought excitement to the quiet town of West Chester. Excitement!

West Chester is a college town, full of kids whose parents encourage them to enroll in West Chester University so they can attend classes, get an education, and become more well-rounded. What the parents are really paying hundreds of thousands of dollars for is a four-year party.

The college girls I met were complete sluts who didn't have to be talked into anything. College gives some women a license to sleep with anyone, drink as much as they can, do as many drugs as they want to. After all, when they graduate, they'll move away to a place where their reputation is a clean slate. Then they can settle down with the right guy who will never find out they were dirty, filthy, disgusting whores for four years of their lives. Their college years are a period when the consequences of their actions will never catch up with them. Not that I am any better than them: I slept with every one who threw herself at me.

The guys were even worse. Insecure, unworldly kids, they haven't figured out what they want out of life. They desperately want to fit in and belong, going through the motions, floating from one identity crisis to another. Their idea of a meaningful experience is smoking pot and listening to the Beatles' *Sgt. Pepper's Lonely Hearts Club Band* or tripping acid and watching the film *Pink Floyd The Wall*.

To these kids I was cool, mysterious, and they got to live vicariously through my stories. At parties and the bar, I was the center of attention. Ludicrous as it seems, it was an honor for them to keep my company and a privilege to buy me a drink. I made people feel special, as if they were learning something from me. As if, by befriending me, they were accomplishing something that allowed them to go to class the next day and brag that they had hung out with a Heroin addict! Ha!

Every day I would sit at the bar and wait for classes to let out and the barrage of free drinks to begin. The kids would swarm around me. I'd look at their books. Psychology. Sociology. Ethics. These kids resented their professors who worked for years to achieve their degrees in order to teach them valuable knowledge. Here I was, a junkie at a bar, a hero. I was like Jesus, with his apostles sitting at his feet, holding their breath for the next gem of wisdom. I looked at the naïve faces, hanging on to my every word.

STUDENT #1: So Novak, you were addicted to . . . *heroin?*

ME: Yep, since I was seventeen years old.

STUDENT #1: Oh shit! What was that like?

STUDENT #2: What's the craziest thing you ever did?

ME: *(clearing my throat, as if ready to make a speech to promote world peace)* Did I ever tell you guys about the time I shot bleach by mistake?

STUDENT #1: You shot what?! *Bleach?!*

STUDENT #2: Oh shit, man! That's fucked up!

STUDENT #3: How? Why?

ME: Well, I used to know this junkie named Kaitlin from Park Heights, Baltimore, who would score Heroin for me when times were tough. She used to rip me off and pinch from the bags she'd score for me, so she would always come up with some bullshit reasons to pick up the Dope without me.

STUDENT #1: Was Kaitlin *black?*

STUDENT #2: Did you know a lot of black people?

STUDENT #3: Shut the fuck up and let him tell the story! I wanna hear this. Go ahead, Brandon.

ME: One day she had me wait at her house while she scored. I started rooting around in her stuff and found a small bag of heroin that looked like she had once hid but forgot all about. I didn't have a needle, so I found hers and started to clean it out with bleach—

STUDENT #1: Why bleach? Why did you do that?

STUDENT #2: Does bleach get you high?

STUDENT #3: No, you stupid asses! The bleach was to clean out the diseases like AIDS that she might have had. Stop interrupting the story! Go ahead, Brand.

ME: So, there I am, cleaning out Kaitlin's dirty needle with bleach. I was sick and strung out at the time, and real nervous because I had no idea when Kaitlin would come home. And I panicked! I did the wrong thing, and mixed up my bowl of bleach with the water I was supposed to use in the cooker, and I ended up shooting up a needle full of heroin and bleach by mistake.

My audience is speechless. One asks, "What did it feel like?"

"It felt like my veins were on fire for about three days," I tell them.

They sip their beer as if they had just experienced an alternate reality.

As I tell my story to Guy Leeper, I explain, "So I was in this crazy position. I mean, my whole life, everyone despised me for being a drug addict, and now, the tables had turned, and it was like, I was now being *rewarded* for it."

Guy tried to provide insight. "This is what is called positive reinforcement, when someone is rewarded for their behavior. It is dangerous when a person is given positive reinforcement for negative behavior. So you were in a position in which you no longer had anything to dissuade you from your addiction."

"Almost anything," I tell him. "But that's where Bam's friends and family stepped in."

chapter twenty-eight
Paradise Lost

The enabler is a best friend of no value, a living paradox. He nullifies the aid that he gives to the addict by maintaining the lifestyle that makes addiction possible. He is the junkie's greatest asset, more valuable than the needle itself.

To the junkie, the world of relationships resembles a chess board on which Heroin is in full control of the game. The pawns are all those who have ever cared: parents, brothers, sisters, aunts, uncles, grandparents, old friends, old girlfriends, neighbors, friends of friends. Every square represents a place where the junkie has been and can make a move, create a scam, or pull a hustle. To a mind possessed by Junk, friends and family cease to be human. They are simply resources.

The addict and the enabler share a reciprocal relationship. While the addict is dependent upon the enabler, the enabler also needs the addict. It is almost as difficult to break the cycle of the enabler as it is to break the cycle of addiction. One might ask, what's the attraction for the enablers? How do they justify helping an addict? What are the rewards of selflessness? That's easy. Like the junkie, they get to feel good for a while. For one brief, shining moment, they get to feel as if their tiny, insignificant lives actually matter. As if the fact that they ever existed will make a difference in the scheme of things. The junkie is a dreamseller: a mirror on which those who help him can peer into their own souls. The enabler is like a monkey trying to touch his own reflection in the water. But when he does, the image ripples outward, then inward, right back at him.

The best way I can describe this phenomenon is through the following diagram:

The Cycle of the Enabler

Enabler confronts Addict

Confrontation is followed by Emotional Release

Enabler is motivated to enable Addict

Addict betrays Enabler

Addict becomes Enabler's Emotional Outlet

Enabler enables Addict

First, the enabler is motivated to enable the addict, usually out of a sense of obligation or duty. This is why most enablers are family members or friends.

Upon enabling the addict, the addict is forced into a position where he must betray the enabler. He has no alternative. Betrayal is what addicts do.

The addict will then push the boundaries of betrayal until the enabler can no longer tolerate it. Naturally, a confrontation ensues. The confrontation may take the form of a fight, an argument, crying, or screaming, but in any event, emotions are introduced into the relationship. These emotions replace the logic that was once the driving force to help the addict.

After the confrontation dies down, the addict is forced to make some temporary amends with the enabler. He may admit he was wrong, he may promise to never screw up again; he may check into a rehab. But this resolution will give both the enabler and the addict the false sense of security and hope. "I'm sorry," "I love you," and "I promise" are often said during this stage.

Here the cycle of the enabler comes full circle. The enabler has now made an emotional investment and will be afraid to let go. His thought pattern will be controlled by his emotions, and he will cling to his relationship with the addict as does a child to his security blanket. The addict, in turn, will cling to the enabler for dear life. This cycle will then continue until either one of the two comes to his senses or dies.

This is the relationship I now shared with Bam Margera, and it was a cycle in which I couldn't lose. Bam became my enabler, I became his addict, and my life became a continuous stint at the bar, separated by periods of sleep and television viewing.

April began to cramp my style. One argument sticks out in my head. I was watching television when she returned home from shopping. As she made several trips to the car to bring in all the groceries, she looked at me from the corner of her eye. What? Did she expect me to help?

As she put away the groceries, she questioned me. "So, Brandon, what did you do today? Do you have any plans to do anything productive?"

What the hell do you think I did today? I woke up at two, now I'm watching TV. And yes, I have plans. Tonight I'm going to the bar with your son to get drunk and laid. "I'm not feeling too good today, Ape. Do you need any help bringing in the groceries (now that you're done bringing them all in)?"

"Well, you know what would make you feel better?"

"What's that, Ape?" I say with zero interest in what this annoying woman is telling me.

"I think it would make you feel better to go out there and skate. There's a ramp right in the backyard, in case you haven't noticed. I'd think that you would be taking this opportunity to practice every day."

I decided to test my boundaries. "Ape, would you get off my back?! Nag nag nag."

April said, "Well, I don't think I'm being a nag at all. It's just that I think you really need to do something constructive with your time rather than sit in front of the TV all day. It's not like you have a job or anything, or any place to be."

I thought, I *do* have a job! I'm your son's fucking companion. I do whatever he says. I listen to his stories all day long and act as if I care. I laugh extra hard at his jokes to boost his ego. When he gets into an argument with someone at the bar, right or wrong, I back him up. Whatever he wants to do, I go with him and have to act like I'm interested just so he's not seen around town all alone. When he runs out of interesting things to say to people, he makes me tell them stories about my addiction to entertain them. My life revolves around your kid, lady. I'm your son's personal fucking slave, isn't that enough to satisfy you? What the fuck else do you want from me?

Looking back, I really can't understand the mixed emotions that I was feeling. On one hand, I appreciated all that the Margeras were doing for me. On the other hand, I resented them when they expected something in return: for me to be something I wasn't.

And I somehow ended up using this resentment as justification to lie to them, to cheat them, to steal from the very people who were doing so much for me. Why did I feel this way? Why was I so full of animosity and bitterness?

But in the meantime, I had real worries. I had an addiction, and no way to pay for it.

And so . . .

Bam's garage was a warehouse of merchandise, which was replenished monthly by all sponsors who paid him to license his name and image for their products. One entire wall of the garage was stacked with skateboards, ball bearings, skateboard trucks, wheels, sunglasses, sneakers, clothes. The way I saw it, I was entitled to whatever I wanted. After all, Bam had way more stuff than he could possibly use, and I needed money. Hell, he *owes* me, I thought as I would stuff the products into the trunk of Bam's black Audi, drive them to FDR skatepark in Philly, and sell them for one-tenth their value.

With a means to pay for my addiction, I used increased amounts of the drug with greater frequency. No matter how much Heroin I would bring back to Bam's house from my trips to Baltimore, I couldn't seem to make it last. I had no willpower or ability to ration out my stash. Any Heroin I brought into Bam's house was gone within a few days. I began stealing more than ever to cover my habit, and Bam's sponsorship merchandise dwindled.

Bam got pissed at my numerous excursions to Baltimore, and I was running out of bullshit reasons to go. One of the last times I went, I was so high that I gave Bam one of the worst excuses ever offered to a human being for anything, ever.

"Why the hell do you need to go back to Baltimore all the time? I don't get it," Bam asked as he dropped me off at the bus station. "Why do you have to go? Tell me! Why? So far this month you've had to take care of your mother, you've had to take care of your mother's dog, you've had to help your friend move furniture, you've had to help a friend's neighbor paint his house. And those don't include the times you disappeared with my car for days at a time, probably using it to drive to Baltimore yet again. So what's your reason this time? What?"

"I need to go to Baltimore because . . . because I have to get . . . my favorite jeans!" (I can't believe that's the best I could do.)

Bam looked at me. I looked back with an expression of utmost seriousness. He rubbed his eyes from the onset of a tension head-ache caused by the fact that I could even make up such a prepos-terous lie and said, "Wait. Let me get this straight, you're going back to Baltimore to get you *favorite jeans?* What's so special about these jeans? Do they have a mouth built into the zipper and they suck your dick? What the fuck?"

"Bam, they're my favorite jeans! Why would I lie? I love these jeans, Bam. They've been with me through thick and thin, through good times and bad. I'm a sentimental guy, you know that. I get attached to things, man. Just like I'm attached to you."

My welcome at the Margera household eroded each day.

- There was a bottle of prescription codeine in the bathroom medicine cabinet. As per the old junkie trick, I replaced the pills with aspirin. But my mistake was, there were *ten* codeine pills in the bottle and I had replaced them with *eleven* aspirin. By this time, April was keeping tabs on all medicines, and my ruse was discovered. I denied it, but, come on, who else would have done this? *Phil?*
- At this point, it was a well-known fact and almost accepted that I had pillaged the sponsorship merchandise from the

garage. But other items go missing from the house: spoons (used as cookers), a few pieces of April's jewelry (sold at the pawn shop), CDs (sold at the music store).

- One time I shot up in the upstairs bathroom and passed out with the water running. I woke up over an hour later with April pounding at the door. The tub had overflowed and ruined the drywall ceiling downstairs. I woke up, wrapped a towel around my waist, claiming that the bath had relaxed me to the degree that I had fallen asleep in the tub, although my skin was bone dry.

- I would borrow Bam's black Audi to "get a pack of smokes" and then take off for days. Of course, when I returned, the tank was always empty. When I parked, I didn't pay the meters and received parking tickets, which I would laugh at and toss away. When Phil received the unpaid parking ticket notices in the mail, and Phil and April confronted me, I denied it and swore to God that I had never received a parking ticket in my entire life. When they presented me with several unpaid ticket notices from the city of Baltimore, incurred on dates when I had "borrowed" their car, I told them how kids in Baltimore liked to steal parking tickets from cars as a prank, and that this was a big problem there. I never so much as made a half-assed attempt at paying them back for the hundreds of dollars in parking fines. Why would I?

- Bam began to frisk me on a daily basis. Several times, he made me stand by while he searched hiding spots around the house for my drugs. Then he would make me look him in the eyes and lie to him. "Look me in the eyes and tell me if you're on drugs! Go on, lie to me, right to my face!" he would demand. As if I really had a problem doing this!

• One night, Bam, Phil, and April were invited to attend the MTV Music Video Awards. In their absence, I seized the opportunity to take the black Audi to Baltimore, pawn some of Bam's merchandise, and score. By the time the Margeras arrived home, I was shooting up in the garage. Before they entered the house, I turned off the light and retreated to the basement and acted as if I were asleep. Little did I realize, in my junkie mind, they could see the garage light through the window. When Bam called my name, I limped up the stairs, acting as if they had just woken me up.

BAM: Where were you just now?

ME: I was asleep in the basement.

APRIL: Brandon, we just came home and the garage light was on. Now it's off. What's going on? Were you in the garage?

ME: I don't know, I've been asleep.

BAM: Wait, you're saying that you weren't just in the garage?

ME: No, I just walked upstairs just now. I don't see how the light could have been on. It must have been off. You must have imagined it.

APRIL: Brandon, we all saw the light was on. All of us.

PHIL: That's true, we did, we all saw it, there's no way we all could have imagined it.

ME: Really? Are you sure?

BAM: Dude, we're fucking sure!

ME: *(so obviously lying)* Oh! I know what happened! I was getting something to drink in there so I had the light on. Then I turned it off.

BAM: But you *just said* that when we came home you were sleeping.

ME: No, I was, but I meant *before*.

BAM: Before what?

ME: Before you came home.

BAM: *(frustrated as hell)* Dude, your story isn't even making sense.

APRIL: *(trying to catch me in a lie)* Well, let me ask you this, if you were thirsty, why didn't you get something from the refrigerator in the kitchen? Why did you walk all the way to the garage refrigerator?

ME: Oh, I really wanted a soda, not water, so I went to the garage.

BAM: *(opening the kitchen refrigerator)* Look! There *are* sodas in here!

ME: Oh, I didn't think to look there; I just assumed there wouldn't be any. That's why I went to the garage to get my soda, just like I said.

BAM: Well where is it?

ME: Where is what?

BAM: Your fucking soda! The fucking soda you told us that you got!

ME: Oh, I saw you guys come home and I wanted to ask you about the awards, so I shut the light out and didn't get it. That's when I turned off the light, remember?

APRIL: But you just came up from the cellar and said you have been sleeping.

ME: No, I *was* sleeping, but that was *before*. Remember I said I was asleep? That's when I got thirsty. Remember? *Then* I turned the light out. Why would I lie? What do you think I did?

BAM: I don't know, but you were up to something. You're obviously lying about this for some reason.

ME: No, you're getting mixed up. I *told* you, I *did* turn the light out, totally. Remember? Why would I lie about nothing when I told you you were right?

By the end of the conversation, the Margeras were so frustrated they gave up and went to bed. I was so fucking high that I believed I had convinced them I was innocent. I envisioned myself as a suave con artist whose superior verbal skills and intellect allowed me to pull the wool over the eyes of the world. Little could my Heroin-polluted brain understand how everyone in West Chester viewed me. April saw me as a lying drug addict who was taking advantage of her son and her family. Phil wanted me to leave and get away from his family. Frantz saw me as a freeloader hanging by a thread to my last friend in the world. Ryan Dunn viewed me as pathetic. All of Margera's friends were disgusted by me and my lifestyle.

Deep down I knew damn well I was a fuckup who didn't deserve this opportunity that was being offered to me. But in my mind, everything was perfect, and I didn't want it to change. I was in my own perverted drug-induced wonderland and I never wanted to leave.

One night, I laid in Bam's basement, chain-smoking half a pack of cigarettes down to the last, in the midst of a Heroin and Xanex cocktail–induced stupor, utterly pacified in my little Dope world.

But it was soon to come to an abrupt halt.

Upstairs, I heard voices as a concerned mother, April, lectured her son. "Listen, Bam, you can't make someone do something they don't want to. You can't make someone be who you want them to be. You can't wish something for someone who doesn't want it for himself. You want him to make a comeback as a skater, but he just doesn't want it as bad as you do."

And of course, fucking Frantz chimes in with his own goddamn self-righteous two cents. "Bam, the guy is *using* you. I know it sucks to admit, but he has no intention of cleaning up. Don't take my word for it, just take a good look at his actions. When you look at Novak, do you see a guy who wants to better himself?"

Bam said, "No." There was shame in his voice.

Frantz continued his little tirade. "And look what he's done to your family! April has to sleep with her door locked and her purse under her bed in her own house."

"Is that true, Mom?" Bam asked.

"Yes," she told him.

Fuck-face Frantz drove his point home. "Look, Bam, I know you feel guilty about this, but you shouldn't. You've given Novak every opportunity here, and he's rejected it. He hasn't skated since he got here, and what's worse is that he doesn't do jack shit to earn his keep. He's never taken out the trash, never picked up after himself, never put his own dishes in the dishwasher. He treats April like his personal maid! Look, right there, sitting on the fucking counter, there's lunch meat, cheese, bread, and mayonnaise from a sandwich that Novak made. Not only didn't he bother to put them back in the refrigerator, but he didn't even put the fucking lid back on the mayonnaise!"

Oops.

April continues. "Bam, I know it hurts you to have to do this, but you have to be realistic. You're not helping him. He's not going to make a comeback. He's made up his mind to stagnate and let his life waste away."

Five minutes of silence followed.

I heard the cellar door open. I knew the sound of Bam's footsteps, having listened for them on many nights while cooking up a shot. But tonight, they were a bit heavier. In my Heroin-infested brain, his skate shoes resonated like a judge marching through the halls of a marble-floored courthouse.

Bam threw a duffel onto my stomach. As I lifted my head he told me, "Here's a bag. Pack your shit, you're going back to Baltimore!" He turned and fled up the stairs, so hurt that he couldn't even look at me.

My old friend Bam. I had taken him, like so many others, on a journey through which he finally realized that the only one who could help me was myself. There was no bullshitting my way out of it this time.

Oh well, it was fun while it lasted, I thought.

I searched my pockets for any drugs I may have forgotten about. Empty. Shit.

No drugs, no money, no cigarettes, and no home.

How did I end up in this position, once again?

I looked at the empty bag Bam had thrown on my stomach and wondered how much of the merchandise from the garage I could stuff into it prior to my departure from West Chester, Pennsylvania.

"So, Guy, they finished the movie *Haggard,* along with a documentary called *The Making of 'Haggard.'* The documentary ended up being about how Bam and the guys dealt with me and my addiction. During one of my sobriety kicks, I showed the film to my mom, and the next day she went out and bought me a funeral plot, and herself a plot right next to it."

Guy Leeper must have sensed that I was exhausted. After a minute, he said, "All right, Brandon, I think we're off to a great start. You've faced a lot here, your guilt, and I hope that through this you can see yourself more clearly, and can prepare yourself to remove your shortcomings. If you put as much motivation into your recovery as you have demonstrated to me today, there's no doubt in my mind you will succeed." He rises out of his seat, walks over to me, staring. I have no idea what's about to go down, but I'm nervous. He reaches out to me, grabs me, and pulls me in for something that resembles a bear hug. I have no idea what to do so I follow Guy's lead and wrap my arms around his body. Affection. I have forgotten it for so long.

"I'll see you tomorrow at the same time," Guy says.

I look above his head to see the old-style black-and-white analog wall clock. Its hands read 2:30. I'm shocked. "Didn't we start this session at eight thirty?" I ask.

Guy stares at me with delight. "Yes," he replies. "This doesn't happen often."

"What doesn't happen often?" I ask.

"A client who ventures so deep into the nature of his problems that he forgets about time, about lunch, about everything in the world except getting in touch with his past, in hopes that he may eventually recover."

chapter twenty-nine

Dealing with Reality

Dinnertime. Pathetic. At age twenty-five I'm standing in a single-file line of men, eighteen to sixty, as we follow the directions barked out by the monitors. Structure.

In this rehabilitation facility, there are three types of addicts. The first are the junkies who are tired of their old lives and desperate to kick the habit. The second are here to convince their family and friends they are trying to clean up, but have no intention of doing so. The third group are inmates on temporary leave from prison, who have arranged some sort of plea bargain that requires them to attend a rehabilitation center. This type of addict enters the Tuerk House in orange jumpsuit and shackles and exits the same way after completing the program. Returning to jail, they wait for their parole board to take their rehab progress into consideration upon their next review.

The guy standing behind me in the dinner line is in this third group. His name is Cecil. He stands six-foot-four, about two hundred forty pounds. His skin is light black, almost white, and freckled. His hair is an enormous semi-curly afro that is matted into uneven sections, perhaps purposely. His teeth are as yellow as piss, and he smells like a greasy cheesesteak with onions.

Cecil's comments have an aggressive tone. "White boy piss me off, rich pussy faggot come here and think all that! Fuck this, nobody here want no rich breakfast-in-bed motherfucker!" The more I ignore him, the worse it gets. "That's right, you don't hear me, right? You deaf now, right? You deaf cuz you know you best be deaf." Cecil's ploy to decimate my self-confidence is working, and I'm getting nervous. This guy seems unstable, and I'm fairly certain he could snap at any moment. I try my best to keep ignoring him, but it isn't easy when someone over twice your weight and a head taller you is delivering threats into your ear.

The amount of food they give us is meager. Each meal consists of a sparse tray on which all the food groups are represented: a piece of meat, potatoes of some sort, a vegetable, a dessert, and a fruit drink. One serving of each, no seconds. Today, the menu offers meatloaf, instant mashed potatoes, corn, chocolate cake, and orange drink. The clients, as usual, are partaking in the daily mealtime barter system: drink for cake, smokes for potatoes, cake for meat, and so forth.

Fruit drink seems to be the most precious item on the barter plate. After all, a junkie going through withdrawal secretes an array of fluids that must be replenished: sweat, mucus, diarrhea, saliva, piss, vomit, and tears.

I spot Dane, Toby, and Sean Williams, sitting together. As I approach, Toby is providing levity and keeping the table laughing while Dane watches over him like a proud father. As usual, Dane, via his connections, has provided extra food for me: a piece of meatloaf and potatoes.

As I sit, one of the guys at a neighboring table reaches for my cake, saying, "You don't want this, right?" Dane snags his wrist, squeezes it tight, and glares into his eyes for about five seconds before letting go. The guy says, "Just shittin', Dane! Shit, man. This place got you, man. You goin' off!"

From the other table, the guys project comments under their breath but audible to us:

"What is white boy paying you for those kickbacks?"

"What is he, Dane, your bitch?"

"So how is that white boy at sucking your dick, Dane?"

Dane sits, chewing his food, degraded as a man, with his street credibility affronted by the men seated at the nearby table. Dane, an O.G., or "original gangster," is now, because of his affinity towards me, faced with a dilemma. He can either bring the situation to the next level and pick a fight—in which case he might lose his street cred by showing that these men have bothered him—or ignore the comments in hopes the other men knock it off. I can tell that Dane is burning to strike out in anger, but knows it is better to exercise discretion.

Toby does what he can to moderate the situation, in his own humorous way. "Now, why are you boys so interested in dick suckin' all the sudden? For a group of supposed straight men, you think an awful lot about a man's dick in another man's mouth. I don't know about y'all!"

During the verbal melee, Dane stares straight ahead at nothing in particular, beaming a look of subdued humiliation and rage. Sean Williams quietly eats his meal.

The last smoke break of the day. It's the time when almost everybody lets down their guard, smiles and laughs more than usual. I always seem to walk away from this smoke break feeling as though life isn't so bad.

Toby is making everyone laugh with off-color sex stories. Dane pays his young protégé no mind and makes eye contact with me. I can tell there is something he wants to tell me. We step to the side where we can talk one on one.

I start off. "Look, Dane, I want you to know, I really appreciate all you're doing for me in here. The extra food, the support . . . and that episode at dinner, I'm sorry if—"

Dane cuts in, "Shut the fuck up! I did what I did because it needed to be done, and I don't want to hear another mention about it." He changes modes. "Did you talk to your mother today?"

"Nah, Dane, why you ask?"

"Just curious," he replies, but I know him well enough to understand there is a deeper implication.

"Why, what's up, Dane?"

"White boy, don't take this wrong, what I'm about to tell you. But, I was cleaning the room up a bit and came across a letter titled, 'Dear Mom.'"

I knew the letter he was talking about:

> Dear Mom,
> I write you this letter for a much more important reason than to let you know how I'm doing. As I am currently in rehab, the question people keep asking me is: Who is your role model in this world? If you had the inner strength, whose morals and values would you like to emulate? My answer came with great confidence and without hesitation, "My mother," I said. I can't quite find the words that truly sum up my feelings. But I want so bad to change. And now I know that this change needs to manifest itself in actions, not words. When blessings arise or nightmares fall, you come to mind. When opportunities are presented or failures occur, Mom, I think of you. Little do you know, truly, my whole

journey, and every decision I make starts with you and ends
with you. Now, in this place, you are my source of strength.
I love you. You will be proud of me one day.

Love,
Brandon

Betrayal! How could he read my personal letters? I'm fucking
tired of this shit. Every time I seem to give someone my complete trust, it backfires in my face. "Why did you read that?" I demanded.

Dane assures me, "Normally I wouldn't have, but in this case,
matters are different. You see, I wrote that same letter to my
mother probably forty years ago, only a month before she was
killed. It's not a time I want to remember. As a matter of fact, I
almost completely forgot until I met you, and since then, for some
reason, I haven't been able to get it off my mind. Don't you see? It
took you coming into my life for me to deal with it. So, I figure,
it's in God's plan that I found that letter, so I could help you deal
with it."

He steps closer and continues. "Don't you see it, white boy?
Look, my mother's gone. And she's gone because I didn't come to
grips and learn from her. And for that reason, I remained a goddamn junkie my whole life. And now, forty years later, God made
me find that note, and maybe even made me go through what I
experienced, just so you would learn from me."

My anger dies away. I am touched by what he has just told me,
and I don't know how to react. Dane places his hand on my shoulder, comforting me. "So check this out, shorty, we're gonna fix
this. Yeah, you heard me right, we're gonna fix this problem, you
and me together. They're always telling us we need to stick together in here. I mean, for real, who else we got? I fucked up my

life, white boy, so I'm gonna do everything in my power to not let you repeat my mistakes. You understand, white boy? Do you?"

I think for a moment.

At once, the situation changes, as I feel someone's shoes stepping on my heels, pinning them to the ground. This is an old street-fighting trick in which the perpetrator might then shove his victim, sending him to the ground, maximizing his vulnerability to a stomp or kick in the face. I half turn my head and see my adversary, Cecil. "White boy! Sup, motherfucker?!"

Cecil's fists are clenched. His chest expands and contracts with every breath, like a huge rubber ball. He lays a fat hand on my shirt. "Pussy, how 'bout this! From now on, you're gonna kick down your meat and potatoes at every meal! What's you think of that?"

I am sure that confrontations such as this are one of the things Cecil lives for. Within seconds, seven years of living as a junkie, eating out of trash cans, sleeping in prisons, hustling for a fix every day, instantly crushes my capacity for rational thought. In a flash, all other problems dissipate, the urge to hurt this man as fast and efficiently as possible becomes my single priority, and I remember my pencil in my right front pocket, sharpened this morning.

I turn, gain a firm footing, bend my knees, and press my hands against his chest, creating a human lever between Cecil and the ground. *Push!* Despite my light weight and deteriorated muscles, I shove him back long enough to go into my pocket, grip my pencil, and drive the shank forward.

In mid-swing, I am grabbed and grappled to the ground, and the pencil is taken from my hand. Disoriented under the choke hold, I wonder how the hell Cecil managed to grab me with such lightning speed. But wait, I can *still see* Cecil. The man who wrestled me to the ground was Dane.

Toby rushes in with a firm right hand directly to Cecil's jaw, stunning the large man and sending him stumbling ass-first to the ground.

Cecil recovers, assessing the condition of his jaw by wiggling it with his right hand. Toby grounds his footing in preparation for round two, when we are charged by a group of monitors and taken down. Dane gets in one final word to Cecil. "Come near this boy one more time, or for that matter even look in his direction, and that will be the last person you'll ever set your eyes on, I promise!"

Dane, Toby, and I regroup as we watch Cecil on the ground, squirming, flailing like a fish out of water. One monitor holds his legs, a second pins his arms to the ground, and a third sits on his head.

chapter thirty
Death and Resurrection

I wake up the next morning as a hand tugs on my shoulder. "Wake up, white boy, get up. It's breakfast time." Toby.

I lie there and take in my surroundings as a feeling of peace and comfort floods my body. After yesterday's therapy, I am feeling very positive and motivated. It's a sensation I haven't felt in years, and one that I thought I would never again have.

Toby puts on a white T-shirt and pulls his khaki pants from under his mattress. "Hey Toby, what's up with putting your pants *there?*" I ask.

"Check this out! When there ain't no iron around, you fold them up neat and put them under your mattress before you go to sleep. And when you wake up, presto! A crease you can cut a stick of cold butter with. Like so." He proudly holds up his pressed khakis.

"Damn. Nice one. But who are you trying to impress?"

"Man, you forget what today is?"

I realize why he's getting so spruced up, and it pisses me off. Today is visiting day, but I have no one coming to see me. I reply smartly, "It's Saturday, it's breakfast time, and we're some of the most pathetic junkies on the face of the earth, stuck in this shithole existence some choose to call life!"

Toby replies, "Stop bein' so negative, white boy! Cheer up, life ain't so bad! You alive, you got a roof over your head, a shower to get into, hot breakfast waitin', and all five of your senses to work with. Remember what Dane always says, 'It could be worse.' "

I take inventory. I am a twenty-five-year-old junkie. I have been to jail and taken into police custody more times than I can remember. I have been involved in petty crimes, armed robberies, shootouts, and drug trafficking. I have pulled more hustles than ten junkies my age put together. The only crime in which I have not taken part is homicide, and I can honestly say that if the price was right, I might have. I have been pistol whipped, shot at, stabbed, prostituted, beaten down, and thrown down flights of stairs. I came from a nice home, lived in a mansion, slept in abandoned houses, and have been homeless. I have dined in five-star restaurants, picked food from trash cans, and gone for days without eating at all. I senselessly threw away my career as a professional skateboarder because I could not handle fame. I have been a successful entrepreneur in the illegal drug business, and begged for spare change on the corner. My reflection in the mirror depicts a person with the worst punishment of all: a waste of life.

Toby tells me it has been about four years since anyone in his family has seen him clean and sober. I am reminded of what life was like a few years ago when I was his age, before I was homeless, when I still had loved ones and a relationship with my family. I can't deny I am jealous, and for some sick reason I take comfort in the fact that although he is intelligent, well spoken, and well dressed, he is nothing more than a piece of shit junkie just like me.

This is so fucking backward. In "normal" relationships, when someone you care about is happy, you should share their happiness. However, in this case, the more excitement Toby expresses, the more depressed I become.

As Toby dances around singing a rap song, he looks in my direction and asks, "So who's coming to see you today, white boy?"

I reply, "No one that I know of."

"For real?"

"Yeah, for real."

"Damn, you must have really fucked up. Now it makes sense," he says.

"What makes sense?"

"Why you look so goddamn down. Anyhow, I can call my baby's mother and get her to bring one of her girlfriends."

A brief pause. "Toby, let's get real for a minute. My own family don't want shit to do with me so why the fuck do you think anyone else would?"

"Okay, if you ain't down, you ain't down, no big thing. But next week I'm tellin' her to come, cuz I know you gonna change your tune after being stuck inna room with me an' Dane's ass for that long!" He laughs.

Toby's funny remark does nothing to lighten my spirit. Oh well, I think, I may as well get up, end my pity party, and get the day going. I know what will cheer me up. A shower. A simple shower, although seemingly trivial, can make a junkie feel as if he's a productive member of society. However, in the bathroom, every motherfucker is singing with joy. Not only do I have to wait for an available stall, I have to listen to every one of these happy pricks gleefully singing a rap song or an R&B ballad. I wait patiently, reciting something I remember hearing in group lecture: feelings pass. One other thought makes my situation tolerable, something my mother had always told me. "Brandon," she said, "no matter what your trials and tribulations are, there's one thing you always have to remember, God never puts more on you than you can bear."

Dane enters the bathroom and begins brushing his teeth. As usual, he looks very serious, concentrating on his thoughts, but picks up on my self-doubt.

"What up, white boy?" Dane asks.

"I'd just rather not talk right now!"

"Whoa, whoa, whoa!" Dane says. "White boy, I've never heard shit come out your mouth like that. What's the fucking problem?"

I reply, "I'm so fucking pissed right now! I've been in more rehabs than I can count on two hands, and I've always had a family, or a girlfriend, or someone there for me on visiting day. Unfortunately, all those times were a game to me, and I fucked up and went back on the Dope as soon as I had the chance. But now, this time I really want to recover, and everyone in my life has given up on me."

"Answer me this. How long you been getting high, white boy?"

"On Dope or anything?" I ask.

"Anything that's mind or mood altering."

"I'd say at least seven years," I reply.

Dane lifts an eyebrow and raises a finger, which he points in my direction, again and again, in unison to the rhythm of his diction. "So let me see if I can get this right. You got high for seven years and expect to gain the trust and honor and respect from your family and friends in a few days? Impossible. If it takes seven years to walk into the woods, it stands to reason that it will take seven years to walk out of the woods."

Dane has drawn his conclusion, and I find myself in agreement.

Unreasonable expectations have always obstructed my judgment. I take a deep breath to calm down and stay in reality.

"Listen, I got somethin' else for you. Now you know I ain't the Sunday school type, but, you remember when Jesus was up on the cross? Now why you suppose he let that happen? You mean to tell me that Jesus Christ couldn't have come down off that cross if he wanted to? Of course he could have. But he knew he had to die, in order to resurrect. You see? He needed to die to become more than what he was.

"It's like a caterpillar who spins a cocoon all around himself. He becomes dormant. But then what happens? When the season changes, out comes a butterfly! Like Jesus, he is more than what he once was, even more beautiful than ever. You see, white boy, that's us. We have to let our old selves die completely, and then and only then can we become this new beautiful person we're supposed to be."

Somehow, his words help me feel that there is much more to life than this place, my addiction, or this day. Dane continues, "And I don't want to hear you say you can't do it, or you don't have what it takes, because I've met a lot of people in my lifetime, and I want you to know you have more heart in your big toe than most possess in their whole body. One thing my mother taught me since I was a kid: give credit where credit's due, and you don't give yourself enough credit. I'm telling you, you're going to make it. You're a fighter. And that's the end of the story!"

We finish brushing our teeth. After we rinse I finally ask, "You got family coming today?"

"Nah, nephew, there's no need for that. I'm only in this joint for fourteen days. I'll be seeing them soon enough. Besides, I don't need my people seeing me in this condition. It's just plain out sad."

"Well, Dane, you have no one comin', I have no one comin', looks like I'm gonna be your shadow today."

He grins. "C'mon, nephew, that goes without saying!"

Back in the room, Toby is putting the finishing touches on his wardrobe. He sprays a thick mist of a knockoff brand of Obsession in the air, walks back and forth through it, looks our way and announces, "Well, well, well, if it isn't the lonely hearts club."

"That's fucking hilarious, Toby, you should be a comedian," I say.

Toby laughs and Dane comments, "Boy, you better thank God you're not in the situation we're in. Remember, Toby, the same thing that can make you laugh can make you cry in a second."

Toby smiles, wiggling his index and middle fingers. "Tell you what, I'll make it up to you. After my girl leaves, I'll let you each smell a finger."

We all laugh. As low as Dane and I feel, we couldn't deny that Toby is one funny motherfucker.

There's a knock at the door. Dane calls out, "Who is it?"

"It's Mr. Leeper, Brandon's counselor."

I go to the door to greet him. "How you feeling today, Brandon?" Guy asks.

"Well, to be quite honest, I feel pretty down."

"Why? What's going on? Talk to me, homeboy." Slang words like that make me feel like I have a friend who cares.

"Honestly, Guy, this might be my worst day I've had here yet. I feel like absolute shit about myself. I'm so fucking depressed. I know I've got to stop getting high, right now that's the only thing that's going to fill this empty hole."

Guy cuts me off. "All right, Brandon, you're a grown man, enough of the pity party. It's time to take personal responsibility for your own actions."

I roll my eyes, but Guy persists. "Well, Brandon, this is what recovery is all about, dealing with life on life's terms. Anyway, I came to talk to you about something."

"All right, man, what's up?"

"Well, I was hoping we could do it in my office," he says. By the tone of his voice, it sounds pretty important.

"Sure."

As we make our way to his office, I worry.

Did my mother not pay my initiation fee? Did she die? Do I have AIDS? What's going on?!

chapter thirty-one
Changes

We enter Guy's office.

He sits, I sit, in the so-called relaxation chair.

Guy tells me, "I have some good news and some news you might not care to hear. Which do you want first?"

"Well, this day has been horrible so far so let's keep it going, I'll take the worst."

"Brandon, I know more than anybody that the world seems to be on your shoulders. When I tell you this information, you're sure to think the world is going to come crashing down. But acceptance is, as I said before, what we recovering addicts call 'dealing with life on life's terms.' "

He pauses. "Brandon . . ."

The cruelest device in all humanity is the preparatory speech. Although this one is intended to inform, comfort and educate, it is instead bringing me anxiety and fear.

"Yeah, Guy, just fucking tell me."

Guy pauses, prolonging the suspense. "All right. You might not recall, being you were somewhat 'out of it' during your time of arrival, but during your admission we drew your blood. It's required upon entering this facility for your safety and rehabilitation. I'm sure I don't need to explain that when you shoot Dope, your odds of catching any number of diseases is much greater than they'd be for a person who uses via smoking it or sniffing it."

My skin goes cold, although I'm hot inside. I've been afraid this day would come.

Guy moves next to me and holds my hand. I'm terrified. I've shared needles, cookers, cotton, and water with other junkies as often as I've shaken their hands. I've entered abandoned houses, found old needles and used them. I've had unprotected sex with hookers.

In the last few months, one of my sources of income was a medical clinic that paid me thirty dollars each time my blood was drawn, and another ten dollars to attend a class that educated addicts on how to avoid high-risk situations that transmit disease. I could make an additional thirty dollars if I picked up the results of my blood test. I always showed up for the check, but I refused to listen to the results. I was aware of the risks of my behavior, but I took no precautions to avoid contracting HIV, "the ninja" as junkies call it.

Guy draws the speech to its climax. "Well, you're fortunate, and honestly quite blessed. You haven't contracted HIV. I wish I could say the same about hepatitis. I'm sorry, Brandon, you have hepatitis C. I know this isn't gonna matter much, but ninety percent of IV drug users in Baltimore City carry this infectious disease. Look at it this way, at least it's not HIV, and there's medication you can take to treat this disease." He hands me a pamphlet to educate me about my new life partner, hepatitis C.

Living on the streets has taught me to take disturbing news with a demented sense of humor. I reply with a laugh. "Fuck you, Guy, I can't wait to hear the good news."

"I haven't lied to you yet, right, Brandon?"

I nod but my grin conveys my distrust.

"Your mother's coming to visit."

And the world just . . . stopped.

"What the fuck, Guy? You call that *good news*? You know damn well I messed up every chance at rehab I've ever had! The last thing I want is to build my mother up to break her down again."

"Well then, it looks to me you have two options. One, you can pack your shit up and catch the next bus to Fayette and Patterson, or two, make a decision right now to clean up your life, and mean it."

I say nothing.

"You ready? Let's go." He stands.

"Go? Where?" I ask.

"To the visiting center."

"You mean she's here? *Now?*"

Soon, I'm face to face with my mother, who, only a few days earlier, I had hurt so deeply. When she sees me, she breaks down in tears. I look at Guy, as if to beg, "Please get me out of this!" But he's nothing but a third party in my bad dream.

"Stop crying, Mom, please. I'm sorry, I never wanted to hurt you. Come on, Mom, stop crying. Mom, I love you. I want you to know I didn't even want anyone to tell you I was here. I'm so tired of hurting you."

I help my mother to a chair. She sits, motionless, as one tear after another falls. She gathers the strength to ask, "What did I do wrong, Brandon? Please let me know, please for the love of God, tell me and let me know."

"Mom," I answer, "you did nothing wrong. You're not accountable for this. You did everything possible to help me. Unfortunately, in the end, I chose this life. The only one who is responsible for my actions is me. Mom, I love you more than life itself! This is why I am telling you, don't get your hopes up, or believe in me.

I wanna show you instead of tell you how I'm gonna stay clean. They're teaching me to be honest, Mom. I'm not gonna lie this time around, so I'm gonna start with the truth. I'm a drug addict. I'm jobless, homeless, friendless, and probably every word that ends with 'less.' They just told me I have hepatitis, and to top it off, there are a few hours in every day that I would go back to shooting Dope if it was available. For those few hours a day, my mind goes through a process of rationalization, as I think of reasons to get high."

This is not what my mother is used to hearing from me. What I usually deliver is a conniving, well-delivered speech that's laced with quotes memorized from NA meetings, calculated to convince her that I am recovered, I will never use again, and I deserve one more chance.

My mother wipes the next tear from beneath her gorgeous blue eyes, which are bloodshot. I continue. "Mom, it really feels horrible to be so brutally honest with you when I say that I have doubts. I love and respect you more than anything in the world, but I guess it's better for me to be honest now than build up your hopes with lies. Although I have to tell you, truly in my heart, this time I feel different. I can't find the right words to explain it; I just feel it in the pit of my stomach. But I can't and I won't even bother explaining this to you, because this time, I'm handling it differently. I refuse to run my mouth anymore. No more words, I would rather just show you with my actions. There. That's what I have to say. Now, it's time for me to go."

I take two steps forward. In my mind, I picture a scene that had taken place over twenty years ago, when a little boy named Brandon Novak took his first two steps and almost fell, only to be caught in the soft, loving warmth of his mother's arms. It feels so good to be held by this woman, the only person in the world whose bond for me is so strong that she refuses to give up on my recovery. Thank you, God. Thank you for my mother.

"I love you, Mom."

"I love you, too, Brandon," she whispers in her sweet voice that has the power to take away my pain.

I wipe away my tears, take a deep breath, and go back into the hallway, where I become one of thirty-five junkies on their way to lunch.

Again, the lunch line. An overweight cafeteria worker serves me a meagerly portioned plate holding two hot dogs, withered and overcooked, limp French fries, and carrot "chunks," that resemble wrinkled-up orange plastic.

Although I should be grateful for this meal, for this lunch line, for this place, I feel humiliated. Why do I feel this way? For Christ's sake, I have been living like an *animal* for the past few months.

I begin to see a pattern. This is my way of rationalizing and creating reasons to justify returning to my old life. These negative thoughts and feelings are my dark side calling me, begging for me to give in. Trying to shake it off, I take my two shriveled hot dogs to the empty seat across from Dane, Toby, and Sean Williams.

I sit and begin eating. Dane senses my turmoil. "What's wrong, nephew?"

"Nothing," I reply, trying to hold the tear dripping from the corner of my eye.

"Nephew, don't even think of taking another bite of that food until you tell me the problem!"

I want to tell him so bad, but something is holding me back. Finally I find the strength to speak. "My fucking counselor just surprised me with a visit from my mother."

"Well, how'd it go?" His brow wrinkles in sympathy, and I

know that it was Dane who told Guy that I needed to face my mother. Somehow, Dane understood that if I looked my mother in the eye and told her the truth, I might gain strength.

I am flooded with gratefulness. I'm grateful to be alive, to have clean clothes, and a clean body, to be surrounded by people who care. Although I am in a constant struggle against my compulsions, I am progressing in my recovery. I've just had my greatest victory: facing myself and telling my mother the truth.

The next morning, I am shaken awake by Dane. The force of his grip on my arms expresses the seriousness of the situation. "What's up Dane, what's wrong?"

"Toby's gone, nephew! He's gone!"

"What do you mean, 'gone'?"

Toby's bed is empty. His dresser drawers are open, also empty. Toby has gone A.M.A., against medical advice.

Dane sits on his bed, crying, as if at the loss of a son. "Late last night, I heard him get up from his bed. I opened up my eyes, and he told me he was just going to the bathroom, and I should go back to sleep. Well, for some reason, I got a bad feeling, and then I had a dream about him."

Dane was in a state that, for such a man, I had not imagined possible. *He* was the one with the cool head. *He* was the one with the ability to calm *us* down. I tried to offer consolation. "Dane, Toby's gone, I guess, but he's not dead."

"No, I'm telling you, he's dead! In my dream, I watched him leave the Tuerk House. I could see him leave the building. And in real life, you can't deny he's gone, right?"

"Yeah, he's gone. And you dreamed he left," I agree.

"Not only could I see him leave in my dream, I saw what he did the whole night. He walked away, feeling alone and beaten by life. He was angry and discouraged, so he felt he deserved a treat, seeing how he did stay clean for a week. I watched him as he bought a bag of raw Dope and decided to experiment with the needle."

As Dane fights to control his emotions, I become afraid to hear the ending of the story.

"Toby went to his girl's house, where she was asleep. He sat in her living room, as quietly as he could so as not to wake her up. In the dream, I watched Toby from above the room, floating—like a spirit or a ghost. I screamed, I begged for him to stop, but he couldn't hear me. Then he put the dope in the cooker. As a matter of fact, he put in the whole bag of powerful raw Dope. My dream ended as Toby laid back, dying, and his spirit left his body, and finally he could see me; we were both spirits. We hugged, and he cried, 'I'm sorry, Dane, I'm sorry.' White boy, I'm telling you, Toby's gone, nothing but a fucking memory. Such a waste! Such a fucking waste!"

chapter thirty-two

It's All Over—or
Is It?

A week and a half later, razor-blade-winged butterflies are fluttering through my stomach, slowly slicing their way through my body. My mind is torn by conflicting emotions. I have serious doubts about my recovery. This is the day of my discharge, and yet I feel the same way I've felt each day of my struggle through rehab: I want to use, yet I am not using.

Today is the final judgment. My fate is still pending. I have interviewed for several recovery houses but haven't received an answer from any of them yet. Please, God, let one of them accept me. If they don't, I have nowhere to go and no backup plan. At this point I am not sure of much but I do know that there's no way I can sleep on the streets without shooting Dope. I need direction and guidance. Rehab has taught me that I have lost the ability to make healthy decisions on my own. My mind needs to be remolded, like an incomplete clay sculpture that isn't turning out as the artist had intended.

My bedroom door swings open. It's Sean Williams and Dane.

"I'm sure gonna miss you," Sean Williams says. "Here's my number. When you get situated, the three of us are gonna go play some golf!"

Dane chimes in, "Shit, white boy, the only thing me and him

know about golf is how much the clubs are worth and who will give us the most cash for a stolen set." We all laugh, and I take comfort in the presence of true friends. While everyone is still smiling, I take one last mental picture. I want to remember this place, the room, bed number 361 B that took me to hell and back, the cold floor I laid on when I was going through withdrawal, and that goddamn window we weren't supposed to look out of.

Dane gives me a firm hug. "You got my number. Use it day or night, rain or snow, just please use it."

Sean Williams lets Dane know they have to be getting back to class. They say their good-byes and I watch them walk out the door.

As I am packing, Guy Leeper enters with his hands on his hips. "Well, now it's time for the real work to begin. You ready for this, Brandon?"

"To be honest, Guy, I'm scared as hell."

"Well, you don't have to be. I just got the call: you've been accepted to Our House. They have a great recovery program; the success rate from Our House is exceptionally high. You'll go there and for the first thirty days you will be on what's called a 'black out.' That means you can't leave the house by yourself for any reason at all. If you do leave Our House, it can only be with a supervisor and you're only permitted to go to a meeting then directly back. This is what you need, a guiding hand to help you resist temptation."

Out loud I answer, "Great, that's fine with me." But my head is somehow filled with doubts.

Guy asks, "Do you have a ride there or do we need to have someone take you?"

And, in that instant, my head, flushed with adrenaline and en-

dorphins, unfolds a plan before me—a way to buy time in order to
score Dope. If I leave this rehab alone, it will be a few hours before
they will start asking questions about me at Our House. It's still
early, and there are plenty of tourists at the port and museum area.
I'm sure I can sell a few dreams that will convince people to give
me a few dollars. After all, I'm smart and cunning. And look at
me! Clean, with new clothes, respectable looking enough. . . . As
a matter of fact, I'll use the time to test my abilities to hustle. I bet
I can bum twenty bucks in an hour. That will leave me plenty of
time to score! I mean, I'm going to be on lockdown for thirty days,
so I should have a little freedom before I enter this place. After
all, I've done so well in the last two weeks, hell, I *deserve* one last
high!

Without blinking, I respond, "No thanks, Guy, I have a ride
already. My mother is picking me up."

Guy tells me, "Okay. I wrote my phone number on the back
of your discharge papers. Brandon, if there's anything you need,
please don't hesitate to call."

"Thanks, Guy, thanks for everything."

"Come on," he says. "I'll walk you out to your mother's car."

I make up a lie. "I told her I'd call her when it was time to leave.
Can I use the lobby phone?"

"Absolutely," Guy replies.

I sit in the waiting room of the room in which I was inducted.

Guy looks at his watch, puts his arm on my shoulder, and tells
me, "I have a session waiting, so I have to go. This is where we
part ways. Good luck, Brandon. I have a feeling about you." We
hug one last time and he walks into the counseling office.

Great! I think. Now all I have to do is wait to use the phone.
I'll act like I'm dialing and talking to my mother, walk out of here,

pull a hustle, get myself a bag of Dope, and make it to Our House in time for dinner. Anticipation surges through my mind and veins.

"Can I use your phone?" I ask the receptionist.

We are interrupted as two monitors enter through the front doors, carrying a young black girl of twenty, who is obviously trying to deal with Heroin withdrawal. She's pissing her pants, throwing up, crying, gasping for air, shaking, and sweating. My heart goes out to this poor girl. She screams over and over, "Lord, why me? Please let it stop!"

The receptionist answers me. "Excuse me, I'm going to need this phone for another few minutes. If you like, you are welcome to wait in the other room."

The receptionist is trying to be considerate, attempting to spare me from this horrible sight. "No thanks, that's okay." Actually, I want to watch. This is exactly what I need to see right now. I watch this poor girl as she slides off her chair and onto the floor. Her pants are soaked with piss, her shirt covered in throw up, the back of her pants seeping feces. Her eyes roll up into her head. This is a human being I'm looking at. This poor, sweet, innocent young girl, living in the hell she created for herself.

"Okay, young man, I'm off the phone," the receptionist tells me.

I stop and think.

epilogue
My Friend Scott

Those who have followed my career know where I ended up. They know I didn't stop using.

You can see a documentary about my addiction in the "Making of" feature accompanying the film *Haggard*. I have had parts on MTV's reality shows *Viva La Bam,* and *Bam's Unholy Union,* as well as *Jackass 2* and *Jackass 2.5.* I have a main role in Bam Margera's film *Minghags.* I have made live appearances here and there and have been a regular personality on Bam's Sirius Radio show. Through these films and programs, the fans have been able to catch glimpses into my life. They have seen my progress and regression, witnessed my promises and pitfalls, and shared in my happiness and misery. But what the fans might not truly understand, what it is most difficult for non-addicts to realize, is the feeling of temptation the addict faces on a daily basis.

November 2007, Mandy's house.

It is a dark, strange, cold, sleeting day, and I find refuge under a thick down comforter as I sit on my couch with my beautiful pit bull, Diva.

Mandy, my girlfriend, is getting ready for work. She's five-foot-six, with jet black hair and beautiful breasts. Unlike the other women

I've been with, she's not the pretty girl in the corner who keeps her opinions to herself. If I screw up, she tells me. When I backslide, she kicks me forward. I can hear her pacing the bedroom, throwing her clothes, cursing that she can't find her bartending outfit and she's going to be late for work. After a half hour of this, she has herself together and stops to give me and Diva a kiss. She murmurs into my ear, "I love you, babe," and whisks out the door.

As is our custom when she works at the bar, she shoots me a text before the night rush filters in. Tonight at 10:30, her text reads, "I'm bored as hell! It's dead in here!"

I'm surprised when she phones me at 11:34.

I answer, "Hey, babe, you that bored?"

My question is met with sobs and choking breaths. She gathers enough air to yell into the phone, "Babe! Babe! I'm coming home! Don't go anywhere, okay?"

A series of nightmare situations flash through my mind in which Mandy has been violated physically or sexually.

"What's wrong?!" I scream into the phone.

"I'm coming home! Just promise me, don't leave the house. Okay?"

"But what—"

"Just promise, Brandon!"

I promise and she hangs up. I pace. Anxious. Afraid. From my body language, Diva senses something wrong.

Although falling sleet slicks the roads, Mandy makes the half hour drive in twenty minutes.

I open the door to see her face wet with tears. Red cheeks. A pained look in her eyes. I grab her and hold her close, petting her hair in consolation for the unknown tragedy. Diva is sympathetically licking our hands, my bare feet, any bare skin her tongue can reach.

I break the embrace and hold her at arm's length. "Mandy, please tell me."

"Haven't you heard? Has anyone called you?" Seeing my blank look, she sobs out, "Scott's dead."

I'm confused. "Scott *who?*"

"Who do you think?"

Scott, my sponsor. Scott, who is responsible for the fact that I am alive today. Without him, I would never have had the courage to go to the Tuerk House, to face my addiction, and to face myself.

Scott has manifested the true spirit of recovery. He overcame the greatest odds in coming to terms with his own addiction and went on to be more successful than any other addict I have ever known. After his recovery, he learned the business of real estate and construction and owned several recovery houses. He made it his personal business to help those who suffered from the sickness of drug addiction. Scott was kind, generous, and understanding. He was my sponsor, my best friend, my savior.

I'm in denial. "It can't be true! Fuck you! Scott's not dead!" I run to the phone and dial, but the call goes right to voice mail. Scott *never* allows his phone to go to voice mail. I drop to my knees and pray for God to have mercy on my friend's soul.

Finally, I try to stand, my legs are so devoid of strength that I fall back down. Mandy rubs my neck and head, whispering, "Baby, it's gonna be all right. You're gonna make it. You can do it, babe. We're gonna make it through this together."

Questions filter through my sadness. I need to know when, where, and how. But as for the "why" of the matter, I already had some idea.

The trouble began about a year ago. A guy Scott was sponsoring had a wife who inherited a great deal of money. She was a recovered addict, but with more money than she had seen in her lifetime, she broke down and bought a large package of drugs. When her husband caught wind of this, he was afraid to return to his house until the package had been removed, in fear of his own weakness. He gave Scott the key to his house and begged him to take the drugs away. Scott obliged.

Driving away from his friend's house, Scott felt the uncontrollable urge to open the package. To his shock, it contained a large bag of pure, uncut Heroin, and another of pure cocaine.

Before this event, Scott had not so much as touched a drop of alcohol in years. He had avoided the parts of Baltimore where he used to score, and abandoned his old crew of drug companions. He had not even discussed drugs unless he was counseling one of the many addicts he sponsored. But, there was Scott, all alone, face to face with his worst enemy. I cannot imagine the mental anguish he must have felt.

The pain was too much to bear. While still driving, Scott began to lick and sniff the bags. And that is all the situation needed to spiral out of control.

Scott was in tears when he shot up a day later. Within two weeks, his personality was destroyed. In the month that followed, his business fell apart. He failed to report to his parole officer or to show up for court.

When Mandy and I heard of Scott's relapse, we said little to each other about it. We knew what had to be done.

That same day I arrived at Scott's door, which swung open upon my knock. I peered in.

The interior of the house was dark. Normal. From the upstairs, I heard a television.

I climbed the stairs toward the sound. In the walls of the unlit hallway I could see several holes, which seemed to have been made by a series of sharp kicks at foot level. Higher on the wall were dents and smaller holes, perhaps two dozen, which seemed to be fist size, as if it had been punched repeatedly.

I took a deep breath. *Knock knock.*

The voice that answered did not belong to Scott. In fact, it was not a voice at all, more like a low-pitched raspy growl from deep in his throat.

"Who's there?" it demanded.

I recognized the tone and knew: Scott had ceased to be. The cocaine and Heroin had subdued him, erased his memories of friendship, love, and affection. All that remained of my former friend was a collection of the undesirable traits that linger after one's human qualities have been stripped away. An unbalanced, incomplete self.

"It's Brandon," I replied.

The door flung open, as if someone had been standing on the other side ready to pounce. The dark figure in the doorway was a shadow of the man I had once known. His once large, muscular frame was emaciated and wiry. His muscles rippled under thin layers of skin. His eyes were framed by the circular orbital muscles that protruded from his skull. The eyes themselves were narrower, more alert, darting back and forth, scanning the vicinity.

His skin was picked to pieces. Bleeding scabs speckled him from face, to chest, to arms, to hands. These sores were the product of a twitching nervous system searching desperately for a compulsive activity to occupy its fitful surges of energy and finding a perverse pleasure in the act of scratching open a fleshy surface.

"Get in!" Scott's hand darted out, clenched my arm, and yanked. With the door slammed behind me, I was in a room that resembled an animal's den. The mattress and blankets lay on the floor in the form of a nest; the floor was littered with empty ice cream containers, cookie boxes, and wrappers from sweets of all kinds. The large color television was gone; it had been replaced by a thirteen-inch black-and-white model I assumed had been pulled from the bottom of a closet storage box when the big set had been traded for drugs or money. On the screen an episode of what may have been *Cops* was barely visible through the static. The set had no antenna. I'm sure the cable bill had remained unpaid for so long that the services had been terminated.

"Hey, Scott, how you doing?" I smiled.

A hollow-sounding laugh contorted his mouth into a sick grimace. "I've been better."

As if it weren't one hundred percent painfully obvious, I asked, "What's wrong?"

As he turned from me, he caught his reflection in the mirror and became entranced, taking a step this way and that, in an attempt to find the image of his former self.

Scott could not hold the first heave of vomit that spurted from his gut to the floor, nor a second gulp, which dripped through his fingers. He picked up a filthy shirt from the floor and wiped his hands and mouth.

"You're using, huh, buddy?"

He, again peered into the mirror, answering as if he were talking to himself, "Nah, man, nah." Then, "Hey man, I'm gonna get a shower. I gotta get this throw up off me."

"Okay, buddy." Realizing that he might not make it to the shower, I placed his arm over my shoulder and walked him, like a wounded soldier, to the bathroom. Once there, I helped him out of his clothes and under the shower head.

Forty-five minutes later Scott is still in the shower.

I am on the living room couch, paging through a women's fashion magazine that had been left alongside a tube of lip gloss and eyeliner by a female companion. In the next room, water from the second-floor shower drips from the kitchen ceiling. And then I hear it.

Scott's moan begins softly and increases in volume and emotion. *"aaaaaAAHHHHHHH!"* This sound repeats, until the screaming groans form words. "Ggghhhaaaaaacomeonnnn! Coooome-ooonnn! Come on, motherfucker! I'm gonna fuck you up!"

From the bottom of the staircase I yell, "Are you all right up there, buddy?"

His response was nonchalant. "Yeah, I'm fine, man! I'll be right out!"

The screams continued, but were accompanied by the unmistakable sound of fists pounding flesh. "Come on motherfucker! I'll kick your fucking ass! Let's go, fucker! I'm gonna fuck you up!" Punching, smacking, slapping.

"Scott, are you *sure* you're all right?"

"Yeah, I'm fine, Brandon! I'll be right down!" His voice is happy. Cheerful. Next, he begins *singing!* "Paint It Black" by the Rolling Stones.

As water pours from the kitchen ceiling, questions filled my mind:

- Could there be a third person in this house?
- Was that person fighting Scott?
- Has Scott gone crazy?
- Is this situation so surreal, has Scott's world driven *me* crazy?

I crawl upstairs and tiptoe to the bathroom. The door is open. A needle and accessories lay in the sink.

Yes, Scott is alone, pounding himself in the chest and legs, striking the walls of the shower. And now, this situation finally makes sense.

Scott's response to shooting up was incomprehensible to me. Where I had always gotten numb to reality, he became ultra-aggressive, paranoid, and sometimes enraged. Judging by the amount of Dope and coke he was presently using, punching himself and the walls around him forced his heart to race, keeping him mentally alert, allowing him to use the maximum amount of Dope and coke without ODing.

I walk downstairs, and suddenly, *Bang bang bang bang!* At first, I don't know *where* the sound is coming from. Then, I realize, it is from the front door.

I go to the front door, open it.

It has never been a problem for me to differentiate an undercover policeman from an average citizen. In their attempt to assimilate with the rest of us, the undercover cops fail to project the personality quirks and mannerisms of a "normal person." For example, take this guy standing in front of me. Obviously, he is trying to create the image of the average slob sports fan by wearing sweat clothes and an Orioles baseball cap. But his hair is meticulously groomed. Why would a slovenly sports fan bother combing and gelling his hair? Wouldn't the purpose of the baseball cap be to hide his messy hair so he didn't have to comb it?

Now his sweat clothes. His pants say "Cats." Not "Arizona Wildcats," just "Cats." His shirt mimics a team jersey but makes no reference to any particular sport, and on it is printed the number "41." Obviously, this cop wanted to save a buck on his undercover outfit and got the cheap knockoff brands at Kmart. No sports fan would be caught dead in this gear! Sports fans pride themselves in identifying with particular teams and players.

Also, this guy is clean. *Too clean.* He is clean shaven. Even his fingernails are clipped. And to top it off, he is wearing cologne! Who the hell rolls out of bed, throws on sweat clothes, and slaps on Brute 33?

Across the street a similarly dressed man stands next to a van in which a third man is seated. Obviously backup. These undercover cops are here for Scott, to take him away for skipping on parole.

"Hello?" I ask.

"Hi, is Scott here?" asks the cop.

"No, he's not. You should come back later."

The cop asks, "Who are you?"

"I'm his friend."

"What's your name?"

"I'm William. What's your name?" I ask.

"Can we come in and wait?" The undercover cop takes a step forward, hoping my instinct will be to say yes.

"No. I'm afraid I can't invite you in under any circumstances. I just can't invite strangers into someone else's house. It wouldn't be right, or legal, for that matter. But you can come back later. I think he's coming back at nine or ten."

"That's okay, we'll wait."

I close the door, climb the stairs, and approach Scott's room. He is now dry and dressed in a pair of gym shorts.

"Scott, listen, buddy, the cops are here, at the door."

Scott grabs my shirt, pulls me close. "What do they want? Are they down there now?"

"Wait, wait, wait. There are three plainclothesmen. They say they want a word with you, but I told them they can't come in and that you aren't home. So, just don't make any loud sounds or go downstairs, okay? They'll have to leave eventually, if they don't have a warrant."

Scott released me and went to the window, looking out of a

small gap in his curtains to the street below. With an index finger, he scrapes the crust from the edge of an open sore, wedging his fingernail between the skin and the coagulated blood and making an audible "picking" sound, which almost seemed to be in rhythm with the gnashing of his teeth. *Pick. Pick. Pick. Griiiinnnnd. Griiiinnnnd. Griiiinnnnd.* As Scott paces in the room, his footsteps become the third instrument in an ensemble of twitching nerves.

"Well, Scott, I guess I should go. That way, they'll think there's no one here at all."

Scott shuts the door behind me. "Oh no! No, you don't! You're staying here. We're not going anywhere. Do they have guns? How many of them are there? What did they say?"

"Wait, Scott—"

"No, fuck them! They're not coming in here, not in my fucking house, no fucking way! We're not gonna let them! No one's fucking coming in here!"

Scott puts on his clothes, still pacing. I've seen him like this before. This is how he reacts when he's getting ready for a fight. He's pumping himself up, breathing heavy and steady. His eyes snap from side to side, looking everywhere, yet nowhere in particular.

I am afraid. Very afraid. When Scott gets like this, he can become dangerous. Is he going to fight the police? Is he going to take me hostage? Does he have a gun?

What the fuck did I get myelf into?

More important, how the hell am I going to get out of here? I have to wait until his attention isn't focused on me. Every few seconds, he examines himself in the mirror.

I wait for the moment when Scott's attention is fully captivated by his image.

"Okay, Scott, I'm going to take a piss real quick." I slip out the bedroom door, leaving him transfixed by his mirror image. In one minute flat I'm climbing out the bathroom window. I drop to the back alley below and run to safety.

So now, weeks later, Mandy and I are dealing with Scott's death. I snatch up the phone and call one of Scott's brothers.

"Hello? This is Novak. Is Scott okay?"

"No, he's not," Scott's brother tells me.

"Is he dead?"

"Well, Brandon, he's not dead . . . anymore. He OD'd, from heroin. He was pronounced dead, but somehow the paramedics were able to bring him back."

Relief. "Who was he with? How did it—"

"No one really knows the circumstances right now. An anonymous source called the ambulance. But now Scott's in the intensive care unit. He'll live, but he'll be dealing with a lot."

Grace overcomes my chaotic state of mind as I snuggle with Mandy under the down comforter, her warm body and mine embraced in peace under the weight of our sleeping pit bull Diva.

Now, if this were a movie, I would write in a FADE TO BLACK, to serve as a visual closure, conveying a feeling that all is well. Unfortunately, the next day is going to bring about an entirely different reality.

We awake to find a steady stream of snow pouring from the sky. The white landscape tells us it has been snowing for some time. Mandy and I dress, preparing ourselves to fight the elements in order to see Scott.

"How you feel, babe?" I ask Mandy.

She looks unsure. "Well, confused, scared, happy, sad, and relieved all in one."

I give her a heartfelt kiss. "It's gonna be all right."

God, I love this woman.

As Mandy and I clean the snow off the car, I am smiling as I envision the scene of us visiting Scott in the hospital. In the fantasy, Mandy and I enter the hospital room, finding Scott in between bites of a hospital breakfast. He looks up and smiles, with his bright blue eyes full of life and fire, and he energetically gives us his usual greeting: "What's up, buddy, how you doing?" This thought gives me motivation to dig the wet snow twice as fast as before.

As Mandy drives us to the hospital, I become fixated on the snow and how beautiful it is, and I picture Scott watching the winter scenery from his bed. I wonder how he feels the morning after he was brought back to life after dying from a needle full of Heroin that he voluntarily stuck into his arm.

From the parking lot, into the elevators and past security, Mandy and I cling together, holding hands as we make our journey to Scott. The hospital is a strange place, where tragedy brings together families and friends in sadness, hope, science, religion, and every so often, miracles.

We are alone, and share a moment.

Mandy asks, "Why are you shaking?"

"I'm not shaking."

She gives me a look. "Stop lying; I can feel it in your hands."

"Well, I guess I am a little."

The elevator takes us to Scott's floor, the ICU. The waiting room is packed. Nurses, doctors, visitors. We wander through the commotion to the receptionist's desk. She is wrapping up phone calls, answering others, placing a dozen people on hold. In five minutes, she asks, "May I help you?" We give Scott's name and she gives us his room and bed numbers. We thank her. I grab Mandy's hand and we rush to Scott's room, open the door.

Scott's bed is empty. A million thoughts and emotions bombard me. Uncertainty. Sadness. Disappointment. Disbelief. Panic.

A voice behind us breaks the silence. "May I help you?"

"Where is Scott? The guy who is registered in this bed?"

"That young man discharged himself over two hours ago," she informs us.

I hear her, but it takes time for the words to register. "Discharged himself?"

The nurse continues. "Yes. He left in such a hurry, he didn't even have his shoes on. That young man has a real battle on his hands, and if he doesn't surrender soon he will be lucky to make it back here again."

"Did he say where he was going?" I ask.

"No," she replies. "But I don't think it was anywhere positive."

I grab Mandy's hand and take one final look at the hospital bed that might have saved Scott's life. As we turn and head for the elevator, I can see a vision of Scott, running barefoot across the snow-covered hospital parking lot. Although the windy chill of the snow-filled air must be stinging him, he is completely numb to it. His eyes are full of despair, his body and mind desperate for his next fix.

Mandy searches through her purse for a tissue, in vain. I wipe my tears away with my sleeve, overwhelmed by an unsettling emotion that bears no name.

That night, Mandy is back at work and I am again alone, in contemplation of Scott and his addiction. There is never a moment in an addict's life when he can honestly say that the flames of his addiction have been completely extinguished. Addiction is a smoldering fire, subtle yet fierce. Through his years of sobriety, Scott could only pretend to assimilate into the normality of the real world. He had prayed for the strength to avoid dipping into his friends' medicine cabinets while using their bathrooms. He had hoped for the will power to avoid street Dope shops on his way home from work. He had abstained from taking up offers for free hits offered to him by old acquaintances he had met by chance. But although he had successfully resisted one temptation after another, moment after moment, day after day, in the end, Scott couldn't hide anymore. Heroin had sought him out, taken possession of his person, and claimed his soul.

Now I face a painful and disturbing conclusion. Through Scott's struggle, as well as through my own, there has been no epiphany, no catharsis, no transformation of character. And this uncomfortable feeling, this emotional void, this uncertainty that I am experiencing *is* the essence of addiction.

I drift off to sleep, with the knowledge that, although the time and place have changed, my life remains the same.

I am a twenty-nine-year-old junkie, lying in my girlfriend's bed, in a quiet suburb of Baltimore City. My eyes close.

If you're a Brandon Novak fan, be sure to check him out in these movies and TV shows:

Movies

Element's *Bam's or Bust* (2009)
Minghags: The Movie (2009)
The Making of Minghags (documentary, 2009)
Bam Margera Presents: Where the #$&% Is Santa? (2008)
Dreamseller: The Documentary, series (2008)
Jackass 2.5 (2007)
Jackass Number 2 (2006)
Haggard: The Movie (2003)
The Making of Haggard (documentary, 2003)
CKY 4: The Latest and the Greatest (2002)
CKY3 (2001)
Powells' *Chaos* (1992)

Television

The Dudesons (2009)
Travis Pastrana's *Nitro Circus* (2009)
Howard TV (performing the most outrageous "Stern Show
    Moment" of 2008)
Fuel TV's *Daily Habit* (2008)
Bam's Unholy Union (2006–2007)
Cribs (with Bam Margera) (2005)
Viva La Bam (2003–2005)